MAN AND BALL

My Autobiography

Stephen Ferris

TRANSWORLD IRELAND

TRANSWORLD IRELAND PUBLISHERS
28 Lower Leeson Street, Dublin 2, Ireland
www.transworldireland.ie

Transworld Ireland is part of the Penguin Random House group of companies
whose addresses can be found at global.penguinrandomhouse.com

Penguin
Random House
UK

First published in the UK and Ireland in 2015 by Transworld Ireland
an imprint of Transworld Publishers

A CIP catalogue record for this book
is available from the British Library.

ISBN 9781848272163

Typeset in 11.25/16pt Berling by Falcon Oast Graphic Art Ltd.
Printed and bound by Clays Ltd, Bungay, Suffolk.

Penguin Random House is committed to a sustainable
future for our business, our readers and our planet. This book
is made from Forest Stewardship Council® certified paper.

FSC
www.fsc.org

MIX
Paper from
responsible sources
FSC® C018179

1 3 5 7 9 10 8 6 4 2

PICTURE ACKNOWLEDGEMENTS

FOREWORD BY RORY McILROY

Growing up in Northern Ireland, Ulster Rugby was a big thing. I followed the team from around the age of eight, but the first game that really stands out was the 1999 Heineken Cup final. I was nine and counting down the days to my tenth birthday. It mattered little to me that it was four months away. That game was a big deal. My dad took me to Holywood Golf Club to watch it. I was out practising with mates but was constantly in and out of the clubhouse bar to check the score. The bar was packed and I remember the place erupting when the final whistle blew. Ulster had become the first ever Irish team to win a European Cup title.

Rugby became an even greater part of my life when I went to Sullivan Upper School in Holywood. A big rugby school, it was there that I became good friends with Darren Cave. I only started going along to Ulster games when Darren made his breakthrough to the senior squad. By that stage, 2007, I had turned professional.

Rugby was, and is, another sporting outlet outside of golf. Being on the road so much, I like to have that connection with home. Ulster Rugby allows me to do that. Wherever I am in the world, I will turn on my laptop and catch up on a game. If I have an early round, on Fridays, I will get back to my hotel room and try to watch a game.

Stephen Ferris had already made quite a name for himself by the time I got to see him live. It was 24 April 2009 and the season was coming to a close. I was enthralled to see how a guy so big and powerful could be so fast and cause so much trouble. He was such a danger. It was taking two and three Cardiff guys to drag him down. I got to meet him after the game and his persona was entirely different from this wrecking-ball character on the pitch. He was a friendly, gentle giant who would go out of his way for you.

Around that time, I was privileged enough to spend a bit of time with the Ulster lads – Stephen, Darren, Paddy Wallace, Niall O'Connor. A few of them were keen golfers but mostly it was a couple of great lads' nights out. Great fun. I got a lot out of it. Being a golfer is a very solitary pursuit. It is completely different from being in a team. They made me feel part of their group; their team. I followed Stephen's career closely after that, as it reached peak after peak.

When Stephen was on form, he was the best number 6 in the world. Only Jerome Kaino, the All Blacks blindside, could challenge him. Back in his heyday, with Ireland, he teamed up with Sean O'Brien as openside and Jamie Heaslip at Number 8. Even to this day, that is one of the best back rows in world rugby.

Many of his stand-out matches were in an Irish jersey. He was immense; so many game-changing contributions. Picking up Will Genia and charging him back down the pitch, during Ireland's 2011 World Cup win over Australia, was one of his career-defining moments. However, as any Irish fan will tell you, that was the norm for Stephen. He was a dominant figure in Six Nations matches and against the world's best – New Zealand and South Africa. It was a great time for Irish rugby. He was part of that Grand Slam team, in 2009, that proved to be a real catalyst of the success that was to come. Ireland has evolved into the top northern hemisphere team and one of the best in the world.

I always felt it was inevitable that someone so physical would end his career earlier than others. It is more likely that players like him – who make the big plays, land the huge hits – will suffer a physical toll. I would liken Stephen to a finely tuned Ferrari or a racehorse. They are likely to break down more but it is only because they perform so close to the edge and are pushing limits all the time.

I have caught him on TV a couple of times in the past year and feel he has the makings of a good pundit. He is very natural and tells the game as he sees it. He will be successful at whatever he puts his mind to. We have played a bit of golf together recently. Rugby players, I find, are so anterior – built-up, tight around the chest and shoulders – that it is hard for them to make a full shoulder swing. Stephen is no different, but what I will say is this: he has a very good five iron off the tee.

Looking back, there are so many fantastic moments from his rugby career – big plays and hits that I will never forget. But there is one overriding feeling that sums up the type of player he was. Whenever you saw him run out on to that pitch, whether it was in a white or green jersey, you were immediately filled with a greater confidence that the team would do well. Stephen Ferris is in the number 6 jersey – we're going to give it a real go.

CHAPTER 1

'CHOPPER!'

Seventeen months away from the game but I know the call. We are going to put up a high bomb. Johann calls a five-man line-out, Rob finds his jumper and we feed back.

Ruan lets rip and spirals one into the night sky.

My eyes light up, legs already pumping. Scarlets' Kristian Phillips is under it but he must catch a glimpse of me coming, full tilt. Shoulder lowered; almost on him.

Almost on him. He braces for impact.

Bang!

I hit the guy hard and keep leg-driving, leg-driving, leg-driving. Before I know it, I have dragged him back 15 yards. The boys come flying in behind me. The roof is coming off Ravenhill. The roar is a wave. Right in my eardrum and all around.

Somehow we do not get the bloody turnover but the impact feels unreal. To feel my shoulder searing. For ten seconds, my ankle, my feet, mean nothing. They are forgotten. Play spills on but, for a brief moment, it is just myself and Phillips lying on the ground, side by side.

'Welcome back, mate, that was a good hit.'
'Cheers. Ya alright, mate?'

Four hundred and ninety-seven days have passed since I wrecked my ankle on that pitch, under the weight of two Edinburgh players. One year, four months and twelve days since I was carried off to the sideline with my head raised to the heavens: 2 November 2012 until 14 March 2014.

Ulster have played forty-three times, Ireland sixteen. I have been under the surgeon's knife three times and spent countless hours, either by myself or with Jonny Davis (JD) by my side, in rehabilitation. Inching closer only to slide back.

The Lions tour to Australia came and went. When I missed the 2013 Six Nations, I knew I would not be travelling. At that stage, it was far from my thoughts. I was struggling to get a contract extension. I had few chips left to bargain with, save my reputation, work ethic and vows from coaches and doctors that I could return as the same player.

Initially, Ulster Rugby projected my comeback at six weeks. The time frame doubled, then tripled. Six weeks became six months. Eventually, I was excluded from the squad updates. No point in depressing everyone.

That changed yesterday – Thursday, 13 March – when my name appeared in the match-day squad to face Scarlets. Still, most people will only believe I am back when they witness it for themselves.

On match-day, many of the Belfast-based players would be out in town for a bite to eat or a coffee. The very odd time, if I fancy a wee trip into Belfast or I am up early and need to get out of the house, I would do likewise. Mostly, I try to sleep as much as possible. I usually get up around ten a.m., have breakfast, sleep again, get up, have a sandwich for lunch, and take the dog for a dander – to get the blood flowing in the legs. I have often been caught cold that way – running out on the pitch, getting a shock to the system. Legs have not woken up yet. I go for a walk before the game. That always helps me. It has become a distracting habit throughout my career.

Just about every player will have a pre-match ritual, one way or the other. Mine is to bring Bailey Frank Ferris for a walk. BFF. He is one of the few that understood my frustration during the last couple of years with this injury, because he was the one who sat beside me every frigging day, wagging his tail while I tried to get some positive thoughts in the head.

The last four weeks have finally brought progress and, with the help of JD and Kevin Geary, Ulster's strength and conditioning coaches, I underwent a pre-season of sorts.

The latest in my long list of targets is our Heineken Cup quarter-final against Saracens. The lads have won all six of their pool matches to top their group and the European seedings. We have a rematch with the same Saracens team that knocked us out in 2013, only this time the game will take place at a sold-out Ravenhill. Win that and we have a semi-final at the Aviva Stadium in Dublin.

The match is three weeks away so my sights are set.

Mark Anscombe is my fifth head coach at Ulster. Everyone calls him Cowboy.

During my recovery, he always came to me on a Monday and asked, 'How are you feeling? How's that ankle feeling? You'll be good to go this week?'

'Hopefully, Mark. Hopefully.'

Then the medical staff would say, 'Stevie's not training today.'

Mark would then turn to me. 'Are you not training today?'

'Nah, I'm not, Mark. I don't think so.'

Even though the medical staff had told him, he was hoping I would say yes, so he could get me out for a couple of sessions. That happened a lot. Of course that is what your head coach wants – their best players playing as much as they can. I missed too many training sessions. Mark has not seen half the stuff I am capable of doing.

I love training. I hate it when it's pissing down and you have to go through defence sessions. 'Why is somebody trying to teach me how to tackle when I've been tackling since I was eleven years of age? I know how to tackle.' Otherwise, I cannot get enough.

Everybody has training drills or exercises they hate doing. Tackling or rucking drills, especially when the army net is out and you have to run at a crouch, do my head in. I enjoy the line-outs, mauls and scrums. There is always good banter between the lads and genuine friendship between the forwards; fighting for one another during every game. There is usually a bit of niggle in training though, a few cheap shots and big hits going in. Some of the younger lads try to get the upper hand on the older ones.

I have always been a chirper. I run around with a smile on my face and give a lot of talk when play comes my way. A younger guy sees me loping about and decides to stick a shoulder in on a tackle. It hurts but it is enjoyable. Great to be back out there. That is not to say I am just running around, grinning away. If someone gets out of hand with a cheap shot, I am liable to let rip.

'Oi, dickhead. Do that again, I'll rip your head off.'

'Do what? Do what?'

'I'll rip your head off and stick it up your arse, see, if you do that again.'

'OK, OK.'

The niggle, I have no issue with. Especially when you are attacking defences. You take the ball into contact and next thing, smack. You get a shoulder into your chest. 'Ohh, what are you up to?' It is the same the other way and I can dish it out too. If someone runs into me, hard, hit them back harder. A 'hold on a minute' hit.

I am such good friends with the lads – Chris Henry, Robbie Diack, Iain Henderson, Roger Wilson, Nick Williams. Nick is a bollocks for it. He tries to level you with a hit then breaks into a smile, jogging off. 'Hee hee, hee hee. Don't hit me back, don't hit me back.'

Working closely with JD and Kev, I now weigh in at 109 kilos – five down from the guy that was injured back in 2012. The aim is to keep me as light on my feet as possible while maintaining that explosive power.

The speed drills are a rush. I am setting personal bests again; pushing beyond.

Three weeks before my comeback game, I set a club record for fastest speed.

Usain Bolt runs 13 metres per second. Even for a world-champion sprinter, that is just crazy. In terms of any professional rugby player, I do not think 10 metres per second has ever been done in an international game. It may have been done in training but I would not say any back-rower has done it.

Myself and JD are in training, doing some progressive build-ups into some sprints. Chris Hagan, Ulster's sports scientist, is not there so we have the GPS units on ourselves. JD is a former Northern Ireland 60-metre sprint champion and he is not holding back. He takes the first couple but I turn it around. Once I get to my top speed and start to slow down, I am limping to get stopped. My ankle is screaming. I push on through. It is great to be competing again.

We think we have clocked some good times. Driving back round to Ravenhill, I say, 'Here, mate, I felt good out there. I think I have some great times.' He is not having it, mainly because I was beating him – just edging him – in the sprints. It is not much. Half a metre per second would probably work out as an inch or two in the distances we were running.

'Mate, I feel like I was getting some speed up.'

'Yeah,' he replies, quietly. 'I'd say 9.3, 9.2. Maybe not even 9.0 on the button.'

I go into the changing rooms and start icing my leg; trying to prevent any swelling.

JD takes the data chip out of my jersey and hands it to Chris.

I am in the shower when Chris bursts into the changing room, shouting, 'Mate, ten metres per second!'

'I knew it. I told JD.'

I dry off, quick as I can, and find JD. 'What did you get?'

'9.48.'

'Ah, unlucky, mate. Unlucky.'

None of the lads have ever run that speed, not even Andrew Trimble or Tommy Bowe. So for me to run that, it fills me with confidence. I am going to get there. I have it in my head. Because it was 9.98, it gets rounded up to 10 metres per second. I want to go back and get it over, to 10.01, or better.

A couple of days later and Mark comes over for another chat.

He has been talking with the medical staff and the consensus is to give it a rattle.

'Stevie, let's give it a go.'

Mark is really pleased I am able to get on the bench for him. He has seen me play two halves of rugby before, more or less, but does not know how good a player I, potentially, am for him. With the season nearing its climax, he needs all the able bodies he can get.

I am grateful to have been spared media interviews. The idea is to leave me be until I get back on the pitch. Hopefully, after a successful comeback, I can then chat away all day. For once it will feel good to talk about my injury and the long, long road to return because I will have reached the other side.

The drive to Ravenhill usually takes about half an hour. Car park space number 28 was always mine. I had parked there on the night I injured my ankle. I have owned cars of all shapes and engine sizes over the years, but 28 was always my space. It's gone now, though. Ravenhill is nearing the end of a major redevelopment. I park in Aquinas Grammar School. I have had more time than most to observe the ongoing changes to the stadium but tonight, on match night, the difference sinks in. I walk in, then around, the changing rooms. The new rooms will open soon and are oval-shaped, like those used by Manchester United at Old Trafford. Brand-new ice baths.

I take a deep breath. I am excited about playing again.

Gareth Robinson (GG), our physio, arrives and sees to me. It takes five or six minutes to get my knee done – a precaution ever since injuring it in 2007. I already have my feet done. I run the padding along, covering just about every part of my feet, then strap it on. If you strap it on too tight, your feet cramp, very quickly. It is a nightmare. I always strap my feet to get rid of any nerve pain I might have.

It is time to really test this ankle, under duress, in a match setting, and see how it holds out. Or not. It might not all fall into place tonight but twenty, thirty minutes should give us an idea.

Both feet padded up, my right ankle lightly strapped, my left knee strapped unbelievably tight, my left ankle well strapped, my left thumb strapped. I look at myself in the mirror. I am like Paddy Johns from the old days. He used to go out strapped from head to toe. I still need my line-out strapping.

'Flipping hell, I'm just strapped together here.'

The nerves arrive as the game draws near.

I have played in front of 82,000 people at Croke Park and would not have felt a flicker. The new stand at Ravenhill is not fully complete so they are expecting 14,000 in. My legs are twitching, non-stop.

Cowboy approaches. 'Stevie, just go out and do what you do.'

'No worries, Mark.'

I am an experienced enough player not to go out and do something silly or get myself a yellow card or something like that. All I want to do is get my way into the match, make whatever impact I can and get a bit of game time under my belt.

Ten minutes into the second half and Mark tells me to warm up. The ankle is playing on my mind as I am running on my toes. I do not want to close the front of the ankle joint up by keeping my foot flat as that causes it to bite, snapping at the tendon. I start hitting the few bags Kev is holding when the nerves wash back. My feet are killing me. I have been out of the game for so long.

'What's going to happen here?'

I have to have a word with myself. 'Right, just get on the pitch, do what you normally do and see what happens.'

We are winning the game pretty comfortably, 21–10, so there is not much pressure on. Kev pats me on the back. 'Right, big man, you're up. Best of luck.'

'Right, OK.'

I jog back up to the touchline and the crowd starts chanting my name. People often ask, 'Can you hear the crowd singing? Can you hear what they say?' Tonight, I can. Every word. It embarrasses me, slightly.

'One F in Ferris, there's only one F in Ferris . . .'

'Oh shit. Let me be the guy they remember.'

I take off my woolly hat as I wait for play to stop. The last thing I do before I go into a game is put on my head-gear. I scan the plays; try to get myself up to the speed of the game. I have another few words with myself. My feet are sore but I am feeling good.

A break in play. I pull my head-gear on, tighten the straps. A couple of slaps on the head. Here we go.

I walk on to the pitch, then break into a slow jog.

Big Nick is coming off. 'Best of luck, chief. Welcome back.'

'Thanks.'

The 'Chopper' play, moments after I come on, involves Johann Muller's call, Rob Herring's throw, Johann's catch and Ruan Pienaar's garryowen. The three lads do their job perfectly just to set me up with a target. It is that teamwork and brotherhood – working for one another – that I have missed most.

The reception I receive at the final whistle is astounding. Our fans stay on to applaud us off, many still chanting my name.

I take longer than I usually would to leave the pitch. Hands criss-crossed on my head, I draw some deep breaths and take in the sights and sounds. The Scarlets players form a guard of honour and my number 20 jersey is almost slapped off my back. I walk up the tunnel but am encouraged back out. An encore.

Back in the dressing room, and Cowboy grabs hold of me.

'Jeez, it is good to have you back, Stevie.'

It is strange because my ankle still feels like shite. Even when the final whistle blew, I felt I was limping off. People were probably watching, saying, 'He's not too bad.'

The pain is agonizing.

'It's killing me, it's killing me.'

Having beaten Scarlets 26–13, our next fixture is away to Edinburgh, the same side I had injured myself against in 2012. I miss training on Monday, do a little bit Tuesday, catch a few line-outs on the Wednesday, and take part in the captain's run – a light work-out and a team-talk huddle in the stadium – the following day. This time around, I am named to start. The Saracens game is a fortnight away and I feel ready to get involved from the off.

It is sopping wet; a night for the forwards. Before the half-hour mark, with the scores level at 3–3 and not going anywhere fast, I take a heavy blow. I try to hit their big second row, Grant Gilchrist, high but underestimate how strong he is. I rise to smash him, just as he ducks his shoulder down. The bony point of his shoulder catches me in the temple.

I hit the deck.

Somehow – I am no longer sure of anything – I get up and run back into the defensive line. I finish out the half, scrum, lift at line-outs, make some defensive hits, but not once do I touch the ball. I am running around in a daydream. I do not go looking for the ball; do not want it. When we get our hands on the ball and are passing it out, I am calling the other guys on. 'Hit, Darren. Hit, Iain.'

I know something is not right.

We go in at the break 6–3 up. In the dressing room, Michael Webb, our medical director, comes over to see if everything is OK. Straight out, I tell him about the bang to the head. 'I have been running around for a while and feel OK. I don't feel sick or anything.'

Michael asks who we are playing.

'Edinburgh.'

'What is the score?'

'Uh, 3 . . . 6–3.'

'Who did we play last week?'

Nothing.

'Do you know who we played, Stevie?'

I am trying to process the information but my mind is a jumble. I am thinking, 'Pick a team, any team.'

It is no good. Michael is looking at me; a frown of concern.

I meet his eyes and start laughing. 'Michael, I can't remember.'

Seventeen months out of the game and all I was ever focused on was that first match. I lived for it. Dreamt about it. It was my obsession; my fuel. Now I am sitting here in Murrayfield, against Edinburgh, again, and I cannot remember one of the biggest games of my life. The lads head back out on to the pitch but I will not be going with them. For the first time in my professional rugby career, and after injuries to just about every part of my body, I am concussed.

And then it comes to me.

'We played Scarlets last week.'

CHAPTER 2

Every time I get off the phone with Declan Kidney, I feel no closer to a decision than when our conversation started. Our call on Sunday, 28 October 2012 is no different. Deccie has a marvellously frustrating way of empowering his players.

I have only featured in three of Ulster's games so far this season. I came off the bench in a great away win over Ospreys, from whom we had just re-signed Tommy Bowe. I started the following week, at Ravenhill, as we showed our title aspirations by narrowly beating Munster, 20–19.

The high of that victory was cast aside twenty-four hours later. The club, community and entire country reeled at the tragic passing of the talented, selfless Nevin Spence. Our team-mate. Only twenty-two and destined for a super career with Ulster and Ireland, Nevin died in a horrendous farming accident while trying to rescue his father and brother from a slurry tank.

David Humphreys, Ulster's director of rugby and a past legend on the playing field, admirably kept the lads together and ensured we had all the support we needed. It took weeks for Nevin's loss to well and truly hit home.

He was a lad with a bubbly, infectious demeanour, and

carry-on; we teetered on the brink as we wondered what the next step forward would be. Rory Best's words, at a memorial service at Ravenhill, on a day that was sheet-metal grey, gave us the strength and courage to go on. Nevin was born and raised in Ulster. It was his ambition to play for Ulster and his dream to win trophies with Ulster. His passing had left us punctured but we vowed, as a squad and in moments of private reflection, to fulfil his dreams.

Somehow, the team kept a match commitment in Cardiff only thirteen days later. Playing with the initials N.S. stitched on to our kit, the guys beat Cardiff Blues 48–19. I missed that match due to a back spasm issue, but I returned for another home game as we comfortably saw Connacht off. The spasms flared up again and I missed our Heineken Cup successes over Castres and Glasgow, and a league tie with Newport Gwent Dragons.

We only have one more match – Edinburgh at home – before Ireland's November internationals. A calf injury caused me to miss our three-Test tour to New Zealand in the summer and I am desperate to get back in the green jersey and make up for lost matches.

The Sunday after the Dragons game, I get a call from Deccie. He starts with a recap, to get us both up to speed.

'Stevie, you have been out injured, with your back, in the last few weeks. The Argentina game is coming up. You don't have to play as you are probably going to be in the twenty-three next week. It's your call, whether you want to play or not.'

'Look, Deccie, I haven't played in five or six weeks. I need some game time.'

'Well, it's your call.'

Not for the first time, he leaves it up to me. For once I would love to hear him say 'No, don't play' or 'Yes, I need you to play.' Either would be a relief. Other coaches I have dealt with in my career are black and white, but not Deccie. He often leaves big calls up to the players. 'It's your choice.' This way of dealing with me, with other players, always grates. It should be his choice. He is the Ireland head coach. If he wants me to play, let me play. If not, just tell me.

This has happened a few times during my career with Ireland.

'Do you really need to play this weekend?' he would ask.

'I feel like I do, Deccie.'

'Right, that's your call. I'm not sure if you really need to, but it's up to you.'

I want to tell him to stop beating around the bush but hold my tongue. However, I stand my ground. I need the game time, I tell him, especially if I am going to be starting two of these three Tests. The Argentina game is crucial in terms of us securing straight passage to the 2015 World Cup.

Paul O'Connell would feel the exact same way if he had a Test window coming up and was short of minutes, of match fitness. He would want to play.

'It's up to you.'

'Right so, Deccie. See you next week.'

I feel really good going into the Edinburgh game. My back has settled down. It is a slick, wet night but we are determined to spread the ball wide and make some plays.

Early on, I jump to catch a ball and, on landing, roll my ankle slightly.

'Flipping hell, this is a bit sore.'

I stay down for treatment but thirty seconds later am back on my feet and feeling fine. I hit some rucks and make a few decent tackles. We are 24–17 up after a frantic first half and, just about, on our way to our seventh win in a row.

A few minutes into the second half and the ball comes my way. Jared Payne is on my outside and is calling for the ball. I should pass the thing but I opt for contact – see if I can bust the line.

Allan Jacobsen, their replacement loose-head, tackles me around the neck but the hit from the hooker, Andy Titterrell, does the damage. He hits me around my knees and my ankle gives in on me. He drives me one way and the ankle pops the other way.

Immediately I know I am in trouble and I let out this massive yelp. A couple of the boys are nearby.

'Holy shit, what is going on here with Stevie?'

The referee stops the game immediately and, within ten seconds, I know something is badly wrong. I am carried off the pitch by Davy Irwin, our doctor, and GG.

First thing, David Humphreys is in to me. 'Are you alright, are you alright?'

'I've absolutely wrecked myself. I don't know what I've done.'

Already my ankle is starting to swell; getting bigger and bigger. Before I know it, it is in a protective boot and I am leaving Ravenhill.

The situation looks no better, or the ankle less swollen, the morning after.

The IRFU send up a Game Ready set, which is basically an ice machine, because I am supposed to be going into Ireland camp on the Monday. They want me to try and get the ankle settled down. Ulster do not have a Game Ready – it is on the wish list – so the union pays out €200 or so to get it up to Belfast, from Dublin, in a taxi. It is a reminder of how much I am needed for the upcoming Tests but, preoccupied by my ballooning ankle, the gesture goes unnoticed.

Two days and nights with my leg in the ice machine but the swelling does not go down. It never goes down.

I head down to the Sports Surgery Clinic in Santry, Dublin, as we suspect it may be torn ankle ligaments and a scan may be required. The swelling around the ankle makes it tough for the medics to determine what is wrong. I stay in Ireland camp, out at Carton House, in Kildare, and, with more icing treatments and gentle physio, try to calm the ankle down. Nothing seems to be working.

About ten days later I get another scan and it shows that I have torn my deltoid ligament. It is a significant injury and the medics are talking about six weeks out. That is the autumn internationals out the window. And yet, as soon as I go back to rehab or put weight on the ankle, I get this popping sensation at the back of the joint. It is killing me. The swelling remains. I cannot take my dog for a walk 500 yards up the road without my ankle blowing up.

I am confined to the house. The only times I venture out, risking aggravating the ankle, are for physio sessions at Ulster or medical appointments. Weeks drag into months. Heineken Cup games come and go. I undergo an operation in Dublin but, after two weeks encased in a protective boot, it does nothing to ease the pain or swelling in my ankle. There are low moments, times when it feels like I am getting nowhere. Up against a brick wall, all the time. It is soul-destroying.

The darkest days arrive when Ireland are preparing for the 2013 Six Nations championship and all I am doing is going in, getting some physio, maybe doing some balance work in the morning. All the while, my ankle is throbbing. It is absolutely killing me.

This is not a 'rugby player gets injured' story, however. The support I get from family, friends, supporters, team-mates and Laura, my girlfriend, is insane. It makes me believe I am not fighting to get back just for myself. I have a purpose. Through my rugby, my contribution to the team, I mean something to people. The realization gives me great strength.

During this time, I finally have a chance to take stock and catch up on my career. By rights, and in so many ways, I should not be here. I am unbelievably lucky.

I leaf through the stacks of scrapbooks lovingly put together by my nan, Florence, and recall the quiet, awkward teenager that almost chose to stick with the £200-a-week job in the gelatine factory rather than pit himself against the best schoolboy rugby players Ulster had to offer.

My mum always says I was born with stars in my eyes. At my lowest ebb, I finally begin to understand what she means.

CHAPTER 3

I never knew my older brother, Andrew, but he is still cherished by my family and he played such a huge role in my life.

In 1979, my mum, Linda, married my dad, Rab. She was nineteen and Dad was a year older. Mum was a nurse at the Royal Victoria Hospital in Belfast while Dad was employed in his family's roofing business. Andrew was their first child and he was followed, a little over two years later, by my other brother, Dave. The four of them lived in Lisburn.

Andrew was killed in 1984, in a tragic accident. He was just four years old. Earlier that day, Andrew had picked flowers for Mum and they had taken a trip into town. When they arrived back, near home, Mum was pushing Dave in his buggy. Andrew was a little ahead of them and went on to the road. Mum ran after him but he was clipped by a passing car. He died within a few hours.

My parents were beyond devastated and they struggled to come to terms with his death. As part of the healing process, they decided to try for another baby. I was born on 2 August 1985, to the sheer delight of my parents. We became four again but Andrew was never ever forgotten.

When I arrived on the scene, my mother changed careers and became a classroom assistant. The pay was not as good but she worked fewer hours and was able to look after Dave and me. My dad began to work as a postman for Royal Mail.

As the years passed, I would often ask myself if I would even be here had it not been for Andrew's tragic loss. What I knew for sure, however, was that both my parents were devoted to myself and Dave. We never wanted for anything and, even though they both worked long, hard hours, they always made time for us.

In years to come, my mum would often say to me, 'You are a bloody good rugby player. You are blessed; you're blessed. Somebody has always been looking down on you.'

'Yeah? Then how come I'm bloody injured so much?'

We lived in Lisburn for another six months but my parents wanted to get out of there. It brought up too many painful memories. We moved to Maghaberry. My mum and dad lived at the bottom of the hill, close to the primary school, and life started afresh.

As for the flowers that Andrew picked that morning, my mum and dad still have them in a Bible in the house. They are not religious at all. And yet the Bible, with those flowers, is something that is very close to them.

Mum is walking ahead, chatting with a couple of her friends from the housing development. Our house sits near the bottom of a hill that, to a four-year-old, is the steepest drop he has ever seen.

It is right in the middle of summer so our development, Edenview, is full of children. Laughter and screaming everywhere. There is a good audience for my latest stunt but, with my brother not around, I only want to impress my mum.

My red bike is the greatest possession I have in the world. Dave and I have our little diggers that we use on the muck hills to the side of our house but, lately, I have been all about the red bike.

Once I mastered the pedals, and staying upright, the hill became my next challenge. I have been up and down it more times than I can count, yet each time I reach the bottom I think, 'How can I do that faster?' I have shot down without brakes, tucked low, leaning forward, after running starts and with my hands off the handlebars. Today, I have a new trick.

Mum turns to check on me and her face drops. There I am, smiling away at the top of the hill.

'Stevie!' she calls. 'Stevie!'

Here I come.

After a couple of houses fly by, I start to really pick up speed. I can hear my mum's cries increase as I prop both my legs over the handlebars.

'Stevie!'

My arms shoot up in the air and, seconds later, I flash by Mum, her friends, the younger kids. A bend is coming up.

'STEVIE!'

I somehow scramble back into the seat and grip the brakes. The back wheel sprays pebbles but I stop before clattering into a wall. I spin the bike and, careful to sweep wide past my mum, I cycle back up the hill.

She glares at me but I swear, as I pedal by, I can make out the hint of a smile.

Blessed, so you are.

As soon as I am able to walk, I am out the door, as quick as possible, playing in the muck, in the fields.

Mum comes out, shouting, 'Where are you? Where are you?'

There I am, popping my head up from behind a mud pile, playing with a couple of friends next door.

Mum never lets me out of her sight. She always knows where I am but I am always outside. Always. Rain, hail or snow; always outside.

Some people say we live out in the sticks. Maghaberry is all I know so I cannot say any different. There are four housing developments and Finlay's, a gelatine factory, in the middle of the town. There are a couple of shops, the Maghaberry Arms pub, and the prison is out the road.

The Troubles are words Dave and I hear about on the news but, mostly, it does not affect our lives. We live through them without ever really being fully aware of their true scale and wider impact.

Maghaberry is quite a Loyalist area. The majority of the people living here are Protestant. Years ago, it would have been where the prison officers lived because it was so close to the prison. Each year, on 12 July, the Union Jack and Ulster flags go up. There is always a bonfire, every year. Neither of my parents have much to do with religion and I have taken their lead. I am not a Loyalist or a Unionist but I love getting involved in scavenging for, and building, the bonfire. The older boys do most of the work but never refuse the offer of free help, or firewood.

My school, Maghaberry Primary, is up the hill and right across the road from our development. The school itself is small – it has about 150 pupils – but the grounds are massive. We go over there to play golf, tennis, American football. Whatever we want to do, we have the space to do it. Football is the main sport of choice. The school is heated by gas and there is this massive wooden box, to the side, that covers the boiler. Six metres wide, over two metres high. We use that as our goal.

There are potato fields right behind the school grounds and there are trees, at the far end, that are perfect for putting up swings. The field is protected by big gorse bushes but there are a couple of pockets and holes you can fit through. On the rare days we are bored with playing sports or cycling our bikes, we climb a tree, jump into the fields and have potato fights. If you get caught with a potato on the side of the head, it is bloody sore.

If one of the guys can get hold of matches from the shops, another has to run home to steal a pot. We start a wee fire, peel potatoes, put water in the pot and boil them. Here we are, aged eight, sitting in the middle of a field with a fire going, boiling potatoes.

'How brilliant are we?'

'This is unbelievable.'

My dad works night shifts and has done for as long as I have known him. He usually gets home from work around five a.m. As my school is close enough to home, I am allowed to walk over for lunch. When I get in, I wake Dad with two rounds of toast, marmalade and a cup of tea. We have a catch-up before I nip back over for a game of football with the lads. The games continue when school finishes up. Some days it is rounders or running. At certain times of the year, all on the school grounds, it is tennis or cricket.

June and July mean Wimbledon so the tennis rackets come out. We bring across two of Mum's old PVC patio chairs and tie a net up. Once that is done, we go into the potato field, get a couple of pieces of flint and draw our lines out. This is tournament tennis, of course, so we take our time and pace out the steps to get all the right measurements.

Although he is three years older than me, myself and Dave have a fierce rivalry. He has a slight height advantage but with every passing week I am catching him. A couple of my closest, life-long friends, Stephen Williamson and Darren Gamble, are involved. My group of friends would be about ten boys and two or three girls that hang around. Many of them take part but the most brutal, bitter matches are often fought out between myself and Dave.

By the time Wimbledon usually wraps up, we are right into the Ashes and we hunt down any cricket balls and pads we can find. I steal a petrol lawnmower from Samantha Pearson's parents' shed and wheel it, fast as I can, up the road and get it across, into the school. We mow our own cricket strip and, while we are at it, a couple of putting greens. I get the lawn-mower back and the shed key slipped into the kitchen without getting caught.

Stephen Williamson, who only lives around the corner from me, is mad into his cricket and has all the big pads, the shoulder-guards, helmets and a 200 lb bat. Trying to lift that bat is tough enough but we get the swing of it and think we are Brian Lara and Darren Gough.

If there is a World Cup on, the footballs are never far away. When the Olympics come round, we get out the stopwatch, run 100 metres and time each other. See how far we can launch potatoes like the Eastern European shot-put throwers.

Every day brings a different adventure. I have a big brother who plays with me, looks out for me, and a great group of friends. Our whole world is within a space that surely cannot measure a

kilometre from one tip to the other. If Mum needs me for anything, all she need do is walk 100 metres up the hill and find me
playing one sport or the next on the school grounds.

My dad works every hour going just to get food on the table.
Although Mum is employed as a classroom assistant at
Ballycarrickmaddy Primary School, she takes shifts as a cleaner
there too, to get extra money in.

Some afternoons, if Mum is working late at the school, Dave
and I head over. The school is like ours and has big grounds. We
go in and lift the cones and beanbags. There is a small football
pitch so we play there, play hide and seek or chase around the
school itself and jump up on top of the prefabricated classrooms,
which we call mobiles. Mum is buffing the floors and we are
running about for a couple of hours.

My proudest footballing moment arrives at Maghaberry
Primary as we beat Ballycarrickmaddy 9–0. I score four goals and
set up another two. Mum is at the game but is not upset at all
that I helped beat her school. I play up front for the school team
but, because of my pace, I am occasionally stuck out wide. It is
rare that I stay on my wing for long. I prefer scoring goals and
taking the glory, so I drift in.

As the weather is often rubbish, our school enters indoor football competitions. We get to the final a couple of times but run
into a school called Tonagh. The school is in Lisburn and tends to
get the best footballing talent. We do well on the way to the final
but Tonagh, both times, have our number.

On the days, or evenings, both my parents are about, they bring
us over to the sports-day running track, out the back of the school.
All four of us race around the track or run relays. Mum attended

an athletics club when she was my age, growing up in Ballymena, and once won a district championship. She must smoke a packet of cigarettes a day and has done for as long as I have been around. My dad says longer.

That did not stop her from chasing me around the front room one day when she arrived back from work and spotted me smoking in there. I tried to flick the cigarette into the fireplace but missed. From that day on, I did my smoking out the back of the school.

Dad is tall, around 6 foot, and wiry. Still, Mum is the main threat. The big race is never the one around the track. It is the one back home, down the hill. On the track, Mum always wins. Sometimes, though, if I jump off to a good start, I am the first one home. When I reach the front door and turn around, beaming, I find my parents just as pleased.

After my eleven-plus at Maghaberry Primary School, my parents have to decide where I will go to secondary school. My mind is made up. Dave has been at Friends' Grammar School, in Lisburn, for the past three years. It takes a little convincing but I get to follow my older brother. It is about six times the size of my old school, holding around a thousand pupils, and on my first day, I am in a daze. I am convinced I have counted ten thousand, at least.

My results in the first couple of years are great. The school has a broad range of sporting pursuits and I pitch myself into athletics, swimming and football. I have Manchester United on the brain and my sporting dreams centre around, one day, playing at Old Trafford.

The first person to throw me a rugby ball, at Friends', is Barney

McGonigle. He is the head of PE and, although he praises me for picking the sport up so quickly, shares my passion for a wide range of sports. He never pushes one sport or another on me but is quick to scold if he catches me skiving out in the corridors.

Elizabeth Dickson is the principal and she supports me when she sees how much I am getting out of sport. My studies are dipping a little but she is encouraged to see me taking an interest in sporting pursuits. A few of my teachers – Misters Gamble, McElheney and Thompson – are also supportive but Barney is key to my progression. He is the point of contact to go to about any sport, yet he knows everything there is to know about rugby. I am not good with remembering names but Barncy knows everybody, first and second names.

'Stephen Ferris, what are you doing over there?'

'I'm a first year,' I think, 'and this guy knows who I am?'

By the time I've reached thirteen I have shot past Dave, who's sixteen. I have a couple of inches on him but, in my eyes, he remains public enemy number one. Oddly, as only brothers may know, he is also my mate and a guy I share so many great times with.

'I'm stronger than you,' I often jeer.

'I'll put you in your place,' yells Dave as he leaps off the couch or away from his homework.

That competitiveness comes out if we are playing darts, pool or soccer.

'I'm going to beat you.'

'No, I'm going to beat you.'

Brotherly sparring is a big part of our relationship. We battle on every front. That includes boxing the head off each other, whenever and wherever. Most of the time it is us rolling around on the couch or swinging away out the back garden. We have bouts in our tiny kitchen. We gather up every pair of socks we can find and bundle them into football socks that we have pulled down to our elbows. The padded socks are taped up and we have home-made boxing gloves. Two or three rounds.

Ding ding.

At Christmas, when our parents are not around, we take all the baubles off the tree and play football in the front room. Dave's goal is the coffee table, mine between the two settees. Mum comes home that evening and finds the tree looking extremely bare. One look into the bin and she discovers about ten broken or flattened baubles. There is no point asking who the bright spark was, as she knows we will never tell. Thick as thieves.

Sometimes, however, the smallest incident, or perceived slight, could spark a full-on slabbering match.

One Halloween, Dave breaks my nose. We are hanging out together and I give him change to buy me some Bengal matches – the sparkler fireworks that glow green and purple. He comes out, minutes later, sipping from a Sprite bottle.

'Did you get me those?'

'Na, na, I didn't.'

'Why did you not get them, you dick?'

'Get lost you arsehole and don't call me a dick.'

'You dick.'

Whack. He hits me with the end of the Sprite bottle. My nose is spread all over my face. Blood everywhere, I stumble home. Luckily, Mum is there so off to the hospital we go. Forty-five minutes later I am back home with a bag of ice on my nose, plotting revenge.

I know it sounds pretty brutal, as if we are knocking the pan out of each other, but at the same time we are so close. If anyone touches me, Dave would go after them. The same goes for me. My dad has six brothers so, when we are not knocking each other out, he is understanding. Mum goes nuts but knows there is little point in keeping us apart. We are best friends.

We learn how to drive together, and it is far from my parents' eyes – or approval, for that matter – if we ever get caught. Our friend Crawford Beckett lives at a place called 'The Bullring' by our gang. It is a car track around a field, so small and tight that you hardly get out of first gear. Every summer, the first thought on our minds, once school is done, is 'Right, where are we getting a field car?'

We ring around scrapyards and try to bargain them down. One summer, Crawford's uncle gives us a silver Vauxhall Nova but, scooting around at such high revs, we run it into the ground pretty quickly. No more cars from the uncle.

We manage to scrape together £30 to get a clapped-out Renault 205. Burgundy colour with masking-tape viper stripes up the bonnet and roof. We find a farmer's field, which has been left fallow for a couple of years, up near the prison.

That works a treat for a couple of days until the farmer arrives in a jeep to clear us off. We clamber over hedges and leave the Renault behind. The farmer moves it off to an abandoned shed in a back yard. We give it a day or two and set off on a rescue mission. No one is about the yard. It is all concrete so we figure we can take a couple of laps around and get the car into second gear. Dave and Darren Gamble have goes, then it is my turn. Dave hops in the passenger seat. No time for buckling up. Foot down, revved up, off we go. The car already has two flat tyres but I feel I am doing 100 miles an hour, burning and skidding through slurry and cow shite.

We come around a bend and, when we hit a straight, I press the accelerator. An old wall is jutting out. It looks half finished – the breeze blocks graduated up, one, two, three. Up to about 6 feet high. We start veering towards the wall and the flat tyres are helping none.

'Watch the wall.'

'We're not going to hit it.'

'Watch the wall!'

The front tyre clips the wall and up we go, like a stunt car from a James Bond movie. We are going no more than 15 miles an hour but it feels like 115.

The car lands on its roof and both the front and back windscreens blow out. Manners be damned: I push Dave out of the way and scramble for the back window. He is close behind. All I can think of are the countless cop movies I have watched, where the fuel leaks out and the car blows. Dave must be thinking the same, as I can hear him panting and heaving right behind me. We must do 100 metres in ten seconds flat, fully expecting an explosion to take us, the car and the farm with it.

Seconds pass, then minutes. We realize the car will not be bursting into flames. We try lifting it, so we can go again. Once that fails we talk about torching it, but opt to get out of there as quick as we can, through the back fields.

We hear, a couple of days later, that the car has been dumped in a ditch on the farm. No police investigations or dusting for fingerprints. Bigger fish to fry, it seems.

*

Every Saturday morning, Mum drops me off for school rugby. She drives off to do her shopping in Sainsbury's or Tesco down in Lisburn town. Once that is done, she comes back and watches the last twenty or thirty minutes of my game. I get changed and we go for a burger and chips at Salt-Seller. I look forward to this time together almost as much as our training sessions and matches.

As weekend rugby is such a constant, and with both my parents working so much, I rarely get in to Belfast, and Ravenhill, to watch Ulster. Before I turned thirteen I had no interest in rugby, let alone an understanding or enjoyment of it. Now that I am playing at school, I get in, either with mates from Friends' or with the youth club.

Most of Ulster's games are on a Friday evening. Sitting in the stands, watching someone like David Humphreys or Derek Topping, I am in my tracksuit, freezing away in the upper corner and taking in the atmosphere.

A narrow win under the lights against Newport Gwent Dragons stands out. There must be about 5,000 in the ground, half full, and the Welsh side are putting up a fight. David Humphreys, the Ulster out-half, is brilliant and almost single-handedly wins the game.

December 1998, and I am watching Ulster's Heineken Cup semi-final against Stade Français in my friend Robert Humpherson's house, eating packets of crisps. Humphreys scores a stunning try after a sprint up the wing. Simon Mason is nailing penalty kicks from the halfway line. The pitch is in a state, so for Mason to make those kicks is even more impressive. There is a real sense of excitement about the team. No one from Ireland has won the Heineken Cup yet.

Ulster are massive underdogs for the final against Colomiers at Lansdowne Road on 30 January 1999. No one expects them to win. If you had backed them from the start, you would have got some amazing odds. But they have picked up some great results, built momentum and – apart from Mark McCall having to retire – kept their squad relatively fit.

Before the match kicks off, the Ulster players bulldoze through the French lads as they are warming up. They get away with it. Colomiers back down with a whimper.

From that moment on, they know they have the game won.

By the time I get to third year, Friends' have a decent rugby team. In an act of stunning democracy, we get to pick our own kit for the coming season. Drunk on power, we choose a yellow number that is absolutely horrendous. At Medallions (Ulster's Schools Rugby competition), we advance to the quarter-finals of the Shield and meet Sullivan Upper School at home.

I start the match at Number 8, the position I have been in since first year. I have my first run-in with touch judges and dodgy decisions. I score a try in the first half and am convinced I have scored a second. The touch judge, who happens to be running the Sullivan side of the line, claims my boot is in touch.

'No way.'

Barney McGonigle is furious on the far touchline but there is nothing we can do. We regroup and, with a couple of minutes to go, get over in the corner for another try. We are now a single point back but our out-half, Nicky Gregg, has a conversion coming up.

The posts are not the full, regulation height but it is clear to us that Nicky has got the conversion. We start to celebrate but one of the touch judges, under the posts, is not lifting his flag. There is a bit of an argument but the guy by the nearest post is not backing down. The conversion goes down as a miss and we are out.

'This cannot happen twice in one match.'

But it does. Sullivan head on to the semis, where they are knocked out.

Once the disappointment dies down, the taste for competition remains.

'You know, I'm good at this. I enjoyed getting to the quarter-final of the Medallion Shield and enjoyed getting stuck into the bigger schools.'

For what it is worth, I am now a rugby player.

CHAPTER 4

Friends' cup run gives me a real taste for rugby. I love the team element – working hard for one another, making sacrifices – but the moments of individual glory – scoring tries, line breaks, making hits – thrill me.

Mum continues to shuttle me around town on Saturdays. Aged sixteen, I have recently discovered alcohol, so the early morning drives to training, or matches, find me in quieter form than usual. We are hardly running wild, my friends and I, but there is the odd morning with a sore head after a night of drinking and games of pool.

Aside from my burgeoning rugby prowess, I excel at the javelin. Though it is a less enjoyable, more solitary pursuit, my competitive spirit kicks in. I like the technical adjustments and improvements I make to throw the javelin further and further. My growing size, and speed, see me reach the district finals up at Antrim Forum during my fifth year at Friends' School.

I hardly embrace the lifestyle of a top track-and-field prospect. Every morning, from about third year in school, I walk round to the bus stop and have a cigarette, get off the bus at the train station and have another. I have at least one more during lunch break and reverse the smoking order coming home. I tell myself I am only having one or two cigarettes but five or six is more in line with the truth.

The night before the district finals was a heavy one for drink – Buckfast and a few bottles of WKD. From what I can recall, there were a few smokes too. Mum is at the bedroom door, banging.

'Right, son, get up, we are going to the districts.'

I am hanging together.

'No. I'm not going, no. I'm not feeling good, Mum.'

She has heard these lines before.

'Get you up out of your bed. You've put all this training in. Get up. We're going.'

Into the car and away we go. My first event is the 400 metres. Thankfully, there is a spot of sun out. Mum sizes me up.

'Right, away you go.'

I am wearing Nike Air Max classics. Big old things with the air bubbles. Laces not even tied. Too cool for school.

Mum thinks I am raring to go. My only thought, as I crouch at the starting line, is, 'Don't get sick out here, in front of everyone. Finish this race, fast as you can.'

Off we go and I bomb through the first 300 metres – leading – before I hit the wall. I am practically walking as I cross the finish line. I finish second. Here comes Mum.

'Well done, son. Well done.'

'Mum, I'm off to the toilet.'

I stagger round to the back of the small stand and lie on my side, boking away. Projectile vomiting.

People must be able to hear my racket as they come round.

'Are you OK?'

'I'm fine.'

There is no way I am letting on.

Mum follows the commotion and sees me still lying down; surrounded.

'What is wrong with you?'

'I'm not well. I must have got food poisoning.'

She is not buying it.

'You were out last night, weren't you?'

'I only had a few.'

'Well, you can run it off in this 400-metre final.'

'No, no, no. I can't.'

'Yes, you bloody can. Up you get.'

She is not far off giving me a boot up the arse. I continue to plead with her: 'There's no way I can run another 400.'

We reach a compromise. I sit out the 400 metres but have to throw the javelin.

'Deal.'

I have half an hour to get my head together and get a couple of bottles of water into me. A light rain begins to fall and Mum heads back to the stand, zipping her coat up. Before she goes, she gives me some words of encouragement.

I go to lift the javelin and it feels so heavy. My head is swimming and my thoughts are far from positive. 'I'm so weak here, I can't even walk, never mind throw a javelin.'

The rain is starting to fall, steadily. I grab the javelin and pad down the runway in my Air Max. 43.25 metres. My stomach lurches but I hold down whatever I have left in me. Water, mostly.

'OK, that is it. I can't do it any more.'

Mum is not having it. I have two throws left.

'We had a deal, remember?'

It is starting to get slippy and, not having a spike on me, I am squeaking and sliding all over the place. I throw 43 metres, then 44.

I am changing out of my gear as they announce the results. The top four will go on and compete in the Ulster Championship.

'First place, such and such. Second place, such and such. Third place, Stephen Ferris.'

'Flipping hell.'

Mum is delighted. 'Well done, son. I'll bring you back next month for the championships.'

I tell myself there is no way I am coming back here with another hangover.

I show up for the Ulster Championship with a pair of running spikes. No more messing around. I pick a javelin from the rack. I feel good. The sun is out. A few of the other guys have recorded throws in the early 40s. I fancy myself to sail clear of that; get close to 50.

I run up for my first throw and release at just the right time. It goes well clear of 50 metres. Holy shit. Now there is a problem, as the markings only go as far as 50. They have to fetch a longer tape. The competition is held up twenty minutes until they finally agree on a distance: 57 metres. It is my only throw of the day. Nobody else comes close and I am named the Ulster champion.

The Irish Championship is four weeks later. A bus is heading down from Belfast but, still shy when I am detached from my buddies from home, I ask Mum to drive me. The event is all the way down in Tullamore.

Three hours, or so, down to Offaly. I have the spikes with me but cannot surpass my Ulster throw. My best lands a few centimetres short of 55 metres and is good enough to win gold.

Back in the car and off home, the Irish champion.

A couple of days later, I am at home when I get a letter from the Northern Ireland Athletic Federation. They want me to come along and train for more javelin competitions under their guidance.

The letter goes straight in the bin. Mum is none the wiser.

Some weeks later, she does ask about the javelin. 'Has no one been in touch?'

'No, Mum.'

Rugby is just about the only thing holding my interest. Dave left school after fifth year and headed on to Lisburn Tech. Seeing him do well and enjoying that more relaxed lifestyle, away from school, I set my sights on emulating him.

Mum is exasperated and half jokes about paying me by the hour to study. I fall behind in a few classes and, frustrated, switch off. The A levels are not on my list of priorities. I want to get my GCSEs done and do well enough to get a place on a Sports Science course at Tech.

It is hard to put my finger on why I slip into a mood, save that I am a teenager and these things, according to my parents, are part of growing up. Falling behind in school does not help.

I find rugby great for getting any frustration or aggression out of my system. Mum says I am a different child during the week if I do not play a match at the weekend. When I do play, and get that release, I am fine. Everyone has outlets for their aggression, or to channel their energies. If I have a hard week, rugby offers a chance to blow a bit of steam off. Especially in school, when I could not be bothered to study or work.

All I focus my energy on is going out and playing rugby. If a game is cancelled or postponed due to the weather, I am seething.

'You're a different child this week,' Mum remarks. 'I know you didn't play rugby but don't be so grumpy. Don't take it out on us.'

Number 8 is still my position. I featured with the fifth and sixth years in the senior team when I was in fourth year. They played me on the wing. Once I reach fifth year, I am back in my familiar position.

Up against Belfast Royal Academy in the first round of the Schools Cup: I relish taking on the bigger schools and doing all the damage. Standing in the changing rooms and I am still a wee, small guy when compared to some team-mates. Darren Hanley, our captain, says a few words. There is another guy on my left, a second row, Mark Enderby. The only other fifth year is Davy McClean, who plays in the centre and is incredibly fast. BRA is one of the top schools in Belfast for rugby. Stuart Olding and Iain Henderson come through a few years later.

There is a big crowd out for the game – two or three deep, all the way around. By my reckoning, there must be about a thousand people there. The way the school pitch is – kind of sunk in slightly – there is a viewing gallery the whole way around it.

It is a wet, cold morning. Not raining, just damp. Your typical morning in these parts.

It is a bit of a tussle early on. BRA start brightly and are attacking in our 22 when I turn the ball over at a ruck. I rip the ball from one of their players and set off. One of their backs comes over to make a tackle but I sit him down. Now there is open field ahead.

I put the afterburners on and can hear the crowd as I race towards their line: 'Owwww, yeaaahhhhh.'

I'm running, springing down the pitch and thinking, 'I'm not going to make this.'

But, of course, my mate Davy, the fastest guy in the school, is jogging alongside me. I pass it to him just before their 22 and he sprints under the sticks.

On the news that night, the Schools Cup gets a round-up and it shows that break. My mum and dad have set up the VCR to record. There I am in my scrum cap, scampering up the pitch. I look so small and skinny. The clip gets another viewing later that evening, when my granny drops by.

'Oh look at Stevie, look at Stevie, he's on the TV. It's unbelievable.'

Then the scoreline comes up at the end. We got hockeyed 37–7.

If a team is put out in the first round, they go into the Bowl or Shield. Two weeks after falling to BRA, we have Coleraine. They were one of the favourites to win the whole thing but were shocked by Methody in the first round, beaten by a point.

We are drawn away and are already thinking, 'Oh my God, we are going to get beaten by 70 or 80 points. This is the best team in the competition. They have a guy called Andrew Trimble who's like Terminator.'

Trimble must be lower-sixth year. He is as good as everyone says.

We head to Coleraine and, next thing, find ourselves 5 points up again as we score the first try. I pick and go for 40 metres and get over the line, but we end up getting beat 65–5. Trimble scores a hat-trick and grabs another for good measure. He plays 13 but, at one stage, makes a break down our wing. He swerves to take himself under the posts, but I run in to cut him off before he gets there. It should make their conversion tougher, at the very least.

He saunters up and is about to put the ball down. I am shadowing him and he lashes into me, knocks me flying. He puts me on my arse. Andrew Trimble, this nice guy I have heard about . . . bang, and I am lying on the deck going, 'What the hell just happened?'

He puts the ball down behind the posts, then turns round, looks at me and runs back to the halfway line.

Back with the Friends' lads, I talk about it the whole way home on the bus.

'That Trimble lad is the real deal.'

Barney McGonigle and Elizabeth Dickson try to convince me to stay on for my A levels but I find excuses to leave. I tell them I want to do economics and business studies but they cannot accommodate both in my timetable.

'Right, so. I'm leaving.'

I leave Friends' School with six GCSEs to my name. I take up the Sports Science course at Lisburn Tech. I feel like a free man and it does not take long to forget about the javelin, forget about rugby and head out partying with my mates. I start smoking dope and getting off my head on nights out, thinking I am the big lad. I am one of the younger ones in my group of friends. I am running around with my brother and his mates, who are all two and three years older.

The nightclub for sixteen- and seventeen-year-olds is the Coach, in Banbridge. Our routine, throughout my year in Tech, is to head along each Wednesday and Saturday. The routine involves heading over to a mate's for a few pre-night-out drinks. We get a bottle of Buckfast in to give us a head start. You have about £20 for the night and that includes taxis. If one of the lads can get hold of a bottle of Aftershock, all the better. Then we have a red or a blue – a shot of blue Aftershock followed by blue WKD, and the same goes for red. Steaming at this stage, we get a taxi to Banbridge and fall in another, a few hours later, to get home. You wake up the next day and decide to give classes a miss.

I am playing underage rugby with Portadown. We have a good Under-18s side but I am not the only lad suffering on the morning of a match. Teenagers gone wild and testing their boundaries. Drinking, smoking, smoking dope. It is easy enough to get dope. Usually you walk out of Tech and there is a lad out by the side, smoking a joint. It seems like everybody is doing it; giving it a try.

I am going through a stage where I find it hard to give a shit about anything. I find I am in good company.

I have no wish to throw any more javelins, rugby is a chore and I do not have any interest in education, or my course. My parents are supportive, concerned, but do not interfere too much. They probably recognize that I need to sort myself out but am not getting there yet. I suspect, however, if they knew half the stuff I am getting up to, they would beat me up and down the street.

On one of my rare days in class, at Tech, my mobile phone rings. I step outside and answer.

'Hello, Stephen, it's Allen Clarke here from the Ulster Academy. I'm coaching the Ulster Youths at the minute. Barney McGonigle was in contact with us. Would you like to come up and have a session with us? We've got a provincial series coming up.'

I tell Allen I will let him know but my immediate reaction is 'no chance'. Playing for Ulster has a good ring to it but it seems like a giant waste of time and effort. No one I know has ever played rugby properly or made any money from it.

I keep my word to Allen and I tell my parents.

Mum says, 'Sure you might as well go up and give it a try. You are a good rugby player.'

'I can't be arsed. No way. I want to play poker here with the lads.'

We leave it at that, but a few nights later we are playing poker in the back room and I get into another fight with Dave. We have both had a few drinks and get into an argument over the way one of us is dealing. It starts off with digs on the shoulder then becomes full-blown. I push Dave against the wall and run upstairs. He follows and it all kicks off again in our bedroom. I fling him on to his bed and jump on him, pinning him down. Whatever way he lands, he fractures his collarbone. It is the same one he had previously broken, coming off a scooter. He is in agony. I realize that pretty quickly and release him.

Mum rushes into the room. It does not take long to figure out what has happened. She orders me out of the house.

'What?'

'Get out of this house now.'

I walk out of the house and into the shed. I sit in the shed for a few hours, just letting the whole situation cool down.

I am apologetic when I come back in but Dave is in bed. He will have to be looked at by a doctor in the morning. I can see the disappointment in my mum's face.

*

Two days later, I give Allen a call and ask if the offer is still open. He asks me along to Jordanstown for some training sessions with Ulster Youths.

I am now seventeen and embarking on something completely foreign to me. I cannot say I ever dreamed of playing for Ulster, as I never would have imagined such dreams as being remotely possible. A lot of people seem to believe in me, so I tell myself I will give it my best and see where it gets me.

Mum drops me off at Jordanstown but stays in the car during my first sessions. She is now a teacher at Parkview, a special-needs school, and gets through some paperwork while I train.

The best players from Omagh, Enniskillen, Banbridge, Lisburn and across the province are there. I am the only guy to have come from a grammar school. I suppose a few of the guys are thinking, 'Who is this dickhead? Who is this arsehole, pitching up here?'

Of course, it being rugby and playing with these guys every week means we forget all that stuff pretty quickly and get on well. My attitude is, 'I'll give this time and attention for four or five weeks and see how it goes.'

A few training sessions, a couple of matches go by and I am selected to start at Number 8. First up, we play Munster at home, in Ravenhill. So 12 October 2002 becomes the first time I play in the famous old ground. There must be all of fifty people there.

In the lead-up to the game, we are told, 'There might be one, two or three, maximum, that are going to make it in professional rugby.'

'Yeah, right, whatever,' I think. 'None of us will make it anyway.'

We beat Munster 17–7 to back up some of the positive words being said, and written, about us.

We have Connacht in Ballina, Mayo, and are up by 3 points when I set off on the counter-attack from just inside our 22. Mum and Dad are at the game so it is a fantastic feeling to know they are there, cheering me on, as I make my break.

I pick the ball up, off the scrum, and steamroll the Connacht openside as he steps up to hit me. I side-step their out-half and tear away, 60 metres up the pitch. Their full-back is sitting deep, for some reason, but I manage to slow my run enough to feint, change direction and side-step him too.

I jog in the last few metres and touch down under the posts. I take some deep pulls of air. I feel light-headed; buzzing.

'Did that just happen? That's the best try I've ever scored in my life.'

All the lads run up to congratulate me and bash me on the back. 'Well done, mate.'

That score gives us an 18–5 lead but we are forced to hang on in the closing stages, eventually winning 18–15.

We play Leinster at Templeogue in Dublin, home to St Mary's. Connacht and Munster's match kicks off slightly later than ours, for some reason, so our best option of winning the Under-18 inter-provincial series is to leave it in our own hands. Tries from Dale Black and Robert Pollock have us 12–6 in front but Leinster answer with a converted try of their own and win 13–12.

Our shoulders sink and heads drop. We shake hands after the final whistle, not knowing how costly our loss will be. It takes about ten minutes but word comes through that Connacht have only beaten Munster 10–7. We win the title on points difference.

I believe my white jersey is the most precious jersey in the land. We are sponsored by Calor Gas and it has their big red logo on it. I sometimes take to wearing it on nights out in Lisburn. A baggy jersey with '8' on the back and muck stains on it from a previous match. I have myself convinced that I am the man. When I get my Ulster Youths tracksuit and zip-up hoodie, it is the same deal. Shoulder raised, chest puffed out. It gets some people talking, from 'Who's yer man' to 'He must be good' and everything in between. It feels quite cool.

Having scored a couple of tries and taken two man-of-the-match awards in the inter-provincial series, I am invited down to Dublin for a weekend session with Ireland Youths. I can see what the call-up means to my family and friends and take satisfaction in seeing their reactions. My overriding feeling, however, is one of nervousness.

I take the train down with five other Ulster lads, including Dale, that were selected. From the station, at Connolly, we take a bus out to Deer Park Hotel in Howth. The Connacht lads are already on board, all of them sitting down the back. The get-together is out at a golf course in the middle of nowhere. I am crapping myself, sitting at the front of the bus while they are all talking and joking at the back.

'Where the hell are we going?'

Forty-five minutes later, the bus pulls into the middle of nowhere and we drive up to this hotel and get out. We unpack our Ulster bags and throw them into this room. I go in and pick my key card up. I enter my room and there are two big lads, props, from Munster and another guy.

I stand in the doorway for the longest time. 'Why are there four or five guys in my room?' I count five beds, one for each of us. I am far from comfortable. 'I don't know these guys,' I fret, 'I'm only young, I'm a bit of a home bird, feel out of my depth here.'

I go to find Dale but he is no use. He tells me I will be grand.

Plan B is to call home.

'Hi, Mum. I'm going, I'm coming up the road. I'm going to get a taxi to the train station, I'm outta here. This isn't for me.'

'What are you on about? Stay where you are.'

I make for the team room and Michael Webb, from Ulster, is there. As the squad doctor, he is giving a talk on concussion, drugs, taking care of yourself.

I go back to the room and there is someone sitting smoking a cigarette out the window.

'What the fuck?'

My room is stinking of smoke. There is one of the Munster props, tattoo on his arm, sitting, smoking away.

'Alright? Do you want one?'

'No, mate, I'm good, I'm good.'

I leave straight away, banging on Dale's door.

'Mate, I'm outta here. This is ridiculous.'

'You'll be alright, Stevie, you'll be grand.'

The prop is caught smoking by one of the coaches and I get my wish, to shift rooms.

It is November so the weather is freezing. The coaches, Colin McEntee and Nigel Carolan, hand out the skimpy training gear. We are put through our paces; run ragged. The coaches tell us how well we have done, give us some stuff to work on, and we head home.

I land back at ours and, of course, Mum asks how it was.

'I'm not going back. No way. That was nuts. Those boys are

madness down there. Didn't enjoy it. Hated it. Training was shite.'

'For flip sake, come on!'

The invitations keep coming and, complain as I might, I take the train down each time.

It feels as if I have been at Deer Park for months. 'If this is the way it's going in professional rugby then no way,' I reason. 'I'm not going to be doing this.'

As the weeks pass, through December, then into January 2003, the squad dwindles: forty, thirty-five, thirty . . . back up to thirty-five, down to thirty again. I am always there. We get to know a few people, meet a few faces, and make friends. The guys that do not give a shit are given the flick pretty quickly. I start to enjoy it. All the training builds towards the Four Nations, which is to be held in Scotland. The team is selected and it is a very proud moment for me – Irish Youth. 'Gee, I am landed here. This is brilliant.'

Around this time, I get another letter in the door about the javelin. My mum writes: 'Due to rugby commitments (Four Nations), Stephen cannot attend.'

Youths is a collection of the best young club players. There is a separate Schools team. Once you get past Under-18s, both sides are brought together. Many of the top schools have full-time coaches in and a strength and conditioning coach on the payroll. It is not far off a professional set-up. It is not uncommon for all the Youths to be cut once the two squads are combined for training sessions, which are effectively trials.

Making that cut, and becoming professional, is far from my thoughts and the thoughts of my twenty-five smartly dressed team-mates as we fly to Scotland. We stay in the Holiday Inn, in Edinburgh, the whole time we are there. It is right beside the zoo and each morning I wake to the sound of the monkeys hollering and screeching. Six thirty a.m., right on cue.

We play Scotland first. They have a mixed group – schoolboys and club players. Stand-out players like John Barclay and Greig Laidlaw. They beat us with a couple of scores to spare. Next up are Wales, and I wish I am back at the Holiday Inn with the monkeys screaming next door as we get thrashed. Wales rack up over 50 points and Aled Brew, their number 13, scores four tries. He is an absolute beast, a freak, and everyone tips him to play for Wales.

Our final game is against an England team captained by Mitchell Hulme. He is keeping a young Kiwi lad called Dylan Hartley on the bench. Hulme takes a run at me early in the game and, as he nears, transfers the ball behind his back to his other hand. Nice trick, but it does not stop me from flattening him with a tackle.

Playing for pride, we go in with the lead at half-time. Shane Geraghty scores a brilliant drop goal from the halfway line. Ultimately, though, we lose. It feels like we are fulfilling the destiny of every Irish Youths team – to lose. The Welsh, Scots and English are all bigger and stronger than us.

I look upon the tournament as a stepping stone. Watching the boys from the other countries, I know I will have to reach, then surpass their levels if I am to stand any chance of representing Ireland again.

I return home to help Portadown Under-18s beat Ards, at Ravenhill. The 27–21 victory means we are Ulster's league and cup champions. We make it a treble, in May 2003, by capturing the Floodlit Cup. The season ends with me having to rent out a suit for a black-tie awards dinner at the Ramada Hotel. I win the Ulster Youths Player of the Year and Tom Megaw from Portadown talks me up to the press.

If my rugby career is picking up, Tech is going the opposite way. I am missing classes due to rugby and have no desire to catch up as I fall behind.

I tell my parents that I am dropping out. They try to convince me otherwise but see my mind is made up.

Pragmatic as ever, Mum says, 'Right, Stevie, if you are not in education any more, you are going to have to start paying your way. You can't just live under the roof of the house here, expect to come in and get your dinner set down in front of you. This is the real world now, son.'

I get my wish and it is time to find a job. Shit.

I phone around a few temping agencies and eventually land a summer job with DM Driveways, run by Davey Mitchell. My friend Andrew Champion is already working there and puts in a good word. DM do driveways, paths and kerbing. As I am still a few months short of my eighteenth birthday, I am hired as a general labourer. If the wheelbarrow needs filling up with sand, I fill it up with sand. If bricks need moving, I carry them over.

To keep motivated, I create a competition in my head. When they need bricks, I see how many I can stack up to carry. I start with about ten, then keep stacking all the way up my chest and past my head. I wobble and teeter around with fifteen or sixteen in my arms. Andrew takes them off me and off I go again – see if I can beat that record.

I enjoy it. It is hard work but the days fly by. I am knackered; get home, sleep, then out the next day for work.

Good craic. Lots of dirty stories told.

I work overtime, whenever I get the chance, as the flat pay is £30 a day. You get paid £10 an hour overtime so myself and Andrew often say, 'Right, we'll stay on the extra three hours and try to get this job done.' It is the equivalent of making £50 to £60 a day so it makes sense, even if some days we end up working 8.30 a.m. to nine p.m. Once overtime is added, I am earning a couple of hundred quid a week, thinking I am a millionaire yet giving my mum £20 a week for house-keeping.

We are down outside Belfast one day, near Holywood, as there is a new development being constructed. We are doing all the flagstones – one-metre-squared. You have to walk them along to get them into place. I am walking slabs all morning long. Walking, walking. We are doing brickwork for the drives, too. It is a tough slog so lunch comes as a relief.

Davey and Steve, another labourer, sit in the front of the DM Driveways van, with myself and Andrew in the back. We are flipping through the newspaper and one of the lads says, 'Come on, what do you say we ring one of these chat hotlines?' Typical builder stuff.

Davey picks up the mobile. 'Hello?'

'Hello,' comes an Asian accent.

He flicks it on to loudspeaker.

'Just wondering, do you do a bit of water-sports? Can we get some water-sport action?'

'Yes, yes. Where do you want to see me?'

I am sitting in the back, thinking, 'Jesus, if my mum knew I was in the back of a builder's van phoning sex lines . . .'

Of course we all start getting brave, shouting different things down the phone.

Getting on like Clampets.

This is the boss of the paving company, having the craic. He hangs up and we have an even greater laugh about what happened. Harmless enough fun, but I am glad I am not paying the phone bill.

Next day, the paper comes out in the van.

'No, no, no, no! That cost me £2.99 a minute.'

After four months with DM, with summer over, the weather turning grey and contracting work easing off, I have to find a new job. I turned eighteen in August and my future is slowly taking shape. Although I am still living at home, regular work and my own money give me a sense of independence. I am signed up with Portadown for another season and can see myself playing there, with the senior team, for years to come. Hard work, Monday to Friday, rugby at the weekend and boozy nights out at the Coach. It is a simple enough plan but it sounds good to me.

This schedule gets messed up somewhat by my inclusion in the Ulster Under-19 squad and a call, late in 2003, to train with an extended Ireland Under-19 squad. This time, the best schoolboy players in the country will be there.

CHAPTER 5

The second job in my short working life so far is a two-minute walk from home.

I sign up with a temp agency and they find me a shop-floor role at Finlay's gelatine factory. Basic pay is £170 per week. I head over for work each morning and throw on my white boots, white hat, white jacket and white gloves. The whole lot.

On my first day there, the lad training me sizes me up and says, 'I don't know if we have a pair of white trousers to fit you. Try those on.'

I wedge the trousers up. They fit my waist. I am 6 foot 4 inches but still skinny enough. I fasten the trousers and look down – it looks like I am wearing three-quarter lengths.

'Ah,' he says, 'you'll have to wear your jeans then.'

I walk on to the main factory floor and can barely see in front of me. There is so much powder sifting around in the air. It is everywhere.

I finish my first shift and, when I get home, blow my nose.

'Jeez, my nose is bleeding here.'

Turns out it is not blood. That is the red gelatine powder I have been breathing in all day. Whenever I get my break, that is the first thing I do – blow my nose.

Everything I eat tastes like jelly.

Everyone is helpful and I meet some real characters there. It is a tremendously boring job. I get a packet of jelly coming my way on a conveyor belt. Zip, stick it under a heat lamp to seal the back. Here comes the next one. Same again. I do that for three hours straight, then get a break. Clear my nose, get some fresh air, eat something. I go back in and fill the bags with these little gelatine squares for three hours. Another break, same again. I finish the day out by packing the bags into boxes.

It won't come as a surprise, then, that getting away with Ulster and Ireland becomes something I really look forward to. I take part in an Under-19 provincial blitz at Barnhall RFC, in Leixlip. We play Connacht in the early kick-off and, after changing back into our gear, catch the second half of Munster versus Leinster. Leinster's scrum-half, Cillian Willis, looks decent and another lad I have heard a bit about, Johnny Sexton, comes off the bench near the end.

Following that, I get invited to the Aer Lingus Social and Athletic Association (ALSAA) facilities, down near Dublin Airport, for an Ireland Under-19 session. Fellow Ulster Under-19 Mark Scott has a car so myself and centre Jamie McGrugan, who is also called up, drive down together.

In a training squad of forty, about fifteen are the top Youths players from across the country, but as the sessions go by, the familiar faces disappear. The lads that have come straight from the Schools Senior Cup competitions are a class above. I am by no means the best in these two-day camps but I hold my own. The letters, inviting me down to train, keep arriving at our house.

The outstanding talents are Billy Holland and Paul Doran-Jones, in the second and front rows. We are captained by Michael Essex, from Cork, and have Cillian as starting scrum-half. Fionn Carr is our full-back and he has a few Ulster lads, former Schools players, for company in the backline – Jamie, Mark and Stewart Megaw. We play some trial matches and have some fifteen-versus-fifteen runs against each other. The way it is shaping up – my take on the situation, at least – I am in with a chance of going to the Under-19 World Cup, in March 2004, possibly as the starting Number 8.

We line up a challenge match against England with two teams for each half. I am stuck with the B team. The A team is all Schools players; my team is mostly Schools, with three other Youths. The A lads get beaten by 30-odd points while we get done by 5. England have Ugo Monye, Dave Wilson, and their main man is James Haskell.

The squad is cut down and we go away to France. We play two games at their training facility. Again teams are split, but this time I am in the A team. We lose, narrowly, but it is a really open game – one of those you do not mind losing because it is so good to play in. It is the turning point for me; I know I will be selected.

Joining myself and Essex in the back row is John McCall. I have played against him once before, when he was at Royal School Armagh. We got opened up because they were such a talented side and he was bloody good. Their best player. He is openly talked about as the next number 7 for Ulster. He is the fittest guy you could meet; a big, physical lad. You cannot miss him, this big red-headed guy. You can spot him a mile away.

As the squad's two Ulster back rows, we are extremely competitive with each other. He thinks he is better than me and

I fancy I am better than him. That rivalry between us is brilliant to have; it drives us both. We were in the same year in school and are a year young for the Ireland Under-19s. He captains Royal Armagh to Senior Schools Cup success as they beat Campbell College in the final.

The squad is selected for the World Cup and both John and I are included. There is a healthy Ulster contingent.

My stint at Finlay's comes to an end, earlier than expected, as I am off to South Africa. There may be more shifts going when I return but I expel such thoughts from my mind. For the next four weeks, the World Cup is my focus.

I am awestruck by the whole journey. We are staying at a big hotel, right on the coast. We throw our gear into the rooms and run out on to the beach. Twenty-five degrees, swimming and massive waves crashing. You are with mates.

'This is unreal. This is top of the world.'

We are not getting paid but this is just insane.

'We're in South Africa, lads!'

I am rooming with Doran-Jones and all the other countries are in the same hotel. Paul knows James Haskell from their school days. Haskell has these massive pecs and Paul is the same. They are hitting the gym every day. Chatting to them, on a walk down to the beach, I feel like a tiny, scrawny little boy.

We are just about to play for Ireland in the opening game of a World Cup. Madness. We sit down for breakfast and are told we can have all the food we want; take as many Powerade drinks as we want.

'Holy shit, what is going on?'

I drink far too much Powerade so that, when I go for a crap, my shit is green. This simply adds to the wonder of the whole affair.

This is amazing.

Our opener, on 27 March 2004, is the toughest game imaginable: we face New Zealand at the ABSA Stadium in Durban.

A little over twenty minutes into the game and there is a line-out. Jumpers from both sides miss the throw. I am standing at the back of the line-out so catch it and set off in attack. I am tackled, and John McCall is the first man into the ruck. We get up and the lads drive around the corner. John remains on the ground.

We keep folding around the corners, inching forward. Peering back, I can see John, immobile.

We keep playing and go through a few more phases until there is a break in play.

Getting my breath back, I wander closer. John has not moved.

'What's going on?' I wonder. 'He must have been knocked out.'

Next minute, the trolley comes out and John is getting wheeled off the pitch.

'Fucking hell, lads, this doesn't look good. He's going to miss the end of the tournament here.'

At half-time we walk into the changing room. Allen Clarke is one of the coaches, assistant to Pat Murray. He is trying to talk us up; encourage us. He says, 'John is fighting for his life in there.'

That hits home. Fighting for his life? What is that about? A coach would never say that. It would be like 'John is in there with a busted knee' or something.

'Come on!' shouts Allen. 'Go out there and give it your all for him. John is in there fighting for his life.'

Those words stick with me. They will for the rest of my life. *John is in there fighting for his life.*

All I can think of is that it must be a really bad condition or, at worst, a broken neck and that he may never play again.

We go back out and play shit. Not well at all. The final whistle blows and we have been beaten with over 20 points to spare. I just want to get back into the changing room to see how John is. He did not show on the sidelines in the second half.

We are called into a huddle on the pitch. One of the coaches says, 'Lads, I don't know how to break this to you, but your team-mate John has died.'

They tell us this on the fucking pitch.

I break my bind with the lads. I break free and sprint off 20 metres with my head in my hand, crying my eyes out. 'What has just happened? What has just happened? I am only eighteen. John is only eighteen. What has just happened?'

Management are probably in shock just as much as we are, so are not thinking straight. Of course they realize their mistake, in telling these guys out on the pitch, in front of the watching world.

'Guys, come in. Come in, guys.'

We all gather ourselves and get into the changing room. Our heads are all over the place. 'What the hell is going on? This cannot be real.'

About five minutes later, a priest comes into the changing room and it hits home. My team-mate has just died. It is the most surreal, crazy, heartbreaking hour of my life.

Some of the lads take it ridiculously bad. Some guys seem OK. Everyone's emotions work differently. I am up and down. One minute, I am completely fine. Next, it comes in a wave – so many questions – and I am bawling. Moments later, I have calmed down again.

A couple of hours pass before we get back to the hotel. Everyone heads straight for their room. Paul steps out so I can call home.

My mum, as always, answers.

'Hello, doll.'

She always calls me doll, for some reason. She is from Ballymena, up north, and it is something they say.

'Hello, doll, how are you? How are you getting on? I saw the result. You didn't do too well.'

I just start wailing like a young kid. It takes me a while to string a few words out.

'You are not going to believe what's happened, Mum. You are not going to believe it.'

'Calm down, calm down. Are you OK?'

'One of my team-mates has died.' I must repeat this about four times.

My mum starts to cry, too. She must feel completely helpless. Talking with her simply confirms the truth, that John has passed away, thousands of miles from home.

Mum composes herself and, by talking, asking questions and reassuring, she calms me down.

I say goodbye. Paul needs to call his family. I promise I will call back, soon as I can. I go and chat with one of the other lads while Paul phones home. I find out, from him, that Ireland have won the Triple Crown by beating Scotland. I later discover that senior management opted not to inform the team about John until after they had won.

*

In the days afterwards, walking down the street in Durban and looking at newspapers, there is John on a stretcher on the front page. The headline reads 'Irish U19 dies on pitch at ABSA Stadium'. Reports confirm John suffered a cardiac failure. All attempts to revive him, on the pitch and within our dressing room – even as we stood there, getting a team-talk – proved hopeless.

'Jesus Christ.'

We remain in South Africa, trying to get to grips with the tragic situation. John's father, Ian, flies over. We go for a barbecue at a clubhouse right next to the ABSA Stadium.

Ian McCall stands up to address us. It must be incredibly tough.

Recalling his words as best I can, he says, 'Look guys, this is just a freak accident that has happened. I don't want any of you to stop playing rugby. I don't want any of you guys to walk away from this tour and say "that could happen to me". This is some-thing that has happened to John. It was his time to go. Everybody is, obviously, really sad about this, but, from his dad, talking to you guys who have known him, John would want you to play rugby and keep playing rugby.'

Amazing words.

I walk outside, away from everybody again. I find I detach myself from situations, and people, if I am finding it tough to cope.

I walk over to the training pitches – four of them lined up, side by side. This is where all the warm-up drills take place before the matches. People park their cars here before the game. I walk all the way to the end of the pitch that is furthest away. I am crying my eyes out. Two days have passed and still I cannot get my head around it.

By the time I get back, a few of the lads are standing out the front. One of them steps forward and gives me a hug.

'It's going to be OK.'

The next day, we go to the funeral home to say our farewells. It is the first time I have been to look at a dead body. A lot of the guys from the south are more used to it than I am – removal services, wakes, seeing the body before a funeral. I am petrified. I have no idea what to expect. I figure the coffin will be in the room and someone will say a few words at a service.

When we walk into the main room, the coffin is sitting at the front, open, and there is a long line leading up to it. I am in the middle of our squad as they join the line but I slip out and go to the back.

I find a seat and drop my head. I ask myself, 'Can you do this? Can you walk up and look at your mate who is now dead in a coffin?' I have never done it before. I never saw any of my grandparents or anybody else in a coffin. Every single other person has done it. I have to do it. I cannot be the only one not to say my goodbyes, as such.

I wait right until the end and walk up to the coffin. John is lying in it. He has this striking ginger hair. The most ginger hair, and an unbelievable, thick head of hair. He is lying in the coffin and is at rest. I put a hand on his shoulder and say, 'Rest in peace.' I touch his chest and walk away. The first and, I swear to myself, the last time I will ever do that. Ever. Even my mum, dad, brother, if they passed away tomorrow, I would not do it. I would prefer to remember them as they lived. I would rather envisage John on the pitch, playing, than lying in a box.

The whole service is tough to take. We take a vote and most of the squad want to go home. There is talk of playing on, in John's memory, but we are in no fit state. We sit in a team room at our hotel. Pat says, 'Look, obviously a lot of people want to go home. It might be some of you guys want to stay and play on. There might be guys here who want to play for John and try and get something out of this tournament. It is up to you.'

About two guys express an interest in staying on, for John, but most, including myself, want to get out of here as quick as possible. We want to be home, be at John's funeral and give him a good send-off. He was a good character. A great talent; a wasted talent too.

We are flown home and attend his funeral, in Armagh. There are more than eight thousand people at the service.

Sitting there, back home, it all starts to sink in.

I realize how lucky I am to be in my position. Some of the lads access the counsellors organized by the IRFU. I feel capable of dealing with his death myself. I am not alone, however. Support comes, in the main, from my mum, dad and brother.

I try to put the tragedy behind me and move on with my life. I try to live out the vows we took to John's father – to play and keep playing.

John's death instils in me a new drive and focus. I cannot explain how. I have always had a competitive streak but I push myself beyond that and start taking rugby seriously. I do my training and put in extra at the gym.

Following the Under-19 World Cup, I get an offer to link up with the Ulster Academy again, with a view to breaking into their Under-21 team. I am not due to turn nineteen for another couple of months so for the likes of Allen Clarke to talk Under-21s tells me the coaches have faith in me. It is a good feeling to have.

The days of being a hallion and a nightmare for my parents, of smoking dope outside Tech and sitting in class like a zombie, are in the past.

Maurice Field is in charge of the running of the academy. He arranges for me to get £340 a month. In truth, it mainly covers travel expenses. Little else. I get the train in and out of Jordanstown every single day, more or less, to do weights and fitness sessions. The work pays off and I start to put some muscle on my frame.

I arrive home one summer's day, full of myself, and find my dad out in the back garden.

'Dad, you would not believe the weights I was lifting today.'

'Aye, son,' he says. 'You know, I think I would be able to believe it.'

He is winding me up – 'There is no way you could lift *that* much.' I fall for it, of course.

I take a couple of strides over and lift him out of his chair. I lift him up, over my head, and he is still winding me up: 'You'll never be able to keep me up here.'

I have him lifted in the air for about two minutes before Mum comes out, screaming. 'Put him down, Stevie. Put him down. Put your father down.'

She probably remembers what happened to Dave and his collarbone. We cannot afford to have another Ferris out of action.

If I want to make the breakthrough with Ulster, and Ireland, I need to get signed up with an All-Ireland League Division 1 side. It is a perfect shop window. The options are Ballymena, where Mum is from, or Dungannon.

Jeremy Davidson, the former Ulster, Ireland and Lions player, is Dungannon coach. I first meet him when he comes to my parents' house and makes his pitch. He arrives in a big jeep. It is not long after his knee operation – he has had reconstructive surgery – so it takes him a while to clamber out and limp in. Immediately, I get a good vibe off him. He asks me to come and play with Dungannon. I have been going well with Portadown, he says, but it would bring my game on hugely if I can play at the top end of the AIL. I click with him immediately. When he leaves, Mum asks how it went.

'There's nowhere else I'd rather be.'

My first AIL game for Dungannon is pure frantic. We are away to Belfast Harlequins and they have some quality players – Lewis Stevenson, John Andress, Andy Ward, Rory Best. Rory has trained once or twice with the Ulster senior team. Supposed to be a handy player, a hooker.

I am in a ruck but am well on the wrong side. All I see is this stocky guy coming in with sort of a baldy head on him. Close-cropped; a few wisps. He bails in and wham, stamps straight on my balls. Instant, intense pain. I roll around like a kid. The sorest thing I have ever experienced. I have a big stud-mark all the way down my leg, an arrow pointing towards my nuts. My cycling shorts are ripped. I am wearing boxer shorts as well. They are torn.

'How did I not just lose my testicles there?'

I remind him of it, soon after, and he remarks, 'I saw you coming. It was a cheap shot but I knew it was you. I knew it was you. This Ferris lad.'

'Fuck it, I'm going to get you back at some stage.'

It is already difficult because everyone is talking me up,

predicting big things. I was the best player in Ulster Youths. I was one of the best players in Irish Under-19s. I am Dungannon's new prospect, hand-picked by Jeremy Davidson. When you start to get a reputation as a top guy, you have to back it up.

I start off like a bullet. I get man-of-the-match awards and garner some media attention. My body is still developing and I come up against some big units, men that have been playing the game for years. An away trip against Shannon, in Limerick, is a dose of reality. Shannon are star-studded and give us the pump. Guys like Tony Buckley, Marcus Horan and Jerry Flannery line out for them on the day. They put a half century of points on us.

I settle in quickly and pack down with a super set of lads. We have Deccie Fitzpatrick and Nigel Brady in the front row, Ryan Caldwell in the second. Oisin Hennessy with me in the back row. Gareth Steenson, a serious young talent, plays out-half. Ulster players like Bryn Cunningham, Paul Magee and Glen Telford in the backline with the experienced Tyrone Howe. We have a ridiculous line-up of talent.

I am playing week in, week out, getting my balls busted; learning my trade.

I am elevated into the Ulster Under-21 team and am chuffed to play a part in our push for an inter-provincial title. I run in a try from the halfway line in a 35–7 win over Leinster after scooping up a loose ball and fooling their covering defenders with a show and go. Our team is a great one – Gareth, Lewis, Oisin and Ryan are all there. Chris Henry is our captain, and I am pleased to finally have Andrew Trimble, Trimby, on my side.

I miss the game against Connacht, in Galway, after injuring my ankle. 'Stevie, take it easy,' the medics say. 'We have a big game coming up next week and someone else is there to jump in. Will you record the game for us up in the stand?'

'Yeah, no worries.'

I go up into the stand to video the game, and next thing my phone rings.

'Where the hell are you?' asks Mum.

'I'm up here videoing the game.'

'Are you not playing?'

'No.'

'I'm standing here at the pitch side.'

She has travelled the whole way to Galway to watch me play and it has slipped my mind to tell her that I am not playing. A four-and-a-half-hour journey, on her lonesome.

'Mum, I'm really sorry.'

She hangs around and watches the game. All I can think of, from my raised position, as I record the match, is, 'Jesus, that guy Trevor Richardson is unbelievable.' He more or less single-handedly wins the game for Connacht.

We need to beat Munster in our final outing, away from home. We overpower them up front and exploit the gaps out wide. Trimby gets over for a couple of tries. The Under-21 title is the first in Ulster's history.

We round out our Under-21 season on 22 November 2004 by destroying a New Zealand Youths side, 'The Baby Blacks'. We prove ourselves a team to be reckoned with, as our pack dismantles theirs and we play some incisive, attacking rugby. Paul Marshall starts as scrum-half and snipes in two great tries. I round out the try-scoring in the closing stages, and Gareth's conversion makes it 34–13. Ulster coach Mark McCall is in the crowd to watch.

The crowd give us a great ovation at the end. I stop, before walking off the pitch, to take in the final score. Nine months have passed since we lost John against New Zealand. It seems fitting that we have delivered such a resounding result against the same team.

Play on and keep playing.

CHAPTER 6

Dungannon have a decent start to the 2004/05 AIL season but our away form costs us. Not due to turn twenty for another six months, in February 2005 I am called into the Ireland Under-21 squad for the Six Nations. Ulster's inter-provincial title means our province dominates the national squad. Beating Munster at Musgrave Park had been our statement. 'We are here to stay.'

We are managed by David Haslett, former head coach at Ulster. But the championship proves underwhelming, as Wales hammer us 32–5 in our final match to claim the Grand Slam.

The Under-21 Rugby World Championship is taking place in Argentina, and I am named as part of a large Ulster contingent. For our opener, against France, I am one of four Dungannon players included in the starting fifteen; I have Gary Maxwell, Ryan Caldwell and Gareth Steenson for company. Joining me in the back row are Kevin McLaughlin, at blindside flanker, and Chris Henry, who plays his club rugby with Malone, at openside. Having witnessed the power and athleticism of Connacht's Trevor Richardson, I am pleased to hold on to my Number 8 jersey. John Andress and Billy Holland are in there too. Being surrounded by such talented lads makes me truly appreciate how far along I have come. I begin to realize that a strong tournament will give me a good shout of making the senior national set-up.

Johnny Sexton is on the bench because Gareth is captain. A great goal-kicker, Gareth had won the golden boot the previous year for being the tournament's top scorer. Johnny is a young kid who talks a good game and can spiral the ball the length of the pitch.

Mark McDermott, Macca, is assistant coach and does not really take to Johnny, even going so far as to slot Barry Murphy on to the bench for a game earlier in the year.

Most of the lads know Johnny has something about him but, at this stage, he has to settle for a sub's role.

Our base is well inland from Buenos Aires, way out in the west of the country in the city of Mendoza.

This is the first overseas Ireland tour where, to a certain degree, we are treated like adults and given some leeway. That means we may head out for a couple of drinks when we arrive, as long as we get back before midnight. Gareth is a top man for an entertaining night out. He is up on stages and poles, taking his shirt off and jumping around the place. The coaches let us away with some things and crack down on others.

There are no real nights out, on the beer, once the tournament is taking place but we all head out for dinners – usually steak – and have a laugh. Argentina is so cheap and our small allowance goes a long way. The CDs must work out at 5p each so I buy up around twenty and have the lads driven mad by blaring the Scissor Sisters out at the team hotel.

The competition set-up is bizarre. We are placed in Pool B-C. England and Italy are in our group but we never get to play them. Instead it is France, Samoa and South Africa.

We are well up for our opener against the French and know a good start should set us up for a semi-final run, at least.

I pop a rib midway through the first half, and injure my shoulder (the AC joint at the top of the shoulder). I feel my rib popping in rucks, during line-out lifts and when I am making tackles. We are beaten, 31–23, France getting a late score to give them some breathing room.

Samoa are next up and I need Eanna Falvey, our team doctor, to inject me with painkillers before each remaining game. At half-time too. But I score a try in each half against the Samoans and our 29–21 win gets us back on track. Our final group game is against the pre-tournament favourites, South Africa. A win will take us through to the semis.

We arrive at the home ground of Liceo Rugby Club for our final training session before the match. South Africa are finishing their session and one of their players is taking kicks at goal. He is a little fella with really thick eyebrows. He does not miss.

'Jeez, he's kicking from the halfway line, no worries. Over the post all the time. This guy's unreal.'

I ask after him and find out, from Gareth, that it is Ruan Pienaar. He will not be starting against us, as South Africa have another kicker. 'This lad Morné Steyn must be pretty perfect,' I surmise, 'as Pienaar is class.'

We give the South Africans a right rattle and go in 18–13 up at half-time thanks to Gareth's six penalties. They hit back in the second half, but we retake the lead when I crash over for a try after their blindside fumbles our restart. I gather the loose ball and sprint for their try-line, side-stepping the covering defender on the way and dotting down under the posts. The successful conversion makes it 25–20 to us but we are not able to halt the

South African fightback. We miss a kick, after seventy minutes, that would have made it 28–27. We do not get another look-in. They manage two tries and a drop goal, for good measure, and we lose, 42–25. Blitzed in ten minutes.

Two days after our defeat to South Africa and a trip to a barber shop in Mendoza lifts my spirits. I flip through a newspaper, as I wait my turn, and spot my name in the listings for tournament top try-scorers.

It does not look as if I will get to add to my tally, as Richardson is being given a start in our match against Canada. Having been knocked out of the main cup competition, we are now playing for the best finishing position. However, shortly before kick-off he pulls up with an injury and I am in from the start. We destroy Canada, 77–3, and run in eleven tries. I get a first-half try when I pick off the base of our scrum and barge over the line. Trimby gets over for a couple and Gareth, playing inside centre so Johnny gets a run-out, kicks 18 points.

My ribs are still killing me and, with our final game coming up against Samoa, again I am grateful to get a final needle jab before taking to the pitch. We are leading 24–5 just after the hour mark when I score my fifth try of the tournament. Samoa nick two late scores in two minutes to leave the game with a respectable enough scoreline, 34–17. Ninth in the world does not exactly have a memorable ring to it but leaving with two wins in a row picks us up.

We head along to watch South Africa play Australia in the final. Pienaar is sprung from the bench after an injury crisis a couple of minutes in. He goes on to inspire his country to a 24–20 win and is named man-of-the-match.

I finish third in the try-scoring charts and Gareth takes home the golden boot for the second year running. To celebrate the end of the tournament, and Gareth's award, we set off to a nightclub and get our fill of a drink called Inferno – Argentinian absinthe; really strong.

Chris, with his blond hair hanging past his ears, is downing shots and looking like a worse-for-wear scarecrow. We do not sleep a wink and fall on to a double-decker bus that is taking the squad back to the airport. Myself, Chris, John and Ryan are all sitting up on the top deck, drinking bottles of red wine. Into the airport and fishing about in pockets, looking for passports. Chris is sitting on his suitcase, smashing back the last of the red wine.

The coaches steam over.

'Right boys, get your act together. We're getting on a long-haul flight.'

Chris passes out and wakes up twelve hours later, back in Belfast, looking fresh as you like.

I start 2005/06 with Dungannon but Ulster, having brought me in to train over the summer, get me in for sessions early into their season. Having done so well at the world championship, I am also offered a developmental contract. I arrive home one day, just before my twentieth birthday, with the news.

'Well, what's the contract?' asks Mum.

'It's £8,000.' I am not happy. 'I can go back and pave driveways and get £15,000 a year. This isn't enough money.'

Some people might call me crazy but it is honestly how I feel. As I said, none of my friends or family, no one I knew growing up, has ever been a rugby player. It is great that I am doing well, I think, but there is no way of knowing if this will ever work out as a career. Ulster Youths rarely make it into the senior team, fewer still carve a career out of it, and no one ever makes it to the Ireland team. I cannot see the path ahead.

'You're driving now but they are paying your fuel,' my mum reasons. 'The rest of the time you're training. All your protein and supplements are taken care of. You might as well just give it the year. If nothing comes of it, nothing comes of it.'

Being younger than most of my set of friends, I see them starting to make real money. I know of a couple of Dungannon lads that had been offered similar deals for a year, two, then nothing more.

I still need convincing.

Myself and my mum sit down with Allen Clarke. He turns to Mum.

'Look, Linda, I'm not filling your head full of magic here. Your son Stephen is going to play for Ireland.'

'Allen, stop that. You're embarrassing him.'

I am lit up, bright red. 'Ah jeez, Allen, right, right, right.'

Allen is such a positive man. He has coached me the whole way through my time at Ulster yet I feel he is just trying to give me a bit of confidence to get the contract signed. We head home and I talk it over with Mum some more.

'Sure listen,' she says, 'stick your name on that contract and give it a rattle.'

I sign the contract and just about double my wages: £154 a week and another step up the ladder.

If my wages at Ulster are less than professional, I fit right in with the set-up of the club. Our gym is an office. It has really low ceilings, with foam tiles, two or three work-out platforms and tiny dumbbell irons. David Humphreys comes in, does dumb-bells, bench, a set of dips, and then walks out. The younger guys are coming in and getting absolutely beasted. The guys that have been around a while – Humphreys, Campbell Feather, Jonny Bell, Tyrone Howe – are getting a bit of slack but, in my eyes, are not giving it as much as the younger guys.

The physio room is a joke. This narrow little room with two beds in it and a masseur that comes in for about three hours a week. You walk in and there is a queue already formed. All us young guys, who have done the weights sessions and extras – and who are playing games for their clubs – try to get a massage slot. You walk up to the room and there is the list: C. Feather, D. Humphreys, J. Bell, T. Howe.

I am hardly going to be able to rub any of those names out.

We train Monday and Tuesday. I love it. It is dependent on the weather so, especially in the winter or when there is ice on the ground, we often find ourselves on the road to Jordanstown, as they have indoor training facilities. The video review meeting comes first, at nine a.m. There is a short look back at the previous match but the focus quickly moves to our next opponents. 'This is what we did against Scarlets. We can't afford to do this against Leinster this week.'

Training on a Monday is always flat out. Rucking, mauling, line-out drills. Most guys grab lunch and head back to Newforge Country Club for a gym session. In the gym, Mondays are always for leg weight exercises, so that by the time you get to a game at the weekend, your legs have recovered. Everybody is different but, for me, leg weights involve mostly squats. That means RDL (Romanian Deadlift), which is good for building up hamstring strength; single-leg Bulgarian; and single-leg RDL. The strength that gives my lower legs is immense. I throw in some further exercises to improve my lower abdominal strength.

Each week, our CMJ (countermovement jump) is also measured. That involves standing still, bending into a squat position and jumping as high as you can. They measure the height you jump and the time you are off the mat. There is some healthy competition around this test but I usually find myself in the top three. My record is 61.4 centimetres. Andrew Trimble pushes that close. I also perform well at concentric squats. These involve lowering yourself and the weights (anywhere between 120 and 140 kilos) before pausing and pushing that load back up as high and hard as you can. An electronic reader measures your output. It is a handy indicator of explosive power. I am miles ahead of the squad and I pride myself on that.

All told, it takes an hour and a half, after which I will make sure to get a protein shake in. If I can get my name on the list, I will look for a massage or a session with the physio.

They swap it around on a Tuesday – upper body weights in the morning and training drills in the afternoon. Wednesdays are generally off but the coaches are increasingly prone to get us in for an extra session if they feel we are lacking in any areas. I know I have a long way to go before I can mix it with the best so I often get along to the gym by myself for some extra lifts, or work on my core. That is not to say that I do not fully embrace a Wednesday off on occasion. Those days could include anything from coffee with the lads, or a game of golf or pool with mates, to a trip to my parents, catching a movie or simply putting my feet up at home.

We play our home matches, at Ravenhill, on a Friday, so Thursdays would be a light work-out – two or three starter moves, line-outs and a jog around the ground – during the captain's run. I try to sleep in later, about 10.30 a.m., on Thursday and Friday. On match-day, I grab a sandwich, bring the dog for a walk and always get over to Mum's for chicken and pasta before heading along to the ground. Playing Friday is brilliant as, unless you hurt yourself or need physio, your weekend is usually off. That said, you still have homework that needs to be done for Monday. Before you leave the ground, after a match, you are given a CD with your video analysis on it.

Match Friday, off Saturday and Sunday. Still fresh on the scene, used to no different, I am in my element. 'This is amazing. Train three days a week and a match on the Friday? Sweet.'

The change at Ulster Rugby during my time there is dramatic. Nonetheless, when we finally set our sights on catching up, we have a few laps to make up.

Having just made my breakthrough into the Ulster squad, and signed the developmental contract, I thought I would stay with Dungannon for that season and play a few 'A' games with Ulster. But it snowballs very quickly.

Most of my team-mates and coaches could not be more supportive. Having cheered on Humphreys as a young Ulster fan, I find him one of the most welcoming of the established players. The fact that he knows me, and speaks kindly about a couple of games he has seen me play in, does wonders for my confidence.

The same cannot be said of my feelings about one veteran in the Ulster ranks.

Campbell Feather, in my eyes, is a dickhead. A New Zealander and a bit of a sour, he is the kind of fella who always walks around with his head down. He does not really like any of the young guys. Nobody really gets on with him, apart from a couple of the older guys.

We are doing a fitness session in pre-season. Running across the pitch with these 50-kilo sleds tied to our waists. Phil Morrow, our strength and conditioning coach, is working us hard. Myself and Campbell are paired together. The way it works is that he pulls the sled over, I jog across with him, we swap around then I pull it the other way.

I am almost ten years younger than Campbell, who will soon turn thirty, and we do not really have much in common. I am a young guy coming in, looking to take his position. I complete my width of the pitch, then swap over and jog across. I go about 10 metres ahead of him and start clapping.

'Good work, Campbell.'

He glares ahead, takes the belt off and tells me to shut the fuck up. Calls me a cunt.

This fella is supposed to be one of my team-mates and here he is, ripping me out in front of all the other guys. He was captain of Ulster the year before.

'Flipping hell. Is this the way it is as a pro?'

The other thing that crosses my mind is: 'This guy is an arsehole.'

I cannot wait to take his place. 'That's it,' I tell myself. 'I'm going to show this guy up in everything I do.'

Campbell is in the final year of his contract and in negotiations for a new deal. We are playing against the Ospreys, on 4 November 2005, and I am on the bench. There is a ball kicked through, near the sideline. I am there in a training top, warming up; so close to the action. Campbell goes down on the ball, 5 yards from our line, but he knocks it on. It spills back over our try-line and Jason Spice, their scrum-half, breezes through and touches it down for a score. Within thirty seconds I am told to warm up and get on.

Campbell trudges off, I sprint on. We end up losing the game, but that is a big turning point. It is one of his last appearances for Ulster. As I run on, I think, 'Right, that's it. That prick is not getting back on the pitch ahead of me.'

His words, hard as they were, gave me the motivation to be better. I never spoke to him after that. Any time I spoke to anyone else about him it would be 'He's a wanker', this, that and the other. But he did me a favour. Maybe he saw me and thought I had a bit of potential and that's why he was worried. I look back on it, now, and say, 'Thanks very much, Campbell, because you gave me the bit between my teeth to push on and declare, "Right, fuck that. You're not getting back in."'

CHAPTER 7

Replacing Campbell Feather against Ospreys was my first senior game at Ravenhill. My Ulster debut, however, had arrived in front of 1,857 people at a ground called Netherdale against a team that no longer exists.

I had been talked up as a decent prospect for the Ulster back row and was getting man-of-the-match week in, week out for Jeremy Davidson at Dungannon. It helped that I was part of a great team and was scoring some nice tries. I was already becoming accustomed to pitching up at Dungannon games on a Saturday morning, walking around for half the game, making a few carries, a few tackles, and getting the accolades. The confidence Ulster had in me was beginning to rub off.

Playing for Dungannon in an Ulster Senior League match against Belfast Harlequins, I landed Andy Ward, the Ulster and Ireland flanker, with a tackle that drove him back 5 metres and won us a turnover. Mark McCall, Ulster's head coach, approached me at training two days later.

'Look, Stevie, you're on the bench against Border Reivers.'

We won 27–0. I was really nervous warming up in front of this small stand but the pressure was really off as we were well ahead.

I ran around like a headless chicken and missed five tackles in my fifteen-minute appearance.

In the dressing room, after the game, Mark said to me, 'Stevie, all you need to do is your job. Don't try to run around doing the other lads' tackles, making errors, stealing their ball-carries.'

To use an Eddie O'Sullivan comment I heard a few years later, I was running around with my hair on fire.

After my cameo appearance, I was sitting in the dressing room and taking it all in. Phil Morrow stuck his head round the door. 'Out ya get,' he said. It was time for fitness work, for all the subs – Isaac Boss, Bryan Young and Andrew Maxwell too.

It was a beautiful night. Still a bit of dew on the ground. We did a shuttle run, 50 metres.

'Right, boys, back on to the line.'

After thirty seconds I was lying on my back with my arms spread. Completely out of breath.

'Phil, Phil, I can't do any more.'

'Get the fuck up! Get the fuck up and get on the line!'

I think I actually was sick. And there was Bryan Young, a loose-head prop, absolutely coasting up and back. It was such a shock to the system.

Years later, Phil told me exactly what he said to Mark: 'Who the fuck is this guy? He's so out of shape. He's terrible. Where did you find this guy?'

Mark had replied, 'Put a bit of time and effort in with this guy. He's got the potential. He's worth it.'

In fairness to Phil, he knew quite a bit about rugby but he would not have known about guys going well in the All-Ireland League. Mark would often get tapes of the AIL games and look at the guys coming through.

It was another lesson. It's all very well having ability, and appetite, but there's no substitute for hard work.

Thankfully, there are no known tapes of my initiation as a senior Ulster player. All new caps had to sing at the front of the bus. I was freaking out beforehand.

'What am I going to sing?'

Every time I started thinking about it, the words of a song totally left me. I needed to sing something that I could actually remember the words to, under pressure. I went with a safe bet: *The Fresh Prince of Bel-Air* theme song, that bit all about my life being flipped and turned upside down.

I got paddled up the bus. The lads called it 'The Gauntlet'. They took off their shoes and whacked me on the arse as I shuffled up the bus with my pants down. I was more worried about the song than the paddling but survived both intact.

Singing a song or haring around against a beaten team meant little in the senior game. I was sent back to play some 'A' rugby and to focus on my strength and conditioning. I never lacked strength in the gym but I needed to get the running, in match conditions, under my belt.

We had Treviso at home the following weekend, in the Heineken Cup. Mark came up to me in training.

'Stevie, look, you did OK off the bench in Scotland but you're not going to be involved.'

I did not deserve to be involved, because I had played shite, but something inside me said, 'Why is he not picking me?' I was beginning to realize how good I was; the potential I had.

I played for Ulster A, against Leinster, soon after. The match was out in Navan and turned out to be one of the best I ever played in. It was hard to keep track of the score but I remember it eventually finished around 43–39, to them. I scored a couple of tries. Jonny Bell was playing in the centre for us. We were up 39–36 and, with the last play of the game, Leinster went the whole length of the pitch to score. It was one of those games, though, where we did not care who won. Nobody got injured, it was a beautiful day and we were throwing the ball around.

After Campbell's mistake against Ospreys, and my opening, there is a prolonged break for the international Test window but I am still there, in the squad, when we get back together in December. We have to get straight back to speed as we are up against Munster, away. I start on the bench and, from my wooden seat, have a great view for Justin Harrison's massive fight with Paul O'Connell and Donncha O'Callaghan. Justin is yellow-carded but we lead 20–3 at the break. Isaac is then sent to the sin-bin but Munster do not break us down until he is back on the pitch and we are back to fifteen men. Jerry Flannery's try sets up a tense finish and I am sent on for the final twenty minutes. We are under the cosh for every second I am out there.

Munster are awarded a penalty, 5 metres from our line. I sit in our defensive line and get ready to hit a red shirt. Denis Leamy walks up to the ball, picks it up and, glaring at me, says, 'I'm going to fucking run over you.'

I figure he is going to take a quick tap.

'Fucking come on then.'

They kick to the corner instead.

We keep them out and get the ball down to the other end of the pitch. I manage to make a big carry, gaining us some ground, but Munster eventually turn us over. Ronan O'Gara kicks in behind us, then, with me chasing back, grabs me by the scruff of my neck.

'You're a fucking young cunt,' he snarls. 'You don't even know anything about rugby. You think you're the big man but you're not. You're a nobody.'

He pushes me and I push back. I try to square up to him but, in reality, I am quaking.

'Oh shit, this is Ronan O'Gara.'

That is Ronan, though. He is a different man once he crosses that white line. A real competitive animal.

Alain Rolland is the referee. I give away a penalty in the final minutes and Rolland turns to me. 'You're lucky you weren't yellow-carded there. That was a professional foul.'

Oh crap. I run back to the line as fast as I can. I have managed to piss off Leamy, O'Gara and Rolland in twenty minutes of my first inter-provincial game.

David Wallace gets over for another Munster try and they have a penalty near the end but they go for the line rather than take the points. We make them regret the decision by holding out, and holding on, for a tight 20–17 win.

It is a brilliant victory. No one expected us to go down, play in that intimidating atmosphere, against proven internationals, and get a result. I do not know whose brainwave it is but, somehow, we get pizza into the dressing room. We fly back to Belfast that night.

We have moved into second in the league but the Heineken Cup is the immediate focus. We beat Benetton Treviso in our first European game of the season but slipped up away to Biarritz. Now Saracens are coming to Ravenhill and from here on out we know winning is our only chance of reaching the quarter-finals.

Sarries have a decent team but they are not the same side as the one that once possessed the likes of François Pienaar, Richard Hill and Thierry Lacroix. We trail 7–3, early in the second half, when I am called from the bench for my Heineken Cup debut. Neil McMillan, our openside, has injured his ribs. Feelings such as pride and satisfaction may wash over me later but right now I am bricking myself. David Humphreys' penalties give us the edge as the game goes into the final five minutes but a brave score from Rory Best settles the tie.

Feeling hard done by, Saracens vow to smash us at Vicarage Road a week later. We front up, and Tommy Bowe scores a nice try, but a couple of Glen Jackson penalties in the second half see them win 18–10. It will take a miracle to advance to the knock-outs.

Defeats to Leinster and Connacht over the Christmas holidays mean we slide down the league table, but we get back on track against Glasgow. I have replaced Neil in five of our last six matches, playing as a flanker each time. Mark tells me, two days before Biarritz come to Belfast, that I will be making my first Heineken Cup start for Ulster.

The French side are a serious outfit – Thierry Dusautoir, Imanol Harinordoquy, Dimitri Yachvili, Benoît August. Sereli Bobo on the left wing. Before the game, flicking through the match pro-gramme, I check out some of the pictures and statistics of the opposition. 'Holy shit, look at the size of this team.'

The guy that stands out is their tight-head prop, Petru Bălan. Big, bald guy; about 23 stone.

I close the programme and catch the eyes of some of the lads. Focused, steely. Ready. We fancy our chances against anyone at home.

Full house at Ravenhill and a pleasant, great January night for rugby. Friday the 13th. I only have one major superstition but it is more a case of habit and getting myself into match mode. I always wear two pairs of socks. It is purely down to comfort reasons as I wear these big, long studs.

Putting my scrum-cap on at the last moment, though: that is my switch. As soon as I put my helmet on, I am in beast mode. Nothing can stop me. I feel like running around, destroying people. That is what I want to do – run around, run over people.

In every match I play, I want to be man-of-the-match. I want to score tries and I want to sprint around, hurting people. Legally. If I absolutely smash somebody and they are down on the ground, winded, I am one of the first to gloat.

'Fucking take that.'

It is by the rules, but it is fun.

Before games, I make sure I am caffeined up to the max and on edge. I like to be on edge. Every time, before I run out on to the pitch, I give my arms two or three big swings out; stretch the chest. My scrum-cap is on my head, and two or three seconds before kick-off I pull it down.

'Bang. Let's go.'

David signals to us, and we set off after his kick.

About twenty minutes in, Biarritz are playing towards the Clock End. Rory scores an early try for us and we are clinging to a 5–3 lead. Biarritz are attacking, wave after wave.

They get to about 5 metres from our line when the pass comes

going and, with David Humphreys pulling the strings, it seems to click for us. David is one of the best players I have ever played with, without a doubt. The number of times I have seen him spiralling the ball into the corner a bit like O'Gara; he is so good to play with, a class act. He runs the ball really well. He likes playing with me and uses me a lot. He once said to me, 'Stevie, you're prolonging my career. Keep making tackles for me and I could go on another couple of years.'

'Cheers, but already I'm wrecked because of you.'

Paddy Wallace is a star for us, at inside centre. Andrew Maxwell is scoring tries for fun while Tommy Bowe is playing full-back for the odd game as well. Anybody who kicks a high ball in the air, Tommy just comes and gets it. All the simple things are done really well.

With three games to go in the season, I come up against Border Reivers again. By the time they arrive in Belfast, on 12 May 2006, I have established myself in the first team. I am by no means a regular but am making it hard for Mark to leave me out.

We have a 7.30 p.m. kick-off but, with summer fast approaching, it is still bright out. A bonus point will put us top of the table. We tear into Reivers from the opening minute. We score nine tries: Andrew, Tommy and Trimby help themselves to two apiece, with one each for Roger Wilson, Paddy and myself. It is my first try for the senior team. We have some good moves during that game but Andrew scores the pick of the bunch as he takes off up the pitch on the right-hand side. Everyone is on top form. Reivers are struggling, but if you are beating any team by 60 points you are doing well. There is a good feeling about the place and Tyrone Howe, playing in his final season, gets a super reception when he comes off the bench for his 100th Ulster cap.

Leinster lose to Cardiff two days after our win, so we know a bonus-point victory over Scarlets will clinch our first ever Celtic League.

We have not won at Stradey Park for a long time. In the changing room, before the match, it is all about getting a win. We go 12–0 up, thanks to Tommy and an amazing try, under the sticks, by Andrew. We are then shaken by the loss of Simon Best, our captain, to a bad ankle injury. Justin Fitzpatrick comes on in his place. Scarlets compound that loss when Phil John squeezes over from close range.

John bullies his way over for his second try in the second half and almost gets a hat-trick, but we do well to put in a couple of hits and hold him up. David misses a penalty kick and a late drop goal and the match ends 12–12. We wanted 5 points but are leaving with 2.

This time it is Bryn Cunningham, our full-back, who has made his 100th appearance for Ulster. Afterwards, one of the suits walks in with a 'congratulations' and a bit of crystal for him. Bryn does not really care for that, all he wanted was to get something out of the game.

We feel we are still in with a title shot. If we had lost the game, we would have had to win at Ospreys the following week, with a bonus point. Apart from Simon there are no other injuries, everybody feels good. That gives us the confidence to go, 'Right, we nearly beat Scarlets, we can definitely go over and beat the Ospreys.'

There is good travelling support heading over to Swansea. At the Liberty Stadium, which is a 22,000-seater venue, with 10,316 supporters present, our 500 Ulster fans make their voices heard.

I play about sixty-five minutes before I come off with a sore ankle. There are loose bone fragments floating around in there and I will need a summer operation to clear it out. It means I will not get a second crack at an Under-21 World Championship.

Matt McCullough grabs us a try in the first half and David kicks 8 points to put us 13–10 ahead. He drops a pass that probably costs us a score, right on half-time, and that rattles him somewhat. He misses two penalties after the break and the score is stuck on 13–10 when Neil takes my place on the pitch.

Jason Spice, the same lad that had scored against us in Belfast, gets a try with just four minutes to play. Richard Hibbard throws it to the tail of the line-out and Lee Beach pops it down to Spice. There is a massive gap and it is like the Red Sea opening. I am on the bench with my head in my hands.

'Oh my God, how did that happen? That's it. Over.'

Spice touches it down by the posts, meaning Gavin Henson simply has to chip the conversion over. 17–16 down.

Justin brings all the lads in.

'Right, boys, we're going to go in and win the restart. We're going to get the ball back and we're going to get a penalty or a drop goal and win this game. Let's do this.'

There is nothing you can do from the sideline apart from shout and rant. We work our way up, to midway in Ospreys' half, and David calls the ball on himself. Forty metres out, he goes for a drop goal. It is surely the hardest one he will ever have to strike.

It hits one post, then the other, drops down and clips the crossbar. There is almost as much drama in watching David's face as the kick itself. You can see him looking and looking and looking at it. Clip, clip, down, over the bar.

His arms launch into the air. Never in doubt, the stance seems to say. On the sideline, we go nuts. Out on the pitch, the lads still have two minutes left and a lot of defending to do. Paddy must make five or six tackles in those final minutes. Ospreys are in our half but are making no line breaks. We are containing them. The final whistle sounds and we are league champions.

Afterwards, I walk around the pitch with the trophy, going over to the fans at the side of the pitch, getting photos taken. Fans, friends and family are bouncing in and out for photos. It is a great day. It pays the Ulster supporters off, too, as they have been backing us for so long without getting anything in return.

At this stage, I do not truly appreciate how important the win is. By my reckoning, I will lift this cup another five times, win a Heineken Cup and try to claim a World Cup with Ireland. The future has other, turbulent, ideas, however.

But now it's time to party. We head out that night and get absolutely steaming in the less than lively city of Swansea. I pick up a hot girl and bring her back to the hotel. When we land back, I sneak her up the stairs without anyone catching me. Upon opening the door of my room, it is dark. The lights are left off for a reason. My room-mate has also picked up a girl in town and is otherwise occupied.

Given the wasted, drunken, joyful state I am in, this development does not faze me a bit. As myself and the Welsh girl take to my bed, I feel that this cannot be my life.

'This is crazy. Is this what these trips away are always like? Was it because we won the league or what?'

My room-mate is young, free and single. My memory of the end of the night is hazy but I do recall seeing lots of shadows on the wall.

I wake at one point, just before dawn. The others are still sleeping so I pull the covers back up. 'If I was in Swansea with a group of mates, this would not happen,' I muse. 'Is it because I am professional? Do women like professional guys who are earning a bit of money? Or is it because I am really good-looking?'

At that stage of the morning the last thought makes the most sense, and I drift back off.

I am woken next time by a loud bang on the door. Myself and my room-mate look at each other while the two girls lie sleeping. We do not know if they know each other. Davy Irwin, our doctor, who used to play for Ulster, bangs on the door again.

'What is going on here?'

He sticks his head in.

'Good night, lads?'

'Shhhh, get out of here.'

We quickly get our stuff together and smoke-bomb it to the bus. We are still drunk as skunks. As soon as we get on the bus, the slagging starts. 'Well, lads?' they chime, knowing fine well that us two had girls back. But, thankfully, there were a few other things that happened that night which took the heat off us. Put it this way, there was a bill of a few thousand quid as TVs and windows had to be replaced and an entire hotel room urgently needed a makeover.

I sleep the whole way home on the plane. At Belfast City Airport there are three or four hundred people there to greet us because we have the trophy in tow. It is a frantic way to finish off the weekend. Few of the other lads are used to it either: apart from the three or four Heineken Cup-winning veterans, they have not won a thing before at this level.

At the end of this first season, having won a league trophy at twenty and run around Swansea like I was David Beckham, I consider my new life. 'How much wilder can this get?'

That is my introduction to Ulster. Eighteen senior matches and one league-winners' medal. A basic wage of £154 a week. When I signed my contract with Ulster, match fees and win bonuses were included but I never factored them in. With my break-through into the squad, and a winning one at that, I end up earning £27,000 in my first season.

The next season a professional contract is placed in front of me, for £35,000. My mum, who handles my finances, is quick with the advice.

'Jesus, son, you're earning more than me and your dad. Get that bloody thing signed!'

CHAPTER 8

I am able to complete a full pre-season after resting up for a few weeks, post-ankle surgery, in June and July 2006. In a team meeting in early August, the lads throw around aims and possibilities for the forthcoming season. No one is getting ahead of themselves but the ambition is there. The consensus is to consolidate in the league – try to win it again – and put everything into reaching the Heineken Cup quarter-finals. Once we get to the knock-out stages, we may talk again.

Backing up our words, we start the season well and by early November are jousting for top spot in the Celtic League. A lot more lads know who I am, and what I am capable of, so I find the barbs, slagging and hits coming harder and faster. I am in my element.

Europe proves to be a frustration. Again. And this after a great start, beating Toulouse 30–3 at Ravenhill. They have a massive second line and Fabien Pelous, an absolute beast, playing Number 8. He normally plays second row but has shifted back. Early in the match, the ball is thrown to the back of our line-out and Neil Best is tackled. I spin round and make for the breakdown. Pelous is beside me and grabs my shoulder. I open my palm out and am trying to slap his arm free when he smacks me in the mouth. My face feels like it has exploded. I carry on, fight free and get to the breakdown. Pelous is not far behind.

'Here we go again. These French guys are crazy.'

The tries we score that day are ridiculous. Trimby runs in a length-of-a-pitch try, Isaac Boss has a cracking score. We absolutely hammer them.

Sitting in the marquee afterwards, all the chat is about a fantastic, unbelievable win. But when you reach 30 points you have to get the fourth bonus-point try. We scored three, and we all feel that, even though we won and played really well, we have left something behind. We were 30–3 ahead at half-time but could not breach them again. I had a try disallowed in the first half but we never really came close in the second. We have killed the three-time Heineken Cup champions but there is a lingering sense that the bonus-point failure will come back to haunt us.

The haunting arrives a week later as we lose, away to Scarlets. We are a shadow of the side that tore Toulouse apart but still have a chance to snatch the game. Unfortunately, Isaac and Neil get in each other's way, the ball is spilled and the game is lost.

By the time we play, and lose, again in Europe, Ulster have a new Ireland international.

Me.

N. Best, R. Best, S. Best, Boss, Dempsey, D'Arcy, S. Easterby, Ferris . . .

Mark gives me the news on the Tuesday morning, the day before the Ireland squad is revealed, but I am convinced it is a wind-up. He shakes my hand, absolutely thrilled for me. I made my Ulster debut less than a year before.

Seeing my name in newsprint makes it feel completely real. My eyes scan down the alphabetical list and there are the other surnames; the guys I have grown up watching on TV: O'Connell, O'Driscoll, O'Gara, O'Kelly, Stringer, Wallace.

25 October 2006. I am in my first ever Ireland squad, and in great company.

Eddie O'Sullivan, the Ireland coach, tells the press he is bringing me in for a closer look. He is aiming to build a wider squad for the 2007 World Cup. No Irish side can ever afford to experiment in a Six Nations. I know I will have to grab any chance I get during the November internationals.

There are nine Ulster players included in the thirty-two-man squad so it will not be quite the same as those daunting trips down to Deer Park and the Irish Youths sessions. That does not mean I am any less than a pool of nerves.

The day after we beat Border Reivers, Simon Best rings.

'Stevie, do you want me to give you a lift down?'

'That would be brilliant. I'm shitting myself about going down. Having someone like you to introduce me to the guys would be great.'

He picks me up and we make it to the Fitzpatrick Hotel, in Killiney.

'Come on and we'll go for food.'

I have no money in my wallet. 'Shit,' I think, 'I need to find a cash machine.'

Simon shows me into the restaurant. 'Here, Stevie, what do you want? Oh, here's John Hayes.'

'John, really nice to meet you.'

'Here's Marcus Horan, here's Brian O'Driscoll.'

'Right, Marcus. Right, Brian.'

O'Driscoll nods the head at me.

'Holy shit, what am I doing here?' I think. 'This is crazy.'

We walk up to the board with all the specials on it.

'What do you want?' asks Simon.

Better come clean. 'Here, I've no money on me.'

'What do you mean? Neither do any of us.'

'What do you mean?'

'We don't pay for anything. You can get whatever you want.'

'So what are you ordering?'

Simon turns to the person taking the order. 'I'll have the calamari to start and the fillet steak please.'

I look at the menu and that meal is coming to €45 or something. Flipping hell. 'I'll just have the same as him please.'

We take a seat and are chatting away. I am reintroduced to John and a perfectly ordinary, everyday conversation begins. The lads are catching up.

The food arrives. I take a bite of calamari.

'This isn't happening,' I tell myself. 'You can't be sitting here, having dinner with John Hayes, a legend of Irish rugby, at a swanky hotel.'

The guys start filtering in. Simon has been really thoughtful. He wanted me to get there early and ease myself into it, rather than walk into a room with forty lads already there.

The meal is finishing up but I am still thinking about the cash machine and am wondering how long it would take to walk into the nearest town.

The waiter approaches. 'Would somebody like to sign this for me please?'

One of the lads throws his hand up. 'Yeah.' He scribbles his signature. 'Right lads, come on.'

It is starting to sink in. I lean over to Simon. 'You don't actually pay any money?'

'No, no, everything is taken care of. This is the way it is down here, Stevie.'

I walk into the team room the next morning and it is massive. Physio beds everywhere and four or five masseuses. No queuing up here. The fridge is full of protein shakes and all manner of drinks. Everything is so professional.

The only glitch is a big one. The pitches, and training grounds, are diabolical. I jog out for my first on-pitch training session and am taken aback.

'What the hell? This is supposed to be Ireland, a top international set-up.'

The grass is so thick that it reaches up past your ankles. There is little or no drainage. Doing scrummaging and live mauls, standing water splashes up against your face. You are absolutely soaking, and stinking. A couple of times during that November, however, we do at least train on the back pitch at Lansdowne Road. The old ground will be demolished at the end of the year but it is still an impressive sight to behold.

During that first week in Ireland camp my body and physique are put under scrutiny. Many of the Irish lads have heard, from the Ulster boys, that I register big numbers in the gym. Up at Newforge, I am nicknamed 'The Horse'.

I have always been tall for my age, and when I took up sport and started to do some manual work I filled out. I have numerous fast-twitch muscle fibres. More than most. It means I have a greater capacity for strength and power exercises. From the moment I began to take my rugby seriously, and with advice from trainers and experts, I took supplements to aid muscle growth and recovery.

Drugs never, ever crossed my mind. I would not have had the first clue about what steroids or growth hormones were, or what they did, when I was in the academy and making my breakthrough.

I am lucky in that I do not have to worry about weight gain or loss. I am fairly steady. I do take on board a lot of calories – around 5,000 a day. Your average male, my age, would consume about 2,500 a day. There are no superfoods I go back to over and over but I do eat decent amounts of chicken, fish and pasta and take protein shakes.

Although they were athletic, Mum and Dad are not really powerful and strong so, genetically, I got lucky. I earned an early reputation as a strong man. That reputation is put to the test during my four weeks with Ireland.

Power cleaning (an Olympics lift) 100 kilos is a rarity. Paul O'Connell could do 110 kilos but not many of the other lads could come close. O'Connell has heard about me and is down in the gym one morning for a light work-out. He is chatting to the other lads and staying close by. As Paulie does some bench-presses, I go through my lift routine. I am lifting 135 kilos, clean. I go through my lift routine and manage another four. By this stage, Paulie is standing, watching. He calls out to another few lads. 'Have you seen how much this Ferris guy is lifting? You've got to see this.'

I have an audience. After my last lift, I step back.

Paulie shakes his head. 'This guy's a fucking freak.'

It is one of the best compliments I have ever received.

The lads quickly christen me 'Freak of Nature'. Of course, I later hear from Brian O'Driscoll that Paulie had had a few more words to say. They were discussing some of the new faces and the conversation turned to me.

'I hope this guy can play rugby and not just lift weights.'

Thankfully, I am able to play rugby.

I am named at blindside flanker for an Ireland A side captained by Simon. Jamie Heaslip of Leinster is Number 8 and Keith Gleeson, a veteran, is openside. We face an Australian side, at Thomond Park, Limerick, that contains the likes of Adam Ashley-Cooper, Drew Mitchell and Stephen Moore. Myself and Luke Fitzgerald, Leinster's highly rated teenage winger, link up for his try, and a couple of Jeremy Staunton penalties have us 11–0 up. Gleeson is yellow-carded in the closing stages, however, and the Aussies get two late, converted tries to beat us 24–17.

Ireland beat Australia's first team 21–6 four days later. They had defeated South Africa 32–15 in the first game of the Test window. There is a real sense of momentum going into 2007, a World Cup year. Eddie wants to keep that up by putting the Pacific Islanders away. The match will be the final international at the old Lansdowne Road. Eddie is keen to win it with new blood.

The squad he names is a mix of established players and guys that had done well in the A game. I am named as openside flanker. My ability to slot in, across the back row, is paying off. Jamie, Luke and Paddy Wallace, at out-half, also get their first starts. There is plenty to talk about but, first, we have to settle a minor debate.

Nine hundred and ninety-eight players have represented Ireland since their very first Test match. As Jamie, Luke and myself are all set for debuts, a journalist asks who will be the 1,000th Irish international. Caps usually go in alphabetical order, I learn, but Jamie will be the 1,000th. I am number 1,001. I could not care less. I am desperate for number one. The first second of my first minute of my first Ireland cap.

Luke is just out of school and the most nervous out of every-body. I know I am a long way off being a professional rugby player but, in that match, I feel like a boy against men. The Islanders are so big and strong. I am this young Irish kid who is trying to make it to the top level.

Ma'ama Molitika has a good game for them. He takes some shifting at the rucks. Tusi Pisi is a handy 10 and they have some real danger men on the bench. Epi Taione is one of them. A monstrous player. A Tongan back-rower and a guy that can play centre and will go on to star in Super Rugby and the Top 14. I have to tackle him a few times and, days later, will sorely remember each one. He wears a massive forearm guard, with five rolls of duct tape around it. He looks like he is coming at you with a metal bar on his arm. I have to jump on his back at one stage, just to pull, or slow, him down. Whatever works.

I am happy with my performance and am so tired coming off – knackered, and cramping up really bad.

I have never cramped up before.

'Whoa, *this* is Test rugby.'

Paddy plays like a dream that day. He had played out-half in the Ireland Under-19 team that won a World Cup in 1998. He had been their star player. Brian O'Driscoll had simply been a team-mate, a cog in the wheel. Injuries stalled his career but on this day, 26 November, he looks ready to make up for lost time. He lands nine out of ten kicks at goal before he hits the post with the last one, as well as scoring a try. He has a terrific game.

We win 61–17, with Rory Best also getting over for a try and Shane Horgan finishing off a nice team move. He claims a couple of nice cross-field kicks. We vary our tactics and that, combined with our greater fitness, sees us through.

Simon Raiwalui is the Pacific Islanders' captain. He presents me with his jersey and I plan to frame it, alongside my own, for my house. A lovely gesture from their captain to Ireland's 1,001st player.

The long-standing tradition in the senior Ireland team is to get the guy that made his debut steaming drunk. The post-match dinner usually involves good food and some wine. You go up and accept your first cap, say a few words and get off the stage. The fun begins after the meal. Each of your team-mates gets you a drink but you have to drink whatever they are having. It might start off with a whiskey and Coke, a bottle of beer, but it usually escalates. A shot of tequila, more wine, five shots of vodka with Red Bull.

The Pacific Islanders are great fun that night. One of their players brings in an old acoustic guitar, flips it flat and starts finger plucking. Real happy, lilting music; all their boys singing along and laughing. They find out it is your debut so it is more drink to be drunk.

Luke does not make it as far as the music. Not a big drinker, he has one or two and slips off early, much to the annoyance of the senior players. They swear they will get him back at some stage.

Such a crazy night, a proud day, and hard to take it all in. But, at the same time, I am itching to get out and do it all again.

*

Ryan Constable came on board as my agent ahead of my first full season with Ulster. Having agreed to the £35,000-a-year basic contract, Ryan had Ulster include a clause that would see a new deal being worked out if and when I won my first Ireland cap. Within four months of signing that deal, myself, Ryan, Ulster and the IRFU were back around the table.

Two months after my debut, I walk into our house and say to Mum, 'Ryan Constable just phoned me. I'm going to be earning £100,000.'

'What?! Oh Stephen, Stephen, ohhhhhhhh! My heart, my heart.'

'Mum, a hundred grand, a hundred grand, a HUNDRED GRAND! I'm twenty-one years of age and I'm going to be earning a hundred grand!'

Of course, when you play for Ireland and you win, you also get bonuses. This is all new to me.

Life is going to be different. I am not going to be a regular, jobbing rugby player that earns £35,000 for the next ten years. I am going to make £100,000, maybe £200,000 or £300,000 a year if I continue on the road I am on – if I reach every goal I set for myself.

I know that the real work is only about to start.

CHAPTER 9

As soon as I return to Ulster from my time with the Ireland squad, my goal is to help us reach the Heineken Cup knock-out stages and force myself into the 2007 Six Nations squad. Fate has other plans.

I come off the bench in the second half of our home draw with Leinster and damage my thumb. I do not notice it at the time but my thumb has swelled significantly by the time I get back to the dressing room. An X-ray shows a lateral ligament tear and I am on the operating table by Monday morning. Seven weeks out is the prognosis. I travel to Reading and watch, helplessly, as our European ambitions are trampled by London Irish. I return towards the end of January 2007 but that is too late for Eddie O'Sullivan. Jamie Heaslip and Keith Gleeson are included in his squad while I have to content myself with an Ireland A match at Ravenhill.

Two days before Ireland play their first ever rugby match at Croke Park, I am part of an A side with three other Ulster lads, Tommy Bowe, Bryan Young and Roger Wilson. Michael Bradley and Allen Clarke are coaching us but Eddie has selected the team. We are 8–5 down at half-time, our try coming from Rob Kearney.

England bring the likes of James Haskell and Andy Titterrell off the bench in the second half. They open us up.

Midway through that half, the Irish pack is in a maul. I have my head down and am driving forward when Dylan Hartley comes in and uppercuts me. It is for no reason other than him being a dirty bastard. I come out of the maul with blood gushing from my nose, and he just laughs. They are winning by 20-odd points at that stage.

'Ha, ha, you're shit.'

I want to chase after him and pummel him but restrain myself. Little good it does, as we lose 32–5.

'Any opportunity I get to play him at senior level again,' I tell myself, 'be sure to put in a good hit.'

I have no issue with guys playing hard against me. I have come across tough tacklers in my career. Guys like Dan Lydiate and Sam Warburton have hit me hard and dumped me on my arse. I do not mind that. It is the dirty players and the cheats that annoy me. A couple of months later, Hartley is hit with a twenty-six-week ban for eye-gouging James Haskell and Johnny O'Connor in an Aviva Premiership game.

After losing that opener at Croke Park, Ireland go on to win their final four games of the Six Nations but are pipped to the title, on points difference, by the French. Eddie has a settled back row – Simon Easterby, David Wallace and Denis Leamy – so I remain with Ulster. Mark McCall gives me some run-outs at Number 8. I am happy to be back in a role I enjoy so much. I tell myself that my chance will arrive in the summer. I will be ready.

In May, Eddie names me in a thirty-man squad to tour Argentina. It is fantastic to be back in the senior set-up but it is not the tour everyone thinks it is going to be.

Many of the frontline players – the guys that had starred in the Six Nations – are staying at home and are placed on gym routines. While 'The A-Team', as we call them, are back at home, we are away, slogging it out in Argentina in one of the worst tours I have ever been on.

We stay in Buenos Aires and more or less live out of McDonald's for two weeks. We then have to play in Santa Fe and undertake a nine-and-a-half-hour journey there just to get beaten. I come off the bench for my second Test cap. Brian Carney, who has recently converted from rugby league, scores a try on his debut. It is a close-run match. Geordan Murphy misses a drop goal, to win it, in the last minute. There is a sense among the lads that they are in Argentina to make up numbers. As much as guys may not admit it, many still believe they will be the ones to force their way into the World Cup reckoning.

Tomás O'Leary and Tony Buckley are on that tour. Everyone recognizes their potential. You have senior lads on tour too. Malcolm O'Kelly, Keith, Geordan, Jerry Flannery and Simon Best, our captain. Our squad has plenty of caps and experience but we do not play at all well.

Four of the lads – Brian, Tony, Tomás and Barry Murphy – make their debut in the First Test so, that night in Santa Fe, they have to go through their rites of passage. The city itself is not much to speak of, but it has a giant nightclub that serves us well. Our team bus pulls away from Estanislao López Stadium and ten minutes later arrives at the club. All we can hear is this dance music, pumping.

Doh, doh, doh, du du, doh, doh, doh.

There is a red carpet lined with promotional girls leading into the club. No formal ceremonies, no speeches, just both teams in there to socialize with each other.

Tomás is the first of the new caps to be carried out. Tony, for such a big man, gets into all sorts of trouble. We are back drinking shots of 70% proof Inferno again – 'You drink one, I drink one' – until, ten drinks later, you are well on. We are in the nightclub dancing away with what must be fifty stunningly beautiful Argentinian girls. It is heaven.

'Has it only been two years since I was first here with the Under-21s?'

Myself, Bryan Young and Tommy get a taxi to another night-club. Next thing, the taxi stops. We get out and start walking towards the nightclub. I turn around, looking for Bryan.

'Bear, Bear? Are you coming?'

He is hanging out the door of the taxi boking all over the place. We end up paying the taxi driver a few more quid.

We are in that nightclub until all hours of the morning and some guys are out even longer. It is one of those tours where the food is crap, everything is crap, but we end up having a couple of good nights out. It makes the end-of-season grind tolerable.

We have so much kit and training gear. The day after the First Test, myself and Neil Best walk out the front door of our hotel. There is a homeless guy lying asleep in a doorway across the road. It must be minus one or minus two and here is this poor chap in his sleeping bag, freezing. We go back to our rooms, get shorts, T-shirts, coats, trainers, and cross back over to give them to this guy. He wakes up as we are giving him the clothes and his eyes light up like he has won the lottery. He only has a few words of English but is grateful. 'Gracias, gracias.' We can understand that much.

We jump on the bus and head to the airport. To this day, there is probably some guy walking about Argentina with a frigging

Ireland coat on. If anyone ever sees him, tell him Bestie was asking after him.

On that tour, during our gym sessions with Mike McGurn, the strength and conditioning coach, I am clean-lifting 140 kilos. I am in really good shape, strong and fit. I am really looking forward to the Second Test but we get blown away. Argentina get off to a good start and their out-half, Federico Todeschini, puts away a couple of penalties.

I do not make it to half-time. I tear cartilage in my left knee. That is my tour done. I am booked in for another operation to repair the cartilage (it is a damaged meniscus). I have a fight on my hands to get myself fit, well in advance of the World Cup. There is only going to be one Test match, against Scotland on 11 August, before Eddie selects his squad.

Within two weeks of the operation I am back in the gym and doing lengths in the swimming pool. The guys at Ulster are a great help to me and I am straight down to our pre-World Cup camp, in Killiney, in late July. My knee is still stiff but I tell myself I simply need game time and the problem will sort itself out.

The camp is intense during the day, and Eddie is eager for us to go on a few nights out in those early weeks. We are in a Chinese, in Killiney, one night in early August and, as things in groups of lads often go, some messing about rapidly escalates. Something gets thrown across the room and the handkerchiefs get dipped in the red wine, rolled up into balls and flung back. Next thing, the white wall in the room is covered in red wine and bits of tissue. More or less like a school cafeteria food fight but with wine and Chinese food. It is brushed under the carpet. We give them a couple hundred quid to paint the wall and get out of there.

Eddie often joins us for a few beers. He is that kind of guy. He is very good on nights out as he makes sure there is security for the guys. Brian O'Driscoll and Ronan O'Gara are under serious pressure from the public but the security is brilliant. On the nights Eddie is out, drinking with us, he sits at the back of the bus, smokes a cigar and sings songs.

The good vibes within the squad do not mean there is not a real edge to training. Eddie has selected a large training squad, forty-eight lads. With only thirty places up for grabs, there are lads having pops off each other.

There are always scraps at Ulster. Neil is a mental case. In training, in playing, he is so physical. Ryan Caldwell and Bryan Young fight each other all the time, throwing digs at each other. Bryan and Justin Fitzpatrick often stand toe-to-toe and start boxing. When a big fight breaks out the best thing to do is let it happen, let the boys get it out of their system. There might be a bit of rolling about for ten seconds but then that is it. Done and dusted.

There is one incident in the World Cup training camps that shakes us. Paulie O'Connell and Caldy get into it during a break-down drill down on the back pitch at the University of Limerick. The pair have been at each other all day. Ryan has dropped a couple of sly shoulders on Paulie. They clash again, with Ryan dropping the shoulder, and both fall to the floor. Paulie springs to his feet and lamps Caldy in the gub.

Paulie literally knocks him out. Bang, out cold.

Neil is a yard away and grabs Paulie in a bear hug. 'Whoa, whoa, whoa.'

As Paulie is yanked out the road, he flicks a boot out, trying to shake himself free. It catches Caldy in the cheek and opens him up.

As soon as it happens, Paulie puts his hands on his head and starts walking off the pitch. You can see it in his face. 'What the fuck did I just do?'

There is quite a bit of blood pumping from the cut on Caldy's cheek but Gary O'Driscoll, the team doctor, is over immediately. Within ten seconds everybody has cleared and Caldy comes to. He is all right but has no idea what has just happened.

That changes Paulie. He saw red that day. When he turned round to smack him, he did not mean to drop him out like a stone. Those things can happen at training. There are fisticuffs all the time, there are niggles all the time. But this incident is above and beyond bad. We go to see Ryan afterwards, in hospital. The medics keep him in overnight, as a precaution. We later discover that he had swallowed his tongue after the punch. Paulie is so apologetic. They are both big enough men. Caldy accepts his apology and they both move on. Paulie is a good man. He never loses that competitive streak or that will to win, but I never witness him do anything like that again.

The only real shot I have at getting myself selected is Scotland at Murrayfield. Brian Carney starts in front of Tommy. Shane Jennings' thumb injury helps my case and Eddie selects me at openside. Keith and Alan Quinlan are on the bench so getting the start means nothing, yet, in terms of a World Cup spot. I am only supposed to play fifty or sixty minutes but Neil picks up an injury and I switch to blindside. I play the full game and, as we are under the cosh for most of it, land twenty-seven tackles. Many newspaper articles are putting it down to myself and Jamie Heaslip for a place in the squad. We lose 31–21 but I am happy with my performance and feel I have the edge.

The squad is named two days after the Scottish match. I make the cut. Keith and Jamie miss out. Quinny sneaks in as he is covering second row too. Eddie has only selected one designated Number 8 in his squad, Denis Leamy, but he tells me that I am his cover there.

I am one of seven Ulster players selected but it should be eight. Tommy is extremely unlucky not to make it. He briefly travels to France with us, as injury cover for Shane Horgan, who eventually gets the all-clear. Eddie does not seem to rate Tommy as a player but I find his omission strange, as everyone else does.

Eddie has zeroed in on getting his players bigger and stronger for the World Cup. All the focus is on strength and conditioning for the tournament, not on skill. Eddie's frontrunners play only one Test, against Italy at Ravenhill, before setting off to France. We get away with a win, by the skin of our teeth, but the mood is less than buoyant afterwards. There is a lot of talk that the boys are undercooked – that they do not have enough games going into it. They are gym-strong instead of being fit, quick and sharp.

We dismiss such notions. 'Once we land in France,' we say, 'we will hit our stride.'

As a team, we know we have the potential to go far. Although I am new to the scene, we have, essentially, the same squad that beat Australia and South Africa in the November internationals and only lost out in the Six Nations on points difference – a last-minute French try against Scotland. Both Eddie and Brian, as our captain, openly state that we are going to France to win the World Cup.

I never felt like such a rock star as I do for that flight over to France. Arrive at Dublin Airport, no passport control, straight through and on to a private plane. Upon landing we hop on a bus that takes us to Bordeaux. The rock-star feeling soon fades.

'Where the frig are we staying?'

We are based at a big hotel in an industrial estate outside Bordeaux. The remote location means you cannot walk outside the front door and into town. We arrive in good spirits. It is 24 degrees and we are sunbathing by the pool. Five days later it is 5 degrees. It is a twenty-minute taxi journey into Bordeaux and the drivers are ripping everyone off. It is horrendous. But the worst thing about the hotel is the food. We laugh and joke about it but we live on Nutella, toast and cans of Coke. I fly over there 112 kilos and come back 104 kilos. That tells its own story.

Mike McGurn is working us hard in the lead-up to the tournament. From the training drills and plays we run, a set of us cop, fairly quick, that we are the outsiders when it comes to selection. Myself, Bryan Young, Alan Quinlan and Brian Carney. We dub ourselves 'The Bordeaux Four'. We train together, go out for dinner together and nip out for a few beers together. To be honest, without that group, the monotonous camp existence would be even more of a struggle.

For the main lads, the going is tougher. In the warm-up game against Bayonne, Drico gets sparked out, by Mike Te Whata, and fractures a cheekbone. Then, when the World Cup gets going we play Namibia first and scrape through with a 32–17 win. We look flat. Eddie decides he has to stick with the same team. He was probably hoping to get a good win against Namibia and to experiment a little for Georgia, but the same team is wheeled out for that, the same team for France, and the same team for Argentina. For me, from the outside looking in, I feel I will never get an opportunity because the lads are not performing well. Eddie is hoping they are going to come good, but they never do.

The performances on the pitch reflect the atmosphere off the pitch. In the team room there is not much craic. Everybody keeps themselves to themselves. The team room is 500 metres away from our rooms so a lot of guys just spend time back at theirs. It is not like other team hotels we have been based at, like Carton House, where everybody comes straight down and has dinner in the team room. It is very awkward.

The Bordeaux Four are the only ones who come out of the whole thing looking well because we do not play. We never get a sniff. It is hard to say if the four of us would have made a difference but the frustrating part is the realization that you are not going to get the chance.

There is an open training session, the second week in, and I am pumped for it.

'Right, I'm going to fucking prove a point here. I need a game.'

I am running about, smoking everybody, carrying balls and sitting anybody that comes near me down. I am off the leash, running through the boys and fending people off.

There is a drill that goes tackler, tackler, tackler, tackler, tackler, tackler – three defenders on each side. You run up, get the ball, and have to beat them. Then you come round the corner and do the same again. There are three or four hundred people in the stands and it is pissing down, wet, soaking. Every time I get the ball I sit somebody down and every time I am in the defence I am smashing ball-carriers. We are wearing these padded suits and I am cleaning boys out. You could hear the wet smack, the impact off the suits, up in the stands.

I make one mistake, and that is trying to smash John Hayes. He very rarely gets the ball. Our coming together is a bit like mine with Petru Bălan. I try to pulverize him but we both thwack off each other. Shockwaves through my body. We both bounce back and I look him in the eyes.

'Go on ahead, John.'

I am not doing that again.

I believe I have done everything I can. In the training sessions, open and closed, I am scoring tries all over the place. The boys are openly chatting about how well I am doing but I never get a look-in. I cannot do much more; that is the best I have, but it is not enough for Eddie.

I sit down with him once during the tournament.

'Is there any chance of giving me a shot?'

'You're putting the hard work in and you are doing everything right. But I have to stick with the boys at the minute and hopefully we will get a performance.'

Neil is on the bench and Simon Easterby is starting. That is how it is. It is tough but it stands me well, going forward, as I know what I want out of the next World Cup, if I make one.

Walking along the pitch as the boys were warming up against Georgia, there was this sense that we were not in a good place. I will never know how Georgia did not beat us that day. There was a Georgian try disallowed in the end and it was always a try.

It was one of those ones. As soon as we got off to a bad start it got worse and worse and worse. The performances reflected that and the atmosphere reflected that. My brother, Dave, and friends

Adam McMinn, Andrew Fraser and Stephen Williamson travel over to the World Cup from Dublin in a Ford Fiesta. They head to Dublin, have a night out and get up the next day going, 'Shit, we are late for our boat.' They drive the wrong way down one-way streets trying to get to the docks. They just about make it to the boat, travel to France and drive to Paris. They expect me to play or feature in one of the games. That is disappointing, as I want the lads to see me play. I get them tickets to the France game and I am sitting more or less directly across from them in the stand in my team tracksuit. They have an absolute ball and I meet them on a couple of nights out. But it is difficult when people make the effort and make the trip and you are not able to repay them with a performance.

France demolish us, 25–3, but worse news is to follow. Simon Best is rushed to hospital following a heart scare. It is worrying for the entire squad, but hits Rory, his brother, hardest. Having captained us in Argentina only three months before, Simon is one of the leaders within the squad. Once doctors have discovered there is no immediate threat to his life, the decision is made to get him home as soon as possible. As players, we are kept informed of the situation but pretty much cocooned. Given the seriousness of his situation, group visits are not advised.

Four days later, and chasing tries to stay in the tournament, we run into an in-form Argentina side. They know they can slow us down illegally as we have no use in penalties. They beat us 17–12 and we are out. Eddie has, pretty much, selected the same squad for each game with nothing to show for it. Eddie is all about the big players and he sticks with the big players. It is, to a degree, more about individuals than assembling a good team. The talk, before any ball was kicked, was, 'If Ireland don't have Brian

O'Driscoll fit, they have no chance. Shane Horgan is injured? Ireland are out!'

In time, the lads opened up and talked about how tough it was but it was a touchy subject for a while. Donncha O'Callaghan used to joke that it was like *Fight Club*. The number-one rule about being at the 2007 World Cup was you are not allowed to talk about the 2007 World Cup.

When I get my World Cup medal, for taking part, it is almost left out of the suitcase for home.

'I don't want that. Frigging hell, I didn't even play in it. I was there, but what did I do?'

I tell myself that I will go to another World Cup and that it will be nothing like this. I use my disappointment as a positive in my career but it feels far from positive at the time. It is terrible; so unenjoyable. The only thing I can take out of it is that I have got better at table tennis.

Any hopes I have of taking my frustration out on the opposition are super short-lived. In November I play against Glasgow, but we are lit up at Firhill. We lose 25–6 and I struggle throughout. My knee is giving me lots of grief. The operation has not fixed the problem. Mark McCall makes a brave call, to pull me out of the line of fire. I am scheduled in for more surgery to repair the ligament. This time, with no World Cup looming, the recovery period is drawn out.

I return in mid-February 2008 and take home a couple of man-of-the-match awards. The repaired knee feels great. I am unable to force my way into Ireland's match-day squads for the Six Nations, but there are call-ups for training squads.

In terms of the national team, it is a frustrating period. When it is a thirty-five-man squad I am called down, but when it is cut to thirty I am out. We are training at Bray and it is absolutely horrendous. The only reason I am there is because David Wallace and Denis Leamy are sitting at the side with their beanie hats on. They are taking it easy, as they have put in a hard shift the week before. I am just down for scrum training and line-out opposition. It gets tedious, but I keep working hard in the gym and try to have the craic with the lads. Not that there is much of it around. Ireland are struggling in the Six Nations. The World Cup pall has yet to lift.

Eddie is struggling to get any extra out of the lads.

I used to love his wee sayings.

'Get out there and set your fucking hair on fire.'

'Don't put the cart in front of the horse.'

'The egg in the hot basket.'

In the changing rooms he is a good motivator and somebody I like playing for. He is a good guy, and I have a good relationship with him. I know all the lads do as well. Ultimately, though, his time runs out.

Eddie departs the scene in March. There is talk of Declan Kidney, the Munster boss, coming in. Adapting to a new coach is something I am getting used to. In the space of three months, with my province, I have played under three head coaches. Ulster are imploding.

CHAPTER 10

During a training session at Newforge, I am in with the dirties. It is October 2006, and we have a big Heineken Cup game coming up, at home.

Kevin Maggs is training with the first team, as is Tommy Bowe. You are not going to let the boys run through you so, when the lads run their set-play, I tackle Tommy really low. When I tackle him, I roll and take Maggs out. He goes down as if he has been shot. Mark McCall freaks out. He thought Maggs had really hurt himself. I have taken two players out with one tackle.

He turns to me. 'Stevie, get off. Get the bloody hell off this training pitch and don't come back.'

I stand up, a young kid with my tail between my legs.

'What?'

'Get off this pitch right now and get to the changing rooms. Piss off.'

'OK.'

I walk off, and into the changing rooms. I throw off my boots, thinking, 'Was that uncalled for? That was really bizarre what just happened.'

Of course Mark must have been feeling the pressure. He was

Left: I came into the world in the summer of 1985 – already inquisitive!

Below left/right: Lounging around with my dad, Rab, at home in Maghaberry and then (literally!) looking up to my brother Dave as he headed off to school.

Bottom: Christmas 1990, with my mum Linda in the picture too. My other brother, Andrew, has never been forgotten by our family.

Above: I eventually grew into my Manchester United T-shirt. I've been a lifelong fan of the Red Devils.

Below: The javelin was my best sport before I chose a life in rugby. This was at the Districts Championships in 2002, before I became Ulster and Ireland champion.

Above: The Friends School squad with me already in the back row (*centre*). I played number 8 but was bitter to lose to Sullivan Upper at Medallions.

Below: There was more success though when I made it with Ireland Youths. This was in Italy in 2003 and I seem to be in the same position again!

The World Cup in South Africa with Ireland Under-19s in 2004 should have been fantastic, but will be remembered only for the tragic loss of John McCall.

Two years later I was winning the Celtic League and named Ulster Player of the Year. I look so young!

A proud moment: making my senior Ireland debut against the Pacific Islanders in the final international at the old Lansdowne Road.

Above: The Ulster boys – me, Rory Best and Paddy Wallace – after winning the Grand Slam at the Millennium Stadium in 2009. It was an unforgettable day and night.

Below: The Ireland squad was invited up to Stormont for an official congratulations ceremony; meeting the Queen was a big honour.

Above: The infamous eye-gouge by David Attoub of Stade Français caught on camera by Oliver McVeigh. He was bang to rights.

Below: The Lion at full speed. Scoring that try against Golden Lions at Ellis Park was my proudest moment.

Above: Unfortunately, injuries became a constant theme throughout my career. What might Ulster have gone on to achieve with a full-strength squad?

Below: There were plenty of brilliant days too, with the highlight probably beating Munster at Thomond Park. Just look at ROG's face!

freaking out about losing two of his star men. Kevin was an outstanding international. We had started 2006/07 well but results had tailed off.

Phil Morrow comes in to see me.

'Are you alright, big man?'

'What the fuck was that about? I'm hardly going to let the lads run through me.'

'I know, Mark was out of order there. Don't worry about it.'

I shower, get a bit of lunch and go to the gym. Next thing Mark taps at the window. Am I going to get another bollocking?

'Look Stevie, I'm really sorry. I lost the head there. I thought we had lost a couple of key players there. I apologize for it and for bawling you out of it in front of the players.'

'It's grand, I'm only a young fella.'

'Listen, just put it behind you.'

The season before, our league win came out of nowhere. We put together a great run and started getting in crowds of more than 10,000. We were getting eight and nine lads called into Ireland squads. Expectations shot up. We did not have the squad to cover the international call-ups though. We were stretched thin. Europe was over for us by January.

The following season was even worse.

The IRFU had persuaded Mark's assistant, Allen Clarke, to manage its Elite Player Programme. This guy called Steve Williams came in. We called him Turkey. He replaced Allen, who was an Ulster legend and someone I had looked up to when I was younger. Ulster through and through. From that, they brought in Steve, who is a great fella but who arrived from Pertemps Bees. Division One in England. This was Ulster Rugby, who wanted to create this professional set-up, make strides in Europe and win more trophies, and they brought in a guy nobody knew. Six months in and they realized, this guy was not cutting. We fell away badly in the league and could not retain our title.

I arrived back from the World Cup in early October 2007 and could tell something was up. The atmosphere was off. People were sniping at each other. I came in after a bad defeat to Newport Gwent Dragons and it was rock bottom. In the gym I looked the boys in the eyes and thought, 'We are in a bad place.' Fingers were starting to be pointed. In professional rugby, the results are never blamed on the players.

'Ulster are shite. Get rid of Mark McCall.'

It is not just him, it is the players' responsibility as well. But the players do not get sacked. I played in away defeats to Scarlets and Glasgow and a home draw with Leinster. All the while, my knee was in bits. I was heading in for more surgery, in November, when Gloucester beat us at home in our first Heineken Cup game of the season. They were scoring tries for fun in the first half. Two days after that loss and word came out that Mark was resigning. We already knew. He had told the squad after the Gloucester game. It was incredible. Yes, we had lost a good few games in a row and professional sport is a cut-throat business, but Mark had led us to win the league in 2006. It was not that long ago.

Mark would often say to us, 'You don't become a bad team overnight.' That is what we tried to say to each other as well, after he left, but there is no improvement after Steve Williams is somehow placed in charge of the team. In my opinion, he is not good enough for Ulster. It is tough on the players. All we want is a coach with a bit of a name, a good reputation. Somebody who can come in and fill us with confidence.

We cannot put our finger on how everything has turned on its head.

Our Heineken Cup hopes are said and done a week after the Gloucester defeat when Bourgoin turn a 17–9 half-time deficit into a 24–17 win. We are out on our arse.

There is no respite in the league. We are getting beaten so regularly. If Munster or Leinster are not in town, Ravenhill is doing well to get about 7,500 people through the gate.

'What the hell is going on? How can things go so wrong, so quickly?'

Steve is completely out of his depth. He is in charge of a professional team, the only professional team in Northern Ireland. A guy who came from Pertemps Bees. None of the players believe he is good enough to do it

The Ulster board must agree with us, as they are scouting around for a new head coach already. They eventually settle on Matt Williams, the former Leinster and Scotland coach. The news filters through in December but Mattie will not officially take over until February 2008. The wider squad is again underwhelmed with the appointment.

Before Mattie arrives, Tommy Bowe breaks it to us that he is leaving for Ospreys in the summer. It is a big blow to lose one of our star players. There is a bit of money floating around the Welsh club right now, and Tommy is offered a good deal. He has only been contracted to Ulster, not the IRFU. Ospreys are a good side, with Mike Phillips, Alun Wyn Jones and Shane Williams in their line-up. He can picture success with them, whereas we are on a downer.

You can see where he is coming from – earn more money, play for a better team, and, hopefully, play for Ireland. Being left out of that World Cup squad has probably played on his mind. But Ulster are losing a player of the highest calibre and I am losing a mate. We are sad to see him go. By the end of the season we also lose Roger Wilson and Neil Best to Northampton.

Mattie's arrival at Ulster coincides with my return to fitness after my second knee operation in six months. This time I feel stronger than ever. Mattie pulls out all the motivational stops for his first game, against Dragons. Before the match, he has Ulster legend Mike Gibson come in for a speech and to hand out jerseys. It is a nice touch but we are fortunate to be playing such a poor team. We win 38–13, blaze in six tries, and I am named man-of-the-match.

For the rest of the season, and into the next, I produce some of my finest performances for the club. If I am fit, it does not matter who we are playing against, I know I am in with a shout of being man-of-the-match. Every single week.

That is a good way to feel.

David Humphreys used to say, 'Right, let's make sure we get the ball into Stevie's hands.'

When you have someone that has seventy-two caps for Ireland and he is calling on guys to get the ball to you, as you are the best carrier – the player to get the team moving forward – it fills you full of confidence.

I walk into a team meeting on a Monday morning and one of the coaches says, 'Right, instead of taking the ball there, passing it into midfield and hitting up Paddy Wallace, we want Stevie to take that ball up.' The confidence gets another boost. There is a real belief in you.

I want those man-of-the-match awards. The crystal vases after Heineken Cup games or bottles of champagne after league clashes. With Ulster, we also get a £100 voucher for Shu restaurant, up on the Lisburn Road. I must eat at Shu about ten or twelve times over three seasons.

'Alright, Stevie? Same again?'

That is what I love.

Playing well brings with it that extra attention and time in the spotlight. People begin to know my name. I do not need to wear my Ulster jersey into nightclubs any more.

You always get dickheads or drunken arseholes coming up to you on nights out. As I am a big lad, they puff their chests out and tell me I am nothing special. Now settling into my role as a senior player, albeit still in my early twenties, I learn to walk away from these people. For the most part, people could not be nicer when they approach, usually asking for an autograph or a picture. I am happy to oblige and still find it a complete novelty. For every request I get, Tommy, whenever he is back home, gets ten. He is pestered.

In school, I dated a good-looking girl. I had no chat in me and was a bit shy. Growing up, I hung around with a group of fifteen lads and two girls. The two girls dated a couple of the fellas in the group. There were never any single girls in our group. As soon as I left school, and was single again, I was never able to go out and get girls.

Starting at Ulster Rugby, I had to learn the ropes of trying to pull.

The more famous you get, however, the easier it gets. You no longer need to approach a girl; they come and chat to you. For some of the lads it is a nightmare. I am young and single and enjoying every minute of it. A professional rugby player, aged twenty-two, earning £100,000 a year. I am on top of the world and cannot wait for more.

As a team, and a set of players, we have our encounters with groupies. Does Ulster Rugby have groupies? One hundred per cent. We win a match at Ravenhill on a Friday night and head into Ollie's nightclub. I see the same girls in there from when Ulster won the last time. With Belfast being such a small place, it is very difficult to find a girl from home who has not been with one of the rugby players. If you do get up to mischief, word gets back and around very, very quickly.

There is no doubt being successful and earning good money attracts good-looking girls. I cannot tell if those girls consciously show up where we are. They are probably thinking, 'There is a good crowd tonight, the rugby guys might be in town, we'll go over for a few laughs and a few free drinks.' As a young guy, if you and your mate were both single, were going for a beer and heard there were supermodels in Ollie's, you would go round for a look. You might even run.

I remain very close with my friends from back home. When I go out partying at the weekends, I am usually with them instead of the Ulster team. I do not spend a lot of time socializing with the rugby lads. If I go out and pull a girl, it is somebody the rugby players have never heard of. The rugby players never go out in Banbridge. Rory Best is a good country guy. He is still dating his childhood sweetheart, from home. None of the guys ever seriously date any of the girls who are in that group. Nothing comes from it, apart from good craic.

The biggest temptation I face is cars and trying not to blow all my money on them. One of the first things Mum wanted me to do when I started on the £35,000 contract was to open up a Credit Union account. I did, but soon found myself pouring much more money into my obsession with cars. In my first full season, I went from driving my mum's Renault Clio, a 1.5-litre turbo diesel, to getting an Ulster Rugby car, a champagne-coloured Ford Mondeo. I picked my brother up and took him on a lap of Lisburn, thinking I was a high roller in this 2-litre diesel Mondeo.

At the age of twenty-one, the very first car I bought was a BMW M3. It had a 3.2-litre V6 engine. The only way I could get insured on it was through Ulster Rugby. So, when it came down to negotiations, I made sure I had free insurance, through their fleet deal, included on my contract.

A mate of Rory's, a guy called Greg Mitchell, has a car place in Strabane. I gave him a call one day.

'Greg, I want an M3. I want it blue, Estoril blue. I want black leather interiors and it has to be Tiptronic.'

Two weeks later he said, 'There's one coming in, I got you one.'

'Has it got everything I need?'

'Yep, it's got everything.'

I drove the couple of hours over to Strabane and met Greg.

'Come on and we'll take it for a rip up the road.'

Jumped in. Vroooom. Raced up the road and this thing was doing 130 miles an hour just like that. Nought to 60 in 4.5 seconds.

'Right, it's mine. Gimme it.'

I got the windows tinted and rocked into training a couple of weeks later, and the boys were like, 'Holy shit.' Rory and David already had M3s so I was only following the trend.

Tiptronic, tinted windows, black leather interior. Still, it gave me some problems. I was on the M1, driving into training in my lovely M3, thinking I was the dog's balls. Out of nowhere these lights started flashing on the dashboard. I drove another couple of miles to Sprucefield and next thing, bang, the car cuts dead. It was rush-hour traffic and I was in the fast lane.

Within minutes there was a five-mile tailback on the M1, with the main suspect sitting in his car, behind his tinted windows, embarrassed as fuck. What could I do? People always warn you not to get out on to a motorway. I could have easily got out a couple of guys and pushed it on to the hard shoulder. Instead, I phoned 999.

'Hello, I'm stuck on the M1. My car has just cut out.'

Ten minutes later, nobody had come. Another ten minutes went by and traffic was going berserk. Cars were crawling by because of the tailback. All I could hear was beep, beep, beep, beep.

These guys in a white van cruised by with the windows rolled down.

'Ah, you fucking wanker. Look at you in your flash car.'

They were giving me the fingers.

This would be some excuse to pull at training. 'Did you hear about that five-mile tailback? Yeah, that was me.'

Half an hour earlier I thought I was some Billy Big Dick in this class car. But there I was, sat holding up traffic coming from Dungannon. I kept the head down with the hazard lights on until the police arrived. We pushed it on to the hard shoulder and I rang a crowd to get it towed. I had to get rid of it after that experience.

Six weeks into Matt Williams' reign, he calls us all in for a meeting and, when we are seated, dims the lights. He starts up a slideshow.

'Boys, we're playing the Red Stags this weekend.'

'Who?'

'The Red Stags.'

'Munster.'

'You're not to call them Munster. All week, it's the Red Stags.'

'Why? We're fucking playing Munster. We're not playing the Red Stags.'

He has it in his head that if we call them the Red Stags all week, we will play better and beat them on the Saturday. We are grown men. We are not fucking sixteen.

'Yeah, let's call them the Red Stags all week. Let's see if it works.'

We play Munster and are impaled on their horns. We lose 42–6.

The next week, he calls us in for another meeting.

'Alright boys, close your eyes.'

Thirty grown men sitting together in a room, looking at each other.

'Right, close your eyes. I want you to think about winning this weekend against the Ospreys.'

We close our eyes.

'Right, now I want you to sit in silence and think about the first tackle, the first carry you are going to make.'

'OK.'

This goes on for about fifteen minutes until the talk is over, our eyes are open and we walk out of the room.

It starts with a few jokes.

'Here, what were you thinking about? You thinking about riding your missus?'

It starts like that.

Ospreys throttle us, 32–7.

The next week, we go in.

'OK, boys, close your eyes.'

I take a glance around. One of the boys is on his phone, another lad is lining up a punch on his mate with his eyes closed. Four other lads in the corner laughing.

'This is fucking pointless,' I think.

Matt is standing at the top of the room, thinking he is a sports psychologist that is going to turn Ulster Rugby around.

We walk out, and the chat begins.

'Is this guy cracked in the head? Is he not right or what?'

Matt had been out of full-time coaching for about eighteen months when he landed the Ulster job. He had won the Celtic League with Leinster but that was back in 2001. He had coached Scotland for two years and had a ridiculous record: he had won three matches out of seventeen with the Scots, and they were against Italy, Japan and Samoa.

How can Ulster then employ someone with that record?

A few of us had been chatting to the Leinster lads, down at Ireland camp.

'What is he like?'

'Yeah, yeah, lads,' they said, their faces breaking into big grins. 'Good luck with that.'

They knew; they had worked with him at Leinster. We already had our doubts after chatting about his Scotland record. Talking to the lads confirmed our suspicions.

Matt came in and talked this unbelievable game. He should

make his living from public speaking. He walked into a room, at the start, and left with every one of us thinking he was a god.

'Jeez, this guy really knows his stuff. He knows what he's talking about.'

But he seemed to me not to have a clue. Not a notion.

In one of our first sessions he walked out on to the pitch and went straight over to Paddy Wallace, our number 10. He started showing Paddy how to kick a conversion. Paddy must have thought, 'I've been here ten years. I've played international rugby. You're not even a rugby player and you're trying to tell me how to kick?'

Another time, he approached Rory as he was taking line-outs.

'This is how you should be holding the ball.'

Rory had played for Ulster about seventy times at this stage.

Matt was the master of appearing to know everything but, as it turned out, he did not seem to me to know that much. Again, I got on well with him. I believe he is a decent fella. You could have a good laugh with him. But, in terms of a rugby coach and bringing Ulster Rugby to where they wanted to be, he should never have been employed. Never. That responsibility came down to Ulster chief executive Mike Reid.

I was in training one day, early on. I was coming back from that knee injury. We were running drills. Mattie had been showing us clips, earlier that day, of James Hook, from Ospreys, catching at pace, at full speed, behind his back. That is the skill he felt we were lacking. We ran a few set-plays and one of the lads threw a pass behind me. I tried to catch it, behind my back, but failed. Mattie chirped up with his take on how I should have caught it.

I whipped around.

'Shut the fuck up, Mattie. Fuck off!'

Everyone stopped what they were doing. Time for the coach to rip me a new one.

Silence. I was standing there, glowering. A couple more seconds passed. Mattie was sizing up his next move.

'The Horse is back!' he shouted. 'The Horse is back!'

'What is this guy at?' I asked myself. 'This guy is doing my head in. There he is, trying to be one of the boys. Everyone just looking at each other.'

It became a catchphrase at the club, whenever I walked in the door. In a bad Australian twang: 'The Horse is back! The Horse is back!'

Near the end of 2007/08 and we are sitting eighth in the table. Matt may have inherited a mess but the situation has not improved a jot since his arrival. We have one more game left, against Cardiff. Matt has one last slideshow for us. The lights are dimmed and up goes the first slide.

'Boys, last week we got beaten by five points but we got a bonus point. If we had won that game, we would have had another three points and we would be into sixth.'

'Right.'

Another slide.

'Three weeks ago, we got beaten by Cardiff. We got beat by thirteen points. If we had've converted those few penalties and scored a try in the last minute, we'd be up to fifth in the table.'

Next one.

'A few weeks before that, the Ospreys beat us . . .'

It gets so bad that he goes way back; months.

'Boys, if we had've beaten Leinster, in the RDS, we'd be sitting top of the table.'

We can only shake our heads, but all of us are thinking the same thing. 'You can't go "What if?" If we had've won the last fifteen games of the season we would have won the league. Right. We get it.'

These fucking slides. In his head, he can probably see the league table changing with each win that never happened. We are sitting there. We know we are eighth and in trouble. We do not need to be told that if we had got some last-minute tries we would be sixth.

He starts to become this laughing stock. Nigel Brady perfects an unbelievable impression of him and that, in a way, sums him up. Mattie seems to me to be just one of these characters that believes that whatever he is doing is right. That, for some reason, we deserve to be top of the table. But that is not the way it works.

He strikes me as a bluffer. Yet Ulster say he is the man to take our team forward. It is not Matt Williams' fault. It is the people who employed him. We had a good coach in Mark McCall. We had won the league with him. Next thing you know, a few bad results and Allen Clarke was gone, then Mark. They did not give them enough time. That is the problem with Ulster and will be for the next three or four years. You do not know who is coming or going. It is the same for players too. Just look at Tommy going to the Ospreys, Roger and Neil heading to Northampton. David retires at the end of the season. Four quality players out the door. For me it is a case of 'Why are we getting these coaches that aren't capable of bringing us to the next level?'

*

Following a summer tour with Ireland, I sign an improved, three-year deal for 2008/09. If I stay fit and in form, I will be earning £200,000 during the third year of the incremental deal. David Humphreys moves upstairs and becomes director of operations, but we all know it means director of rugby. We shore up our squad but it is nowhere near as strong as the likes of Leinster, Munster, Ospreys or Scarlets. The main issue, however, is that Matt is still in charge. We lose our first four league games of the season before edging Edinburgh at Ravenhill. For the second season running in Europe we lose our first two pool games and are goners by December.

The boys just do not want to play for him. Of course, when we are losing, we want to go out the next game and win. There is no league play-off system. You win the league by getting the most points. If you are sitting mid-table at the turn of the year, you have no chance of winning the league.

I, for one, do not believe in the coach and his systems. I know many of the lads do not believe in him. That realization is hard to shake off. Sitting in the changing room and looking at my mate Rory, I catch his eye and we give each other a nod. 'Screw it. Let's go out and give these boys something.'

But if you are not getting the right information to help beat the opposition, of course it is going to have an impact on you. It does not matter how fit or physical you are, if you are doing something wrong out on the pitch it is going to have an impact. Coaching is vital, especially so in rugby, as it is such a tactical game. You only have to look at quality coaches like Joe Schmidt and Michael Cheika to see that. We want to win for each other but we do not want to win for Matt. You need everybody, all sixty people at Ulster Rugby – coaches, players, backroom and support staff – all pulling for the team to win.

January 2009. We are up at Letterkenny Rugby Club. We have heard all of Mattie's speeches by this stage.

He gets up and gives another one, thanking everybody. He goes off on one for about twenty minutes. How good Ulster are, what he brings to the table, his experience, the great players we have, blah, blah, blah.

We all walk out after. 'Yeah, same old shite.'

Everyone else is coming up to us, eyes wide. 'Oh my gosh. Matt is fantastic. He is unbelievable. He's fantastic. Ulster are really going places.'

Four months later, he is sacked. That, in a nutshell, is Matt Williams. Decent fella. Wrong place, wrong time.

CHAPTER 11

My first trip to Lansdowne Road was on 14 November 1998. A bunch of us from Friends' School travelled down, by bus, to Dublin. We played a team down there that morning and headed to the game after. Ireland beat Georgia 70–0, in a World Cup qualifier, that day. Girvan Dempsey scored two tries, with Jonny Bell and Paddy Johns also touching down.

We were part of the crowd that stormed on to the pitch after. We got our hands on these toilet rolls and were passing them like rugby balls; lining up toilet rolls for conversions over the bar.

People were jumping up on big Malcolm O'Kelly, trying to get on his shoulders. I was around 5 foot 5 at the time. He is 6 foot 10.

'God, this guy is an absolute giant. Flip, this is amazing.'

Ten years later, I knock on a hotel-room door in Melbourne.

'Come in.'

There is big Mal, stretched out on the bed in his Ireland tracksuit.

'Hello roomie,' he says with a smile. 'What have you got planned for tonight?'

*

Two days earlier I had packed my bags for a trip to America, with Ireland A, for the Churchill Cup. The prospect of a few weeks in the States, at the end of a hard season, was exciting. Mum dropped me down to Sprucefield shopping centre to get a bus to Dublin. A couple of the other Ulster guys showed up so Mum set off. The bus pulled up, the luggage compartment slid open and I tossed my bag in before hopping on. The door, for the bags, was closing when my phone rang.

'Stephen, it's Sinead here, from the IRFU, are you at Sprucefield?'

'Yep.'

The bus starts to pull out.

'OK,' says Sinead, 'get off the bus.'

'What?'

'Alan Quinlan has picked up an injury. They need you down in Australia.'

'Driver, stop the bus!'

I run to the front, hop off and grab my bag. Mum does a U-turn and picks me up. The next morning I am off to Melbourne, where I meet up with Mal O'Kelly, my room-mate for the next week.

Michael Bradley is looking after the team but Declan Kidney, the former Munster coach, is taking over after the tour. He has flown over to see how things are going. The squad has four fit back rows – Denis Leamy, Shane Jennings, Jamie Heaslip and David Wallace – so I assume I am there for cover. A just-in-case; hold a tackle shield for a week. Mal figures likewise so, along with himself, Bernard Jackman and the rest of the dirties, we go out on the piss for a couple of nights.

Monday, Tuesday go past and myself and Mal have gone out to the Crown Casino in Melbourne, sitting there, drinking away.

Bernard is a bit of a poker head so is in another room, playing cards. Some of the other guys are going in, going for food, sipping away on beers.

'This is amazing. I was supposed to be in America with the second string. I was on the bus to the airport. Now I'm in Australia with the main lads, sipping beers. Brilliant.'

After three days of training and nights out, David strains a calf muscle in training and I find myself on the bench. The panic sets in. 'Oh jeepers, what's going on?'

All of a sudden, I knuckle down, start learning plays, watching video clips.

Mal still heads out on the beers, enjoying himself. He is professional enough, never shirking a task in training. He has been around long enough to know what the craic is.

One of the most entertaining aspects of the tour, away from the nights out, is the battles between Jerry Flannery and Rory Best. Jerry has a real presence on the pitch and possesses this impressive physicality. His line-outs are very good and he is a solid player; fit as a fiddle. Jerry had the edge in the early years but Rory made sure he got to the same fitness levels. He prides himself on that.

Paul Darbyshire is the strength and conditioning coach for the tour. One morning, we all undertake a fitness session on a school pitch. Those two are the last men standing, the two hookers. Fifty-fifty between them. They are running to touch a line between them. I must have dropped out five or ten minutes before. Myself and Quinny, who is still in Australia and doing rehab, are lying at the side of the pitch, cheering them on. It is fascinating to watch, the ding-dong battles they have. There is always the chat that they do not like each other, but that is bullshit. They have a lot of respect for each other. Of course they do not see eye to eye at times but that is because they are fighting for the same position.

On and on the running drill goes until Rory touches the line just before Jerry, and gets back to the next line just before him. Rory keeps pushing it and gets back to the next line a metre ahead of him. Jerry pulls out and Rory runs and touches another couple of lines, just to rub it in. The two of them are absolutely busted.

Rory is named as starting hooker for the Wallabies game. Our team is close to full strength. Rob Kearney is now in at full-back while Tommy Bowe starts on the left wing. We pushed New Zealand close, in Wellington, the weekend before but lost out, 21–11, in the end. That does not stop me from telling the press, after my late call-up, that Australia are 'there for the taking'.

Walking into the Telstra Dome, a couple of hours before kick-off, and heading up and on to the pitch is a memorable moment. It is during these few minutes, before the ground fills up, and during the captain's run the previous day, that you take it all in. Forty thousand people are going to fill this stadium and Ireland are going to take on the Aussies.

I think of Justin Harrison, Ulster's Australian lock. Before every game he walks around the pitch and looks up into the gods of the stadium, at the posts, the corner flags, everything; absorbing it. He makes sure he is totally familiar with his surroundings. Then, when it comes to the match, he is not thinking about that. All he focuses on is the game. He knows exactly where he is, what kind of stadium he is in, exactly the part of the pitch he is playing in. That is something I took from him, that stroll around the pitch to familiarize myself with the surroundings.

Deccie may be in town but Michael is fully in charge. Before the game, he points out Berrick Barnes and Matt Giteau on the Australian team-sheet. He proclaims, 'You know, they have a 12 playing 10 and a 10 playing 12. So you know we have to turn around and attack them.'

So do we. We have Paddy Wallace, who regularly plays 10, at inside centre. Geordan Murphy is our cover on the bench and he usually plays wing or full-back. A few of us look at each other. 'Good one, Michael, but do you actually know our team?'

Brads is not too bad. He lets us get on and do our own thing and we play really well against the Wallabies.

I am sitting on the bench when, about fifteen minutes in, Michael Webb comes up to me. He is the Ulster team doctor but is on tour with Ireland. Shane Jennings has busted a rib.

'You're going to have to go on. Shane's not looking good.'

I just start thinking, 'Oh no.' I have not played openside in ages.

I get myself warmed up and, within two minutes, I am out on the pitch.

'Here we go.'

The Aussies are sensational in the first half but we hold on and batter them after that. Out of all the games I play for Ireland, this, I feel, is one of my best ever performances. It is the turning point of my international career, out playing openside.

As the game heads into the final minutes, with us trailing 18–12, Drico literally passes the ball at Paddy's feet. Paddy ends up knocking it on, kicking it. Chance gone, we lose the game by 6 points. We should have won. We deserved to. I sit in the changing room afterwards and know that was one we let go. At the same time, I am feeling differently from the other guys. I have been given an opportunity and believe I have made it count. 'Hopefully I've got my foot in the door.'

Deccie must like what he sees because I am straight in for the November internationals and am soon a regular starter.

It is only after that week in Australia that I really feel part of the Ireland set-up. Of course, when you stop running to catch up you can finally take a breath. We all go out on that last night in Melbourne and have a great time. I look across the room at some of these men, who are now my team-mates. There are Rory and Tommy, my friends. There is Mal O'Kelly, who I had thrown toilet rolls at only ten years ago, and there is Drico, a guy I looked up to as the best player in the world when I was growing up.

The first game under Declan Kidney is against Canada in the autumn of 2008. I start at blindside and get man-of-the-match. We play really well, considering the atrocious weather conditions in Limerick. We are 38–0 up at half-time and win 55–0. It tees us up nicely for the two big games of that Test window, New Zealand and Argentina at Croke Park.

The following weekend sees me go up against the All Blacks for the first time. By that stage, the lads in the squad have a new nickname for me. In the lead-up to the match, Deccie has us in for a video review meeting and is highlighting just how dangerous the All Blacks will be if they are allowed to get offloads away. He is looking for ways to nullify that threat and throws it open to the floor. I am sitting near the back. There are a couple of suggestions – increasing our line speed, tackling in pairs – but, to me, the answer is obvious.

'Man and ball.'

'What was that?'

'Man and ball,' I repeat, leaning forward in my seat.

'Excuse me, Stephen,' says Deccie, 'could you speak up, please?'

'MAN AND BALL! Just bloody smash 'em. Man and ball. Take 'em both out.'

'Right,' says Deccie. 'Very good so.'

I sit back, pleased with my contribution. I catch Donncha O'Callaghan nodding the head at me, grinning.

Man and ball. That is the nickname. There is only one way of living up to it and it starts against world rugby's most lethal side.

Deccie does not name a lock on the bench and tells me he might need me to cover the position. He wants two flankers on the bench so he can really run the ball and have a go at the All Blacks.

We are level, at 3–3, when we get done by a controversial call by the video referee. There is a high ball chipped towards our in-goal area. Tommy reaches it first but cannot hold on. It flies out of play. Richie McCaw was waiting under it and would have scored had it not been for Tommy. It goes to a replay. The All Blacks get a penalty try and Tommy is yellow-carded.

The referee feels Tommy has hit the ball out deliberately. It is a ridiculous decision and it turns the game on its head. By the time Tommy gets back on, we are 17–3 down. Paul O'Connell picks up a dead leg at the start of the second half but tries to play on for another five or ten minutes. We are attacking, in New Zealand's 22, when we turn the ball over. Ma'a Nonu gets his hands on it and charges for Paul, who can hardly run by this stage. Nonu steps him and runs another 70 yards to score.

Paul attempts to run it off but it is no use. Deccie's plans are out the window. He is forced to put me on in the second row. I have never really played lock before, just once or twice when I had to fill in for a few minutes. Our scrum is under pressure; really, really struggling. I give away a couple of penalties as we are on the back foot so much; scrambling. A tough match finishes 22–3 and leaves us with no excuses. Still, if people ever ask me if I ever played second row, I can reply, 'Ach well, I've played against the All Blacks.' Sounds good.

Truth be told, we barely touched the ball the last ten minutes. There was so much pressure coming on. There are learning curves and then there is New Zealand at full tilt, with their tails up. They are off-the-chart good.

We play Argentina the following week. It is the first time Deccie selects myself, David Wallace and Jamie Heaslip in the back row, together. I have so much respect for David. Even as a player and a team-mate, I look up to him. He is so good; unreal. Very fast and a try-scoring threat. I hate playing against him. I know he is as strong as me, as quick, as powerful. He is just as good a ball-carrier and a tackler. I might edge him in the line-out but that is about it.

Jamie is such a good ball player and I think a lot of people underestimate that with him. Over his years with Leinster and Ireland, he has got the ball away so often. He is a solid player and I enjoy playing with him. You always know he will never let you down. He has no issues. At Leinster, they often use a five- or six-man line-out as he lines up in the midfield. As soon as I come into the Ireland team, he is happy to go into the line-out and leave me with the backline. He never says to me, 'Stevie, you go in and do these line-outs and I'll stay back here.' Maybe he has it in his head that I am the better ball-carrier. He is not selfish; he is a real team player who I hold in high regard. He is definitely one of the best I have ever played with.

The three of us combine well against the Argentinians; make carries, turnovers, beat defenders and do not miss one tackle. We grind out a 17–3 win. Tommy grabs a late try after Ronan O'Gara's cross-field kick.

We let ourselves down against New Zealand but it is a decent enough start to Deccie's tenure. The Munster lads know him well and he was Eddie's assistant at Ireland for a couple of years. Most of the squad are familiar with how he operates but the new faces, myself included, are still getting used to him.

Declan places a lot of faith in the team he has assembled. He trusts them to make the decisions while he oversees everything. Les Kiss, a former rugby league player from Australia, is in charge of defence while Gert Smal, who was part of South Africa's coaching team when they won the 2007 World Cup, looks after the forwards. Alan Gaffney, another Aussie, runs the backs.

Myself and Gert get on really well. He often feels for me as I am injury prone. Every time a really big game is coming up, it seems, I get injured or take a knock the week before. He always says to me, 'Stephen, look after yourself. Look after your body. You're vital for this team to function well.'

He appreciates me as a player because I run around smashing people and bring physicality to games. He jokes that I must have some Springbok blood in me.

He is a fantastic coach. His attention to detail is brilliant. Himself and Paul O'Connell, in terms of the line-outs, mauls and finer details, have everything down to a tee. He is not a big talker but says the right things at the right time.

Deccie does not do much coaching on the pitch. He walks around and makes sure everything is organized. That is one of his biggest skills – the sessions run like clockwork. He has selected a good staff and delegates the workload. Paulie and Les run the forwards in defence. The scrums and line-outs are the responsibility of Gert, until Greg Feek comes in. Declan has nothing to do with that side of the game.

He stands and shouts at people, at rucking drills – 'Get stuck in there!' – but that is it.

In terms of the team tactics, he never turns round and bawls you out for taking the wrong line. That usually falls to Alan. 'What the fuck are you doing?' he yells in reviews. 'You've just taken the wrong line there.'

Mervyn Murphy with his video analysis does not get enough credit. He puts in huge hours. I have seen him fall asleep on laptops in the team room. He takes guys for one-on-one sessions and points out where they are going wrong.

Central to the entire squad, however, is Rala O'Reilly, our kit-man. He has been a key figure within the squad for years. If you ever want a laugh, a chat or just good company, you head to Rala's room. Once there, you often find many of the other lads. His room is a hive of activity. He has developed a habit of delegating just about every job he has to do. The lads love him and are always getting him sweets or smokes. One day, I stroll into a shop, full Ireland gear on, and ask for a pack of twenty cigarettes for Rala. 'Ah, Stephen. You shouldn't have,' he says as he pockets them.

Deccie's style, though, is to have a quiet word in your ear. 'You need to do this or that for the weekend.'

In my eyes, Deccie is a coach that lets a lot of factors get in his way. Instead of making the right decision he ums and ahs and leaves guys hanging about for a week to see if they are getting selected or not. 'Brian is injured at the minute but we are going to give him until Thursday.' It is usually only at the last minute that a player does or does not get selected. You get a small window in which to take in all the information you will need for match-day, so he should be letting guys know by Tuesday, not Thursday morning.

Of course there have to be exceptions now and again. But that happens an awful lot with Deccie – waiting on guys like myself, Wally or Seanie O'Brien to get fit. It irritates people a lot. He often plays that card with key players, telling them they are playing, only to break it to them later in the week that they are on the bench. It happens the other way round too. 'It's not looking good for you this week.' Then he names the guy in his team and tells him he has full faith.

Declan is one of those coaches that tries to be funny and get on with players. He would walk by you in the team hotel and remark, 'Well, how are you getting on, you Nordie bollocks?'

'Ha ha. Great.'

'Oh, did someone get their leg over last night? Is that why you're smiling?'

On he would walk, to the next table.

'Did that just happen? Did he just say that while I'm here eating my lasagne?'

That is his character. He is trying to fit in. Nobody takes any offence to it.

In terms of sitting down for individual meetings, about what is going right and wrong, that never happens. He is more of an overseer.

*

We meet up in Johnstown House, Enfield, in late December 2008. Myself and Rory are driving down together. 'Flip sake, a couple of training sessions in the middle of nowhere' is the general vibe in the car.

We get down there and, as it turns out, there is only one pitch session. There are, however, a lot of meetings. Pádraig Harrington comes in to chat with us one evening. He is only supposed to be there for half an hour but, Pádraig being Pádraig, he is there for nearly two. As soon as he starts talking about something, he keeps going. Folks start asking questions as well and Pádraig goes off on one. Very enjoyable.

As an Ulster player, the famous Rob Kearney comments – the eureka moment – pass me by a little. We are put into discussion pods and get back together as an entire squad.

'Has anyone got anything to say?'

Rob stands up. 'I just feel the Munster players don't put the same effort and the same heart into the Irish jersey as they do the Munster jersey. We need everyone to be playing with the same heart as they do for their provinces.'

Once it is said, it is debated and kept in-house for a long time, until after the 2009 Six Nations. My take on it is, if you are playing for your country, you go out and give it 110 per cent. I cannot imagine any lad approaches a game without that complete commitment. 'Ach, I'm playing for Munster, or Ulster, next week, I won't play as hard.' That is Rob's take and fair play to him for standing up and saying so. It certainly never crosses my mind that the Munster lads play harder for their province than they do their country.

Ulster's wretched run of form does not help when it comes to selection for the national team. Isaac Boss is always in and around the scrum-half position. When Andrew Trimble was fit and Eddie was there, he would have started each time. Eddie loved Trimby. He won a serious amount of caps under Eddie but loses his way a bit when Deccie comes in. Deccie does not have that trust in Trimby, but he likes Tommy as a winger. The Ulster lads are usually myself, Rory, Isaac, Tommy and, then, Trimby in and out.

It is hard to argue for a larger contingent as we are doing so poorly in the league, but I always feel Roger Wilson should be in there. You have Jamie doing a good job, in that Number 8 role, but Roger deserves a chance. Two or three games, at least. I can understand his frustrations at not being selected.

When it comes to internationals, though, you do not care about anyone else. Your only care is for yourself. Once your name is picked, you are happy. Of course you are disappointed for your friends, but not enough to throw you off.

For that first year under Deccie, Rory is not getting in ahead of Jerry Flannery. However, as much as I feel sorry for Rory and believe he should get a chance, when Jerry and I are selected together, we play for each other. That is it. I do not care if Rory does or does not get in. My sole concerns are having a good performance and the team doing well. The next match, if Rory is starting, it will be the same: Rory and I will compete hard and try to win for each other.

Eight caps in and now getting starts at blindside, it is not until we play at Croke Park during the 2009 Six Nations that I think, 'OK, welcome to the big time. This is what it is all about.'

One look at the fixtures and there are England and France at home. You always back yourself to beat Italy and Scotland. It should all come down to the last game, against Wales. The thinking is, get off to a good start, beat these French guys and take it from there.

You never get ahead of yourself and start thinking of 'what ifs'.

It is crucial that we get off to a good start. Our talk is mainly about securing the win but there are a few words about payback – for 2007, when they beat us at Croke Park and at the World Cup. They have so many good players. Sébastien Chabal is touted as the best Number 8 in world rugby, and as an absolute beast, yet they select him in the second row for that match.

The atmosphere stands out. It is incredible; booming. Myself and Tommy are walking around the pitch beforehand, the crowd starting to file in for the warm-ups. I am spinning a ball around the palm of my hand. I look around, knowing 80,000 people are going to be there and I am going to be playing in front of them.

Tommy asks, 'Are you nervous?'

'No.'

'Good. That means you're ready. You know you have what it takes.'

'Suppose you're right.'

It is such a brilliant day. I love playing on that immaculate Croke Park pitch. Playing against the likes of Chabal, Maxime Médard and a heap of quality French lads. Two great sides going flat out at each other and us, thankfully, coming out on top.

About thirty minutes in, Chabal makes a big run up the centre of the pitch. Steam-train stuff. I am trying to chase him down, in awe of the speed such a massive guy can reach. Imanol Harinordoquy, a world-class operator, puts them in front with a try. We answer back when Jamie gets a great try, slicing them open and giving it the old fist-shake heading over. Gordon D'Arcy scores, by the sticks, in the second half. Paddy Wallace started at number 12, with Drico 13, but was split open after twenty-eight minutes. Darce's try gives us that breathing room and we close the game out, 30–21.

We are playing away against Italy, in Rome, second match up, and it is a sweltering, sunny day. Just before the warm-up, I dip into my bag.

'Where's my head-gear? Fuck. Rala, Rala. I forgot my head-gear.'

'There's two spares sitting there, Stevie. Pick one.'

I try them on. One is far too small, the other far too big. Goldilocks. Both look horrendous.

It is the first game I ever play without head-gear. It always feels natural for me. I pop the head-gear on before I run out and, kind of like a pair of glasses, forget I am wearing it.

They kick off to us and we box-kick back. Sergio Parisse catches the ball and Tommy nails him with a tackle. I am next on the scene and counter-ruck, blow two of their guys out and win the turnover.

'Right, that's exactly what we want. Tone set.'

Luke Fitzgerald scores a try after something crazy, like twenty-seven phases. I come around the corner, so, so tired but urging myself to keep the drive on. Peter Stringer lays the ball up for me. One of the Italians is drawn out of the line. I arc around him, make 3 or 4 yards and pop it up to Luke, who is trailing me. He shoots off, straight under the posts, to score. We are right in the game and build on that try.

It is a good game but, despite my contributions, I am still freaking out about that head-gear. Not wearing it plays tricks with my mind. I like that feeling of being cocooned inside that helmet, blocked out to outside noises and weather conditions. Strapped in, ready for battle.

We run away from them by the end. Luke gets a second try and Drico crosses for another. It is a game in which I perform really well; clean breaks, offloads, landing every tackle. Still, I make sure I have the head-gear the following match.

Tickets are going for €5,000, as it is the second and last time we will play England at Croke Park. Beating France has raised expectations. You cannot get your hands on a ticket. People are ringing me, asking for a couple, offering €2,000 apiece. Of course, there is nothing I can do. Make or break. They know, you know. The fans definitely know and they are spending crazy money.

This was our Grand Slam.

Drico burrows over for our try and there is a good build-up to it. The forwards pile in before Brian picks, at the base of a ruck, and dives over.

England are stacked with big lads – Riki Flutey, tipped for the Lions tour that summer, Delon Armitage, Mark Cueto, Mike Tindall. Mike and I have a couple of collisions in the game. I am certain they have that 2007 blow-out defeat to us in their heads and are determined to give us a good game.

It is another one of those days when it just happens for us. No injuries, again. Even though we are well ahead – by 8 points at one stage – we end up under the cosh for the last ten minutes.

Everyone hangs in there and does their job. As soon as we get ahead, it never feels like we are going to lose the game.

Les has been working hard on our defence and, week on week in the tournament, it is improving. We cling on for victory but the scoreline, 14–13, does not reflect how well we played. We give ourselves a couple of frights but have such confidence in ourselves that we knew we were going to win. It sounds really strange but you have the team beat before you play them. It is a great feeling to have.

The closest I ever felt to that would have been my first season with Ulster, 2005/06. You would play on a Friday night and go home to meet up with mates for a few drinks.

'How did you get on?'

'Ach, sure we won again. Yep, we won again.'

Of course, once you feel like that and the wins follow, the ball keeps rolling.

The positivity blooms.

You go into every Six Nations thinking about the Grand Slam. You win your first game and those thoughts pick up pace. As soon as we beat France, I was thinking about it. Friends and family were talking about it too. If I was talking to any of them, it would be, 'We beat England, we're on for it.' Three wins in at this stage and you can be sure everyone is drumming it over in their mind. They may not talk about it but the thoughts are there.

Deccie says it in a couple of meetings. 'Alright, lads, we are obviously on for a Grand Slam but I do not want it mentioned in the media. If we beat Scotland and can set up a decider against Wales, brilliant. Until then, keep those thoughts to yourselves.'

He then plays his trump card of resting, or dropping, lads to keep the squad on their toes. In come Darce, Rory, Peter Stringer and Denis Leamy. Tactically, it pays off.

The Scotland game is my best performance of the championship.

As always, I like to start a game well. It was counter-rucking against Italy, and against the Scots that moment arrives after a spell of kick tennis. They punt long but we put it back to them and it lands with their Number 8, Simon Taylor. Big lad with blond hair, playing his club rugby with Stade Français.

He tries to run it back and I fucking mill him.

There is an 'oooof' around Murrayfield. The guys pile in and we follow that with a counter-ruck. We force them to knock on, spill forward, and get the turnover.

After that positive impact, I settle and play well. I always like playing on hard tracks. It is another sunny day and the Murrayfield pitch is rock solid. We are able to throw the ball around a bit in a good, competitive match. Jamie comes on for Denis after half an hour. We are 12–9 down after fifty minutes when Peter makes a great break off the back of our line-out. He is hauled down just short of the line but offloads for Jamie to score. Once we get ahead on the scoreboard, we are comfortable.

I take to the pitch for the final game against Wales at a jammed Millennium Stadium and get right into it with a couple of carries. I feel strong. For some reason, I feel so explosive, so powerful. It is the fittest I have ever been. Every time I look my opposite number in the eye, I just know that I am better than him.

Six minutes in and the ball spills out of the side of a ruck. I make to dive on it, as every coach would tell you to do – dive on it and secure it – but Martyn Williams tries to kick it. As I jump on the ball, he fly-hacks and connects with my finger.

Compound fracture, dislocated. The bone comes, bang, straight out of the skin. As soon as it happens, I let out a yell.

'Aahhhhh!'

He has managed to hack the ball and it shoots straight up the pitch. I am left there, in bits.

'Aahhhhh, shit. My fucking finger.'

I lie on the ground for about ten, fifteen seconds before I get up. Play is going on and Wales have retained the ball. I rejoin the defensive line but the bone is still sticking out of my finger. I run up to Paul.

'Paulie, Paulie, my finger, get the game stopped!'

'OK Fez, OK.'

Next thing, there is a penalty; a break. I go up to the ref Wayne Barnes, who for some reason seems to hate me. I could not tell you why but he does.

'My finger, Wayne; my bone is sticking out of my hand. I need treatment.'

He is waving me away. 'Back ten yards, back ten yards.'

Paulie jogs over. 'Wayne, he's got a compound fracture of his finger. You need to stop the game.'

Barnes has a look, gives a nod. Michael Webb comes running out.

'Oh no, oh no.'

Not what I want to hear.

He grabs my finger and tries to get it back in. He is pulling away at it, pulling away at it. He cannot get the bone back in so tells me I am coming off. We are jogging off the pitch, slow jog, slow jog, then he stops.

'OK, we'll give it one more go here.'

Pop. He gets it back in but, where the bone has come out, I have a massive cut on my hand. So that is me off the pitch. We reach the medic's room and I'm thinking, 'Brilliant. Right, let's get this sewn up and I'll get back out there.'

I am sitting down, on a bench, when Michael and another doctor walk in. Michael asks if I want a coat.

'No, no, I'm good to go.'

Michael looks at me and says, 'No, you can't go back out on to the pitch.'

I protest. 'I'm stitched up, I feel good. I feel movement in my hand.'

'Listen Stevie, the chances of infection in your hand are huge. You could lose your finger here.'

'It's worth the risk. Get me back there.'

Michael explains that it is a medical decision. He has the other doctor, from the Welsh side, there. He backs Michael's call.

'Stevie, you don't want to be going back out there. There's such a high chance of you losing your finger. The bone was exposed to the air for a good four or five minutes. We really advise you not to go out there.'

At that stage, the realization strikes. Everything is sucked out of me. I say 'OK' but, at the same time, there is another part of me that just wants to run out past them. I still have the adrenalin coursing through me. I am still pumped; ready to run through walls.

They put a massive bandage on my finger and I am left on my own to look at it. It is only a finger injury but it has ruined my Grand Slam hopes. I walk down to the changing room and can still hear the crowd bellowing outside. The volume heaving, up and down. I sit down. You can still smell the Deep Heat, feel the atmosphere, as the boys have only been in here fifteen minutes ago. I sit on my own and burst into tears.

'This is it, my Grand Slam, my championship, my game over. My season could be over.'

I sit there for about ten minutes, bawling my eyes out like a kid. All the emotion hits home. I am trying to catch my breath.

Then I start hearing cheers; hear a few more. I hit myself a few slaps around the face and say, 'Come on, get out and support the boys. The last thing they'd want is you in here, feeling sorry for yourself. Get yourself out there.'

It takes a couple more minutes before I get myself around. I leave the changing room and bump into Rala. He hands me a pair of trainers.

'Here, get those boots off.'

I find the rest of the lads on the bench. For the remainder of the game, it is about getting behind the team and supporting them the best I can. Seeing that chip, the kick across, by ROG and Tommy collecting it; we are right beside that. I am more or less on the pitch when Tommy races over and touches down, under the sticks.

It is a moment in my career when it really hits home: that it is not all about me. No matter what you are thinking, you get out and support them and you can give them an extra 1 per cent. It means a lot for me, that moment. I could have very easily stayed down in that room, went and showered. Instead, I stay out there the whole time, roaring and yelling during those crazy last few minutes. I almost lose my voice screaming when ROG nails the winning drop goal. I am still out there to lift the trophy at the very end. I am hugging the guys, hiding my glistening eyes behind my hands.

That whole week, from the build-up, getting injured and being an emotional wreck, to being on a high again, winning and having an unbelievable night out in Cardiff, is unforgettable. It changes me as a player; as a person.

CHAPTER 12

From a personal point of view, 2008/09 is unbelievable. The Grand Slam success is topped off at Ulster's end-of-season dinner. I am up and down for awards all night. Sports Personality, Rugby Writers' Player of the Year and Supporters' Club Player of the Year. Standing on stage with all these trophies, I feel slightly embarrassed, but, in truth, mostly chuffed.

The springboard was that phone-call in June 2008 and the trip to Australia.

I am out for four weeks while my finger heals, and in April 2009 am right back into action against Glasgow. We win 20–19 but it is the highlight of a shocking season, at the end of which we finish eighth out of ten teams.

As soon as Ireland won the Slam, talk began about what players from our squad would make it on to the British & Irish Lions. I had been asked my first Lions question in December 2008 but answered that it was not on my radar. Starting every game of Ireland's first Grand Slam success in sixty-one years means I am now a huge dot on that radar. Still, I am hopeful more than expectant.

Craig White, the Lions' strength and conditioning coach, had been in touch with Jonny Davis, at Ulster, to say they needed information on two players, myself and Rory Best. That was in March. The Lions squad will be announced on 21 April and I am in the dark, like the rest of the players. No texts or emails. It is all very tight.

I stand outside, on the rugby pitch, and the Ulster boys have the announcement on the big screen, inside, at Newforge Country Club. It is a lovely day, 20 degrees. I am walking up and down the pitch as the announcement draws near.

'I'm not going to watch that.'

I would be embarrassed to be selected and embarrassed not to be in front of all my peers, so I distance myself. I say to JD, 'Listen, if I'm in, come out and tell me, but if I'm not, don't bother.'

JD is not only an unbelievable guy at his job – probably one of the best strength and conditioning coaches I have ever worked with – he is also a mate.

I am pacing up and down and JD comes out. A big smile on his face.

'Ha ha ha.'

He shakes my hand.

The first thing I say is, 'What about Rory?'

'Nah, he didn't make it.'

'Fuck sake.'

I am feeling so much delight, inside, for myself but at the same time I am not looking forward to approaching Rory, shaking his hand, looking him in the eye and saying, 'Unlucky, mate.'

All the Ulster lads are great. Cheering and back-slapping. I feel out-of-this-world happy. I ring Mum and Dad. 'I'm on the Lions tour, I'm on the Lions tour!'

Mum's response is 'Oh my God!'

Ulster are flooded with interview and picture requests. I pose for press photos in my Lions jersey. 'I'm twenty-three and I'm at the pinnacle of rugby,' I declare in one interview.

Life takes on a dream-like quality. I cannot go on a night out without getting photos taken; my profile goes up ten-fold because I have been selected for the Lions. It is absolute madness. I am on a night out with Rory McIlroy and Ulster centre Darren Cave at a nightclub in Belfast, partying and having a few drinks. Rory is a massive Ulster Rugby fan and we have gotten to know each other at a couple of post-match functions. He is on the brink of breaking into the top ten in the world golf rankings and has already won a professional tournament. He tries to get back home as much as possible. All we seem to do all night is get in photos for people; it is crazy. People want photos with me and Rory because I am now a Lion. 'This is madness,' I tell myself, but, at the same time, I am really enjoying it. Once you have success you want more and more and more.

That night out is the exception to a new fitness regime JD has put in place for me. It all starts with that first phone-call from the Lions.

'Stephen, we need your passport and your clothing sizes. You are due in Pennyhill Park on 18 May, Belinda from the Lions will be in touch with you.'

When an email from Belinda arrives, with the flight details, I think, 'Yes, now I can relax.'

JD is not having any of it. 'This is where the hard work starts,' he proclaims. 'You're going over to be the best player there and that's it.'

I do not know how other players approach it but I have never trained as hard in my life. It is insane, five, six days a week. When it is over with, four weeks later, JD reckons I am in the best shape of any athlete he has seen.

The Lions send over a set that, when you put it on, simulates breathing at high altitude. They express-post it in a box: 'S. Ferris. Care of Ulster Rugby'. Upon my first look at it, I ask myself, 'What the hell is this?'

I put it on and hop on a bike, spinning away. JD is shouting at me until I stop. I fall right off the bike. All I can hear is JD shouting again: 'Out on to the pitch.'

It's 20 degrees, another beautiful day, and I am ordered on to the touchline. I can barely speak. JD has me doing 150s: run 150 metres, three-quarter pace, then jog 50. As soon as I hit the line, I have to go again. Thirty seconds on, thirty seconds off. We do six of those in a row and I literally fall over the line on the sixth one.

I get a few words out: 'Can't do . . . any . . . more.'

JD is not buying it. 'Get back in there.'

I get back on the bike, spinning again. We do three sets of that.

Standing in the shower after it all, I know I have been put through the wringer. 'How am I going to keep this up?' Two or three weeks later, I am eating it up. I am jumping off the bike. I cannot wait to get outside and go running. It is the fittest I have ever been in my career. I have no issues with knees or ankles; nothing. The fastest, the most explosive I have ever felt. I know I am in incredible condition.

On 18 May, I board a plane to London. Upon landing, I collect my bag and am walking through the arrivals gate when my phone rings. It is ROG.

'Where the hell are you?'

'The airport. I'm coming down the lift.'

'Come outside the main door.'

I walk out and sitting there is a big Lions-sponsored Land Rover. Big Lions logos on the sides, the back. The tinted window comes down and it's O'Gara.

'We're in here, Fez.'

I am so nervous about meeting up with the Lions squad so it is great jumping in the jeep with ROG and David Wallace. We drive down to Pennyhill Park and meet all the guys. I am rooming with Alun Wyn Jones, the Ospreys captain. I am the only Ulster guy. Ireland are flying but my province is in bad shape. It is not that I feel out of my depth but, in training, I take a step back and let the more senior guys come forward; watching what is going on rather than throwing myself right in. Within that first week, myself and Alun Wyn become good mates. It is like I have known him for ten years. That is rugby for you. It does not matter where you have come from, what level you have played at; if you get on well, there is an instant click.

One guy I am curious to meet is Andy Powell, the Welsh back-rower. About a month before, I had played for Ulster against his Cardiff team. They beat us 11–9 and Matt Williams stormed into the dressing room afterwards.

'You've played that prick Powell into the Lions team.'

I thought it was a strange comment, as Powell had always struck me as a quality player.

Matt continued, 'He thinks he's this and he thinks he's that. You've made him look like the best Number 8 in the world of rugby and he's a hundred per cent not.'

Being able to play with him and train with him every day

reaffirmed my belief that he is a great player and a brilliant athlete.

'More bullshit from Mattie.'

I go on the tour with an open mind. Anybody who makes an effort with me finds I make an effort with them. I get on extremely well with the Welsh guys. There are not that many English guys on the tour but I find Andrew Sheridan, Harry Ellis and Lee Mears to be good fun, very laid-back.

I have not met many of the lads before but get to know them by training with them, doing weights with them and socializing together. Every time I play an international against England, Scotland or Wales after the Lions tour, I tell myself, I will make sure to catch up with the guys. I make some life-long friends along the way.

I play golf at Pennyhill with Andy and spark up a really good relationship with him. We seem to get on really well. We train a lot together, in the gym. He is really, really funny. He only has to walk into a room, without saying anything, and you find yourself laughing. It is the way he carries himself and the faces he makes. A real character. We hit it off really well, play golf, throw the clubs away and go straight to the bar for a couple of beers. The staff lay on a bit of food so that is dinner sorted. All of a sudden, we are standing at the bar at two o'clock in the morning talking about who bench-presses more, me, Mike Phillips or Andy?

'I do 150, I do 160, I do 170!'

Three days ago I did not even know these guys. I had never met them before, just played against them.

Myself, Andy, Mike and, obviously, all the Irish fellas get on so well. We go out on the beers, a couple of weeks before the games, and make sure we get to know each other really well. That is what Ian McGeechan, our coach with the Lions, brings to the table. That whole Lions feeling and making sure everyone is aware of what the Lions stands for. Argentina, Australia, the World Cup, they all pale in comparison.

This is the best tour I have ever been on.

I know nobody, really. There are no best mates like Rory or Chris Henry to walk out to training with every day. Someone you can put your arm around. I have no one like that so it's a case of being open. Walking up to Andrew, who is the strongest guy on the team, and chatting, or catching up with Nathan Hines, Lee Mears. It makes me grow as a person. A lot. It is a tour, I feel, where I go away a boy and will come home a man – 2009 is that sort of a year for me. I go from being a rugby player with a lot of potential to a rugby player who is operating at the highest level and is one of the world's best in his position.

The transformation is not immediate. I go from being Ulster's big-name player to a twenty-three-year-old lad wondering where he fits in. My final game before coming in was with that Ulster team that lost to Cardiff: Alan Quinlan had lost his appeal for a rake at Leo Cullen's eyes while on Munster duty. Still, the Lions have Joe Worsley and Tom Croft – a guy who is supposed to go on and be the best in the world – as blindside options. I wonder if I should target that number 6 jersey or challenge David Wallace and Martyn Williams for openside. Andy and Jamie Heaslip are fighting for the Number 8 role. I know I am in with a good shout with the way I am playing. If you have no belief, going over there, that you are in the mix, there is no point in going.

When we arrived in Pennyhill Park, one thing the coaches said was that everybody was going to get a chance. It did not matter what position you were in, prop, back row, whatever, everybody would get to start one game. I want to impress in training, be physical and show them what I can do. Ian is head coach but the men I primarily work with are Warren Gatland (forwards) and Shaun Edwards (defence). They love that physical aspect of my game and that I am a dominant force in defence. That works to my advantage.

As soon as I get to know most of the lads, and throw myself into a few sessions, the confidence flows back. I only have thirteen caps for Ireland but my sights are set on fifty-plus. There are five players in the squad that could realistically fill in at 6 but I convince myself to aim for 'Stephen Ferris, No.6' on every team-sheet.

The gym work drives home that I am not the top guy in this squad. Some of the Welsh and English guys are really strong; big frames and bulked out. Andy is an absolute freak in the gym. He lifts some serious weights. He is good for the encouragement.

'Jesus, Stevie, you're looking massive, mate, you're looking strong.'

I am throwing around good weights in the gym. Big Adam Jones starts to call me 'The White Samoan'. The nickname sticks for the tour.

At Ulster, then Ireland, I have always been one of the strongest guys in the gym, one of the most physical on the pitch. I jump into the Lions and, when it comes to physicality, I find myself in the middle to higher range. I am not number one. Strangely, I love it. I love the competition, trying to beat people. JD has me in such great shape. I set new targets and push for personal bests.

Once we reach South Africa, we settle into a routine. If you are not selected for the team, you are able to go out for a few drinks.

There are security details who stay with the team all tour. They are in Land Rovers – they pick you up and set you down. There is a bus that leaves venues at one o'clock in the morning and makes sure you get home. A few of the guys miss the bus on certain nights and stay out late.

One night, early on in the tour, myself, Andy Powell, Shane Williams, Mike, Lee Byrne, Craig (the strength and conditioning coach) and James Hook are out. We are in a nightclub, drinking double vodka and Red Bull, standing with our tops off, swinging them around.

'This is the Lions, in a nightclub, pissed out of our heads on a Tuesday night.'

We are not playing this week so we are there with our T-shirts looping over our heads. Andy flings his away and is going mad, dancing. Next minute, I turn round and Andy is wearing my T-shirt. I grab the nearest one I can find; it turns out to be James Hook's. He makes a snatch for another one. It is like musical chairs. No one wants to be left topless heading home.

We party on for another couple of hours. As we have missed the bus, the Land Rovers cruise along to pick us up. In bed at three o'clock and straight up the next day, six hours later, for training. You slog it and get everything out of your system. There are a couple of good nights out but nobody turns up to training pissed or in a complete state.

I am not involved in the first couple of games so have three or four nights out. Ugo Monye is always out on the dance floor, showing off his moves. It is great, pitching up at a nightclub in the Lions bus, covered in Lions stickers and logos. Next thing, fifteen or so boys – sometimes the whole squad – rock into this night-club and the place turns as one.

'Holy shit, there's the Lions come to party in town.'

The girls just flock to Tommy, this magnet for women. He thinks the reception is amazing. Rightfully so. He is a Lion, all his hard work and sacrifice has paid off, and he is enjoying every single moment.

That is what everybody does – enjoys themselves. We are there to play rugby and we take it extremely seriously. Everybody knuckles down when it comes to training. In some of the training sessions, we beat the shit out of each other. That is part and parcel of it but, at the same time, we have a laugh, get to know each other and really, really enjoy it. That is something that will always stick with me – how much fun I had on that tour.

The first game arrives, against the Royal XV in Rustenburg, and I am supposed to be on the bench. I am getting off the bus, the day before, and feel a tweak in a muscle in my lower leg. I approach the coaches and tell them my calf is sore. They are understanding about it. 'Don't worry, there are another three guys behind you. Step out for this week.' They have already lost Jerry Flannery, Tomás O'Leary and Tom Shanklin to long-term injuries. Joe Worsley starts against the Royal XV, with Jamie on the bench. We win 37–25. ROG and Tommy have good games.

The next match is midweek, 3 June, against the Golden Lions. I am named in the replacements. Ian selects a strong side that features many of the lads in contention to start the First Test. Tom Croft is blindside.

We play at Ellis Park, a massive stadium, but it is less than half full. Just over 22,000 people. The atmosphere is different to anything we have found in our first couple of weeks in the country. South Africans love their rugby and are very passionate about it.

This match, though, is very hostile. When we get off the bus, there are people shouting at us: 'You're going to get your heads chopped off. You're going to die tonight.'

We reach the changing room and Ian declares, 'This is what we're going to have to face, guys. This is it for the rest of the tour. We're in the home of South African rugby here. This is what we are going to be facing from now on in. They don't rate us. They think we are a bag of shit. They think we are a bunch of guys who are thrown together and we are not going to play well. We've got to go out and prove them wrong.'

That is really the start of the tour. We kick-start ourselves by blowing the Golden Lions away, 74–10. Jamie Roberts bags a couple of tries and Tom scores too. I come on with thirty minutes to go and relish every second I am out on the pitch.

In the final minutes of the match, we counter-ruck and turn the ball over. I set off up the pitch. Their out-half, André Pretorius, goes for an ankle tap but misses me. I sprint 70 metres to score, holding off a desperate lunge from Golden Lions winger Michael Killian. I barely have a breath left to stand and celebrate my try with the boys.

Ian comes up to me in the changing room after the game. 'Well done. Get your rest. You have a three-day turnaround.'

He turns round and declares that it was great to see a second row run in a 70-metre try. I was wearing the number 18 jersey so it may have thrown him. I just have enough breath left in me to pipe up and tell Ian exactly where I play.

We have the Free State Cheetahs next, just seventy-two hours later, in Bloemfontein. They have a few Springbok internationals in their team but Ian, true to his word, decides to give some lads their first starts. We get off to a flyer. James kicks us into a 3–0 lead before I come on to a ball at pace. I break through the Cheetahs defence to score my second try in successive games. After twenty minutes we are 20–0 up. Keith Earls shreds their defence to score and James adds the rest from the tee.

I am deservedly sin-binned after twenty-two minutes and we find ourselves in a real match. They get two converted tries as I watch on, and we need a penalty from James to leave it 23–14 at the break.

We add another penalty after half-time but do not score for the final thirty minutes. Shane has a pass intercepted with eight minutes to go and the resulting Cheetahs try leaves us clinging on. We have to defend for our lives and are fortunate to see out the victory, 26–24.

Despite my yellow card, I am presented with a gold kruger as man-of-the-match. I put my body on the line in defence and provided us with front-foot ball through breaks and bursts.

We swap jerseys with the Cheetahs and I stand, shirtless, for a few moments as I draw in some deep breaths. The opposition guys walk past, patting me on the back.

'Well played, mate, great game.'

The feeling, as I head back to the dressing room, is sheer elation. The boys give me a warm reception when I arrive through the door. The First Test is two weeks away and I have laid down a real marker. 'Stephen Ferris, No.6' has become a real possibility.

We fly on to Durban later that night. As I have played 110 minutes in four days, I know I will be spared the Natal Sharks game. We spend a down day splashing about in the water at uShaka Marine World. The mood in the camp is good but we know the big challenges await.

Our training session on Monday, 8 June is at Northwood School in Durban. A few of us start with some weights but take it easy enough. We are out on the training pitch by eleven a.m. and a few of the Welsh lads are having the craic. Trying their hand at hurling. We run some scrimmages then get into some heavier drills.

I can tell that people are looking at me differently now. I am talked up, in the press, as a genuine Test contender. Ian, Warren and Shaun have praised my impact and told reporters I am a real consideration for the back row. I am getting called in for more line-out drills and set-plays. Most importantly, I have earned the respect of my peers.

What gets me, though, is not a fired-up Springbok. It is a simple training-ground accident. A collapsed maul. Sometimes you just count yourself unlucky. It is not like I tried to kill somebody in a tackle and got it wrong. It is just a maul. Three or four guys going one way, twists and turns. My leg is trapped beneath a few bodies and my right knee goes. I know straight away. I feel a pop. Gary O'Driscoll, the team doctor, runs over and asks if I am OK. I tell him I am and head to the shade of the stand. I hobble over. Take a seat then try to stand again.

'Oh, shit.'

I sit back down. Gary comes over and tests it; a few knocks on the knee. He can feel the tension is not there. He will take me off soon, he says, for a proper look. I sit on the sideline with ice on my knee. I know the situation is not great.

I go for the scans. It is a Grade 2 tear of my medial ligament. At best, it will be four weeks out. The final Test is in three weeks. For the second time in three months I am in tears.

I do not consider myself to be an emotional guy, but when you have put in so much hard work, time and effort, and everyone else – JD and all the other lads – has too, for it all to go tits up is hard to take. It would not matter if I made the First Test and in the first minute someone came and smashed me and I did my medial ligaments. I would not break down. I am sure of that. However, sitting in Durban, after receiving that news and knowing there is not enough time to get back, I do just that.

'How can this happen to me in training?'

I am a mess. I am rooming with Joe and he is great. He packs all my bags, gets me into the shower, makes sure everything is sorted for me and that I am looked after. He is in his early thirties – an older head. That epitomizes what the team is all about. Everybody looks after me.

I hang around for a week and, near the end, my knee starts to feel better. I am thinking, 'I'm going to be OK. I can play here.' I go to the Sharks game, then fly to Cape Town with the boys. I am saying to the physios, 'My knee is starting to feel really good here.' They have seen it all before and tell me that is natural. I will feel a massive improvement in the first seven to ten days. Then the healing process will get painfully slow before it gets better.

Still, I knock on Gary's door one night and ask him for two minutes. I share with him my conviction that I can get back for the Tests. He gets me to sit down, hears me out, and we have a chat after.

'I'm walking around pain-free. I feel like I'm getting some-where. I've been in the pool, doing lunges.'

Gary nods his head, considers what I told him and says, 'OK.' He reasons, however, that even if everything goes well with my rehab and I can get back for the final Test, I will have played no rugby in three weeks.

'Perfect,' I reply.

I do not care. I have no better plans. I am happy enough to stick around, even if it is just to get on that bench for the last Test. He takes in what I have said and asks me to give it a couple more days.

Ryan Jones, the Welsh back row, is called in as cover. I watch the team squeak past Western Province, in Cape Town. We fly back to Durban and, three days later, there is no sign of progress with my knee. I start to realize that maybe I will not make it back in two and a half weeks' time. My parents are due to fly out for the First Test but I advise them to hold off. I sit down for another conversation with Gary and the decision is made. My tour is over.

I learn that if you get injured on tour, the first thing you do is book your flight home. Do not hang around. As soon as I injured myself and was out of the squad I was sitting round the physio room and was not out with the lads. I did not feel part of the squad and I made it harder for myself. If I had just gotten out of there, I could have said, 'Right, I had a good time, I missed the Test, but that's fair enough.'

That is one thing I say to myself: if I ever get injured on tour again, I will be straight out of there. I will be gone because it is not worth the anguish. Looking on from the outside.

My flight home is booked for the Monday after the First Test. Tom, who played really well against the Sharks, comes in at blind-side. Although I do not look at it like this at the time, just being in South Africa is a sign of how far I have come in the space of a year. In June 2008, I was on my way to America with Ireland A until I received the phone-call to go to Australia. One year on and only injury denied me a starting place with the British & Irish Lions.

*

I go to the First Test. It is a beautiful day in Durban, the sun is beating down. The atmosphere is incredible – very intimidating. I am sitting up in the gods, pretty high. The number of people who have come to the game is insane – just under 50,000, and many from back home. I am roaring with the rest of the Lions fans when Tom scores both of his tries. As the cheers settle down and both sets of fans start ribbing each other, I rap my hand off my knee.

'That could have been me. Maybe I could have put in a couple of big hits and changed the game around.'

South Africa win 26–21 but they are hanging on by their fingernails by the final whistle. I meet up with the guys after and can see how jarred they are by the result. We definitely could have won it.

I watch the final two games at home, on TV. Another close defeat and a blow-out win in the Third Test. By that stage, I am beginning to cope with the disappointment and setting new goals.

Gary and I definitely made the right call. Three weeks on, my knee is not right. There is no way it would have held up to Test rugby.

As the weeks pass, my mobility returns and I catch up with Ulster team doctor Davy Irwin for nine holes of golf. He has played a number of Tests and scored tries for the Lions.

'Stevie,' he tells me, 'you're a Lion but I am a Test Lion.'

He means it as a joke, and I take it that way. However, I also see it as motivation. The next Lions tour, to Australia, is only four short years away.

CHAPTER 13

I make noises about seeking a move away from Ulster, but, as we head into 2009/10, there are some compelling reasons to stay. Unlike my automatic pay bump when I got my first Ireland cap, Ulster will not be topping up my wages now that I have toured with the Lions. I have two years left on my deal, but it is not extra money that will keep me with the club. We need to show signs we can compete with the best in Europe.

David Humphreys' role is expanded to make him a full-time director of rugby. He will now oversee the day-to-day running of the team. Brian McLaughlin is confirmed as the new head coach, with former Ulster players Neil Doak and Jeremy Davidson joining up as his assistants.

Brian is similar to Mark McCall and Allen Clarke, in that he knows what Ulster Rugby is all about and what it stands for. He immediately instils a sense of togetherness; camaraderie. While Matt Williams was trying to be everybody's friend, Brian *is* everybody's friend. You just get on with Brian. He makes some decisions that may not always be right but all of the players get on with it and stick by him. He brings an intensity to training that we never had. One thing that is really, really bad in our game is our rucking.

We are crap at it. He turns us into a brilliant rucking side. Everyone enjoys their time working with him.

Still, guys that are not getting selected by him are not enjoying it half as much as those who are. They are not getting on every week and are left playing for Belfast Harlequins or Malone. Certain lads think they should be playing because they are on £100,000 a year. It is always the way. If a coach is picking you, there are no issues with him. If he is not picking you, you find problems. Experienced and talented lads are not getting a game and there are complaints.

'Brian is useless. He doesn't know what he is doing.'

'No, he is not. You just think he is because he's not starting you.'

Brian is not picking them because he does not think they are good enough.

The appointment of Jeremy is key. I love working with him; there is no better man for motivation. He may not be the most clued in when it comes to preparation. He pitches up to a meeting, late, and whips out a laptop to preview the last week's game. He has no clips cut. Already, at Ulster, we are used to having our clips packaged for us. We are sitting around, looking at Jeremy trying to flick from one line-out clip to the next.

'Could you not have had some clips cut up for us?'

For all of that, he gets results. He really gets our maul working and, technically, makes changes that have a big impact on our line-outs. He is good for us and works well with Brian.

The senior players are consulted more on decisions and encouraged to take more pride and ownership on the direction we are going. We have not played like a team for more than two years. Brian preaches that we must work together, win together and lose together. Before that we were going out to try and get a win to take the pressure off us.

In terms of policing each other, if anyone gets yellow-carded, there are fines brought in. It is seen as unacceptable to be cautioned unless it is something you had to do to save a match. For stupid penalties, guys get fined. Stupid mistakes as well. But paying £20 or £30 a week is not going to make much difference to the lads' pockets. It is more the act of handing over some cash to the players' fund, and being seen to do so. Taking ownership of your actions.

One aspect that markedly improves is how we get on as a team away from the pitch. In my early days at Ulster, all my socializing was done with friends from home. The only regular events I would attend with the rugby boys were the Christmas and end-of-season socials. Under Brian, a social spirit is fostered. A movie club is set up and other lads get involved in the dinner club: each Thursday, they pick a different restaurant and head along. Maybe that is all Campbell Feather and I were missing – a trip to the cinema or a meal out with the lads.

There is a team social every six weeks, where you go out and let your hair down. If I do not know somebody, the best way to get past that is to go out and have a beer, go over a few old stories and have a laugh.

Brian sorts a social budget to go paintballing and go-karting. When the shit hits the fan, you are probably doing the wrong thing, training too much to try and fix it. Rather than training more and doing more video analysis, the logic goes, maybe you should go out and have a bit of fun together instead of stressing out all the time because you are doing so badly. It is a conscious move away from the doom and gloom.

I score a try on my return to the Ulster team, on 18 September 2009, but we still lose out to Edinburgh. A back strain in training, a few days later, rules me out of our 30–6 victory over Connacht, in Galway. By the time I play again, in a high-scoring 45–24 win over Scarlets, I have legal worries dogging me.

It's Sunday, 27 September, and I am out with my brother, Dave, a few friends and my ex-girlfriend at Café Vaudeville in Belfast, partying away. Some friends invite us back to a party in their house, just off the Lisburn Road. Four of them live together and it is a regular party destination. Finishing up in town, I hop in a taxi with Dave, my girlfriend and another girl. We are dropped off at the wrong street, but as it runs parallel to our destination we figure we will walk round the corner.

Dave is smoking cigarettes but is on the look-out for a shop or pub so he can get a light. I ring my friend James, who lives at the house.

'Where are you? We are just round the corner and will be there in ten seconds. Are you home yet?'

'No, we stopped off for food so will see you in twenty minutes.'

'Hurry up, it's freezing. We want to get into the house.'

'Right, grand, we're coming.'

We walk to the end of the street and, across the road, there are two lads standing behind a fence, smoking cigarettes. Dave walks over to them to get a light while myself, my girlfriend and her friend make our way to the house. It is about 80 metres away. I give the front door a couple of bangs, just in case anyone has made it back already. There is no one there. I call again.

'Right, we're on our way. We'll be ten or fifteen minutes.'

As I hang up, all I hear is screaming and shouting. I jog down to the end of the street and, when I get there, see three or four guys, right in the middle of the road, kicking my brother.

I run over and get involved. I clear a couple of guys away from Dave. I get a glass bottle to the side of the face, my eye is cut open. I am held over a car bonnet, both arms pinned down. People must have streamed out of a nearby house as it is bedlam. About ten guys and four girls against myself and Dave. Not all of them involved but it feels like it at the time. My ex and her friend have run down to the end of the street and are screaming and shouting. Chaos. Like something out of a movie. Eventually I break free. My brother is still on the ground, cuts and bruises all over him.

We gather ourselves but one of their guys is lying on the ground, unconscious. We step back from the situation and walk to the other side of the road to wait for the police. The sirens get closer. Someone must have called in the middle of the fight. We stand there for a few minutes until the police, and an ambulance, arrive. Initially, we give a short statement. Because one of their party looks seriously hurt and is being put in the back of the ambulance, the policeman takes us up the road and says, 'Look, get into the car, guys.'

'Yeah, no worries.'

We jump into the car. He turns round to us.

'You're not under arrest but you are under caution and we are releasing you on street bail.'

I look at Dave.

'Why? We were the ones who got our balls rolled there. Why are we getting cautioned?'

The policeman explains that they will gather up numerous statements over the next couple of days.

As soon as I get out of the car I know the fight will be in the press. There is somebody seriously hurt and Stephen Ferris, just back from the Lions tour, is involved. I ring Davy Millar, the Ulster team manager, at three a.m. in the morning and leave a voicemail.

'Listen, Davy, I got into a scrap tonight. It's all blown out of proportion. I'm on street bail or whatever.'

He rings back at seven a.m.

'Right, Stevie, talk me through everything.'

That is the way it is left.

The next day I speak to my brother about it all.

'Dave, what happened?'

'I went over to ask for a light and the guy told me to fuck off.' Dave was very drunk at the time. As he recalled it, he said something like, 'If you tell me to fuck off again I'll hit you a slap.' The guy told him to fuck off so Dave smacked him and bust his nose. The lad he hit ran into the house with blood pishing out of his nose and Dave started scrapping with the other guy he was with. When the ten or so others came rushing out, that was when I heard all the commotion and ran down. I was not even involved in the fight. I was not there when the punches were thrown.

If charges are pressed against the two of us, though, I could face seven years in jail. Dave will get longer. Yet all I was doing was defending my brother from getting an absolute beating. I am livid with him.

'Dave, you're the one that started the fight. If you had walked on round the corner and walked up to the house and waited fifteen minutes for the boys to come home, this would never have happened.'

Ulster Rugby speak to the police and seek advice about the

best way to approach the situation. I believe it will soon be sorted out. There will be no need for a court case. I am mistaken. We are in court four or five times. We have to hire a barrister, visit his house a couple of times and go through all our statements.

The incident remains out of the news, for now, but it is never far from my mind.

As the 2009/10 Heineken Cup opener, against Bath, nears, I convince myself that the fracas was just that. It will go away in time. I focus on Europe and our mission to reach the knock-out stages for the first time since our 1999 cup success. The fact that we are listed as 100/1 outsiders angers us as much as it demonstrates the perceived gulf in talent between our squad and Europe's best-rated sides.

We are too good for Bath, at Ravenhill, but blow a half-time lead against Edinburgh. We face a couple of must-win matches against Stade Français in December.

Ireland's November series confirms that we are one of the world's top sides. I face off against Rocky Elsom, David Pocock and the Wallabies at Croke Park and we are grateful to a late Brian O'Driscoll try, and Ronan O'Gara conversion, in a 20–20 draw. I am reunited with my old Under-21s team-mate Johnny Sexton for our 41–6 dismissal of Fiji at the RDS. He kicks seven from seven and does enough for Declan Kidney to keep him as out-half, at the expense of ROG, for our final Test of the year, against South Africa.

Having missed my shot at them during the Lions tour, I am fired up beyond belief for the Springboks. Ready to rumble. Gert Smal, I find, is even more psyched.

'I want you to go out there and get stuck into these guys,' he tells me. 'Give them everything you've got.'

We are 10–6 down, after half an hour, when I run into BJ Botha, the Springbok prop and my team-mate at Ulster. He hits me hard and I twist to present the ball back. Whatever way I twist, I go over on my ankle.

'Jesus. Here we go again.'

I get some treatment and make it to half-time. The ankle does not look good so Sean O'Brien takes my place. I stay down in the dressing room and Rala knocks a TV up in the corner for me. It is freezing outside. Fog everywhere. I sit and watch the rest of the game in the dressing room, with ice on my ankle and my leg up. Johnny hits five penalties from six and we defend like maniacs in the final minutes. South Africa do not score again. We win 15–10.

I am passed fit for Ulster's Heineken Cup dates with Stade Français. They arrive in Belfast expecting a fight. Instead, we open them up with some superb running rugby. They try their best to spoil a lot of our ball and slow us down but Ian Humphreys makes them pay with a few penalties. After forty-eight minutes, I have a line break and draw in two defenders before releasing Simon Danielli to run in an easy try. We are 21–6 up. Stade are not finished yet but we keep them at bay. Realizing they are not going to turn the game around, they resort to throwing themselves about. I am caught in the crossfire, twice.

People do not seem to understand, but I do not turn round to the referee and say 'Julien Dupuy eye-gouged me.' Sky Sports are covering the match. Their pundits see the incident and highlight it. Dupuy, the Stade scrum-half, puts his hand in my face and pushes my head away, causing me to fall back, over the ruck. I get

Stephen Ferris

up and straight into a scrap with him – both of us rolling around the ground. As far as I am concerned, he does not intentionally stick his fingers in my eye and try to gouge me. Nonetheless, it looks really bad on TV, and because Sky are playing it on a loop, it comes across even worse. Will Greenwood, the former England centre, is on pundit duty and is calling it stupid, reckless.

Many people are saying 'Stephen Ferris has got Dupuy cited.' That is not the case. Not in the slightest.

Later, I will leave a voicemail on Julien's phone, assuring him I was not going to go to the citing commissioners to tell them he had gouged me. There are no hard feelings. He calls back and leaves a similar message for me.

But ten minutes after that incident, about six minutes from the end of the game, I do complain. The barney with Dupuy has sparked the game again and another scrap kicks off. I do not start it but am right in the middle of it, on the ground. This time I do get gouged. David Attoub, their prop, tries to take my eye out of its socket.

'Fucking hell!'

He is not long off their bench and must find my head on the ground. His finger is an inch deep into my eye and is caught around another player's jersey.

If you, ever so gently, push your eyeball back, you can feel the pressure. Attoub jams his finger right in there. The pain is excruciating. It is like someone driving a nail straight into my eye. I cannot budge; cannot get out. I am pinned down by other players. Dupuy is definitely one of the guys that has me locked down. In goes the finger. It must be in there long enough as the match photographers are able to get photos.

At the time I believe Mauro Bergamasco is the gouger because

190

as soon as I open my eyes, he is there. I hop up and am screaming, 'You dirty prick, you're an eye-gouging bastard!'

Up shoot his arms. 'It was not me, it was not me. I did not do anything.'

'We'll see. We'll soon fucking see.'

Looking through the video afterwards, we cannot really see much. But then a guy called Oliver McVeigh sends on some pictures. He was down the far end of the pitch with a long-scope lens and captured the incident. Click, click, click.

Immediately after the incident, though, I do not know that these pictures have been taken. Still, I let the referee know I have been eye-gouged in the seventy-fourth minute and that I want it looked at.

When the pictures emerge, backing my claims up, Attoub still denies any gouging. His story is that he did not intentionally make contact with my eyes and that the pictures have been doctored.

Stade Français then pay someone and set up the same scenario – with a lad acting as me, laid out on their pitch – to prove I am lying and that the way Attoub's finger was positioned, it was not in my eye.

All I can think about Attoub, as the story drags on, is 'Are you for real?' If he just owns up, says something like 'I was trying to poke him in the eye or trying to slap him in the mouth, I didn't mean to eye-gouge him', next time I see him I would shake his hand. Everyone makes mistakes. But he does nothing like that. He denies it and keeps denying it. I have no respect for anybody like that. I could have lost an eye, or my eyesight, and he does not give a shit.

It is a massive talking point in the game. Probably bigger than the actual game itself, because we played really well. The return leg is the following week and we are supposed to play in Brussels. I do not know what sort of tactic it is, but Brussels is forecast to be minus 15° and we are due to play in a football stadium with no under-soil heating. When we arrive in Brussels, there is six inches of snow on the ground. We reach our hotel, get a night's sleep, and the weather is just as bad when we wake the next morning. There is no way this game is going ahead, but there is no word of the game being cancelled. We are forced to wait about. Finally, an hour or so before kick-off, we get word that the game has been called off. We have to play them in Paris, the following day.

We all jump on a train, around eleven p.m., and get into Paris after one a.m. None of us have eaten properly so myself and Tom Court lope off and grab a slice or two of pizza from a corner shop. Most of us end up getting to sleep around 2.30 to three. We get up the next morning and play Stade on a cabbage patch of a pitch. A pitch that has been covered in snow until an hour before kick-off. It is not frozen but is still hard. They have these big industrial air heaters blowing all over the pitch. With all the ice and snow melting, it turns the pitch into a swamp.

When I walk into the tunnel after the warm-up, Attoub is standing there. I trot down the steps and head to our room, on the right. Attoub is standing outside Stade's, staring at me. An expression of pure hatred on his face. I walk on; do not say a word to him.

The silent treatment is definitely not in effect as far as the Stade players are concerned. I get constant chit-chat on the pitch. We lose the game but there are no flare-ups. The referee, Chris White, officiating in one of his last Heineken Cup games, seems to me to be under strict instructions. If there are any fifty-fifty calls or contentious moments, just blow the whistle for a scrum. You carry the ball into contact – scrum. Maul – scrum. He defuses any situation that has the potential to get fiery. Tournament organizers do not want any more mass brawls.

Benjamin Kayser scores a try for them but Andrew Trimble responds with a sensational one for us. There is no intensity to our game, though. We only got four or five hours' sleep and they took the pace out of the game by playing us on that cabbage patch. It is as if they have done this on purpose. It certainly feels that way. The Stade players were in Paris the evening before. They bloody well did not go to Brussels. It is bizarre.

Dimitri Szarzewski is one of the chief culprits of the abuse I endure on the pitch. With the match finished, 29–16 to Stade, I still offer to shake his hand. He comes right up to me.

'Fuck off, you cunt.'

'Whatever, you dickhead.'

I am last out of our changing room and James Haskell, Stade's English flanker, is coming out of theirs at the same time. We start chatting and walk up to get food together. Maybe it is down to us being so friendly together, but there are no incidents at the post-match function.

Eventually, I give my evidence to the citing commission. I make the effort to go down to Dublin with Davy Millar. He sorts a car and we head down. Max Duffy, the citing commissioner, meets us at the door of the hotel.

'There might be a wait for these French lads. Their plane is delayed due to snow.'

Two hours later, we get word that the French are not coming. Were they ever coming?

They set another date and the same thing happens again – they do not show. There is a final date arranged but I do not attend. I am not prepared to waste any more of my time on this.

Attoub gets banned for a year – fifty-two weeks. Dupuy gets twenty-six weeks, but I feel slightly sorry for him. I am so glad for Attoub. He has the potential to go on and be a really good tight-head prop but you do not want anybody like that on your team. A lot of people believe he should have been banned for life. If he had been, that would not have fazed me in the slightest.

All the while, Ulster's form is showing signs of improvement. We avenge our defeat to Edinburgh and beat Bath at the Recreation Ground. Danny Grewcock gets a straight red for stamping on me and we force home the man advantage. We are unable to get the try-scoring bonus point, though, and it proves crucial. Minutes after our game wraps up, 28–10, Stade's losing bonus point confirms them, not us, as quarter-finalists.

Any hope of repeating back-to-back Grand Slams evaporates after thirty-two minutes of breakneck rugby at the Stade de France three weeks later. I miss Ireland's opening-day win over Italy but return for the blitzing by Les Bleus. Cian Healy, who has taken over as starting loose-head prop from Marcus Horan, is yellow-carded seventeen minutes in and I am sacrificed for ten minutes so Tom Court can come on and contest scrums. By the time I am back on, we are 10–0 down and have lost Drico to injury. We try to make it a fight after David Wallace scores a converted try but France have our number.

Szarzewski comes off the bench for the final half-hour. After the game, I try to shake his hand. I try not to hold grudges. Like a child, he puts his hand out then pulls it away at the last moment.

'Ha, ha, ha. You dickhead.'

I offer my hand to Pascal Papé.

'Fuck off.'

And there, again, is Attoub. He is not playing but he is a guest of the French team.

These guys are dicks. Their own team-mate blatantly eye-gouges an opponent, gets found guilty of the offence and is banned for a year, and they are still backing him up. If someone like Tommy or Rory went out and did something like that, I would be having a hard, harsh word with them. The Stade players are your typical arseholes. The rest of the French team would shake your hand and, if they thought you had a good game, would slap you on the back. That is the thing with rugby – there is usually a lot of respect between rivals. With those lads, there is none. I determine that each time I play against them, for Ulster and Ireland, I will put in a big hit or shut one of them down.

The chance has passed me by in Paris.

I am not one for trashing dressing rooms or shouting my mouth off after a defeat. I would be one to sit there, very quiet, analysing what happened. I deal with my frustration by taking a bit of time out.

Paul O'Connell generally sits beside me. If we ever lose, he would be sitting there, talking to himself. He is at it again at the Stade de France.

'For fuck's sake, Paul. Why did you not take that line-out like that, you fucking idiot.'

I am sitting there. I glance up quickly. 'Is he talking to me?'

Next minute: 'You're a stupid fucking idiot. What are you up to? Why did you DO THAT?'

I turn round to Wally and give him a look. What is going on? He is well used to it so gives a shrug.

'Don't talk to Psycho,' he says.

We get our Triple Crown, and championship, quest started in great fashion by defending for our lives against England at Twickenham. We make four times as many tackles as the English and do the damage with tries. Tommy gets two, including the match winner with five minutes to spare. It is a fantastic score as he beats Jonny Wilkinson on his inside shoulder and dives over.

Wales are up next but I am struggling with a viral illness; a chest infection. It drags on for weeks and I am using an inhaler the whole time. I have been given it by Leinster's doctor, Jim McShane, who is covering for Eanna Falvey. I am on antibiotics too, trying to clear everything up.

Eanna comes back in a couple of weeks later and asks what I have been taking. I tell him and he asks if it has been cleared.

'No. I didn't think I had to.'

Eanna gets on the case and makes sure everything is registered.

On the Saturday, after we put Wales away, I get drug-tested. Once I mention what I have been taking, I must take a slew of tests to prove I need an inhaler. It all works out fine but it goes to show you: if I had taken the inhaler and antibiotics without informing the anti-doping agencies, I could have got banned for two years. Jim did not know that that inhaler had been on the banned list but, once Eanna came back in, it was all cleared up.

If you ever had a cold, it was the same. All the way through my professional career, if I had to take a Lemsip or use a nasal spray I was very, very careful. Any time I had something, I was cautious.

I would ring the doctor to check it out and get something prescribed.

Rugby is changing, year on year. You can walk into any sports shop and pick up supplements, some protein powder, and they could be full of stuff. That is why you have to go through the proper channels and make sure you get products that have been tested and are safe. The amount of protein supplements the guys take now, just to keep the weight on and their strength up, is crazy. People taking zinc, vitamin C tablets, Berocca, pre-fuels before a game, to get yourself going. There was a drink called Jack3d – like a Red Bull, but in supplement form. Everyone thought it was a caffeine hit but a couple of guys tested positive for illegal substances.

You have creatine, glutamine, protein before you go to bed at night, beta-alanine. There are so many. I regularly had to take twelve tablets before a gym session at Newforge – swallowing tablets the size of your finger with a protein shake. Do your weights, then take another eight tablets after. By 2010, however, I was reaching a stage in my career where I knew what worked and what did not. Most of these supplements did not make me any better or stronger. Some people swear by creatine. I once took it, for four or five months, to test it out; it did little for me. I decided to simply take protein.

Back on Six Nations duty, and with the chest infection slowly shifting, I have a Triple Crown in my sights.

Against Scotland, we seriously mess up. The game, at Croke Park, is probably one of the poorest I play for Ireland.

To be honest, because we are at home against Scotland, we think we are just going to take to the pitch and win. There is a feeling that we are better than the Scots. We have had the better of them for the last few years. 'We *are* better than them.'

Very early in the game, Johnnie Beattie gets over for a try. It is a fortuitous score. The ball breaks free, I go down on it and pop it back up. It is a fifty-fifty, hangs there for a moment. One of their guys darts in, snatches it and tears off down the field. By the time I am up, off the deck, Scotland have scored in the corner.

'Fucking hell.'

I jog back to join the lads under the posts.

'Right, let's get ourselves back together.'

Dan Parks is kicking really well and lands the conversion. Still, we are not worried.

The number of line breaks we make in the first half is a joke. Tommy is making clean breaks for fun. ROG is putting the ball in behind them. We have these sweeping moves that have them clinging on. The final pass is not connecting. They are making covering tackles. The problem is, we are not putting points on the board. One of the best chances sees a great team move falter at the end, as the last pass goes behind Tommy. He tries to do a flick with his ankle – something Simon Zebo may be watching at home – but he misses it.

Scotland are always in it. We have parity with them in the scrum until a nice piece of gamesmanship by their prop, Euan Murray. He is wearing a scrum-cap, but midway through the first half, before a Scottish scrum put-in, he walks over to the touch judge, gives him the cap and strolls back on, like he is the man. 'I won't be needing this.' Next thing you know, he wins the penalty at the scrum. Parks knocks it over.

'What is happening? Is this happening?'

Tommy finally scores after bursting through two men but

Parks keeps nailing kicks. The final whistle does not feel real. 23–20 to Scotland.

'This can't be it.'

It is one of the most disappointing moments I have ever experienced in Test rugby. The dressing room is a desolate place. We played some really good rugby in that first half.

I cannot get my head around it. The big players did not perform, and I include myself in that group. I did not show up. It is another trophy – the Triple Crown – that we all could have won. You have to give Scotland credit, though. They deserve the win.

I chat to Ruth Gorman, of UTV, after the game. She tells me I look devastated.

'When you can't go back and fix something,' I reply, 'it is very hard to take. If I could run out, now, and play the game again, I would.'

We were so off the boil. Those things happen, but you are always going to get results like that.

The fact it is the final game at Croke Park makes it worse. We have such great memories of the place – we sowed the seeds of our Grand Slam there. The place was rocking during that first half.

People may have thought our motivation was lacking as there was a Triple Crown, not a Grand Slam, up for grabs. That is not the case. To win any trophy in the Six Nations is something to cherish. To end the championship a distant second, after our achievements the previous year, is a let-down.

Narrowly missing out on the Heineken Cup knock-out stages is the height of it for Ulster. From 19 February to 16 April, we draw once then lose five on the spin. I score a try as we stop the rot by bloodying Edinburgh's nose at Murrayfield with a 37–25 win. Our final game of the season is a home match against Connacht, with only inter-provincial pride to play for. Ireland have a summer tour to Australia and New Zealand coming up but it is not until June. I am bristling for some action.

On the Tuesday before the match I am in the starting team, at training. Nevin Spence is in the other team, the dirties. We are running a few plays and boys are boshing. In the dirties there is always the chat.

'Right, boys, we aren't letting these boys get through us. They might be starting this week but let's not let them make us look like dickheads. Give it to them, stick a shoulder in.'

In the other team they are saying, 'Boys, take it nice and easy.'

Next thing you know you are getting smacked back.

I have been riled up a few times. I take it upon myself to try and smash somebody from their side. It is a bad idea. They have a scrum and I come around off it. I never do that. I always stay on the blind side. Nevin takes a short ball off his out-half and steps inside. I go to clothesline him. Whatever way Nev ducks, the top of his head hits my cheekbone. I hit the deck. I have never felt pain like it. The nerve has been hit.

'AHHH, AHHHH, AHHHHH!'

The boys think I am messing. I am not crying so much as roaring. The pain is blinding. My cheekbone has sunk in. After about a minute, I stand up and look at Jeremy Davidson.

'Stevie, you may go up and see the physio.'

Nevin comes over. 'Are you alright?'

'This is killing me.'

I have fractured my cheekbone and my eye socket. I stumble into the physio room and lie there. Alan McCaldin is in there.

'Alan, I need some pain relief, now!'

'Settle down. The doctor is on his way. Chill out.'

Alan is working on a lad's ankle. I am on the physio bed and cannot sit still. Up, down, up again. The pain is insane.

Davy Irwin comes over from his practice (Ulster do not have a permanent on-site doctor). He comes in and gets straight to it.

'Pull your pants down, Stevie.'

I turn over and get morphine straight into my arse. 'Ahhhhhh.' Within five minutes I am sleeping on my good side.

Later, David Humphreys drops in. 'You'll be alright. Take it easy. You'll be back in six to eight weeks.'

I see a surgeon and am operated on the next day. Nice scar, biggest black eye you have ever seen. The summer tour is off the table. Another lesson learned.

Sometimes it is best to let the dirties do all the hitting.

CHAPTER 14

August 2010. For the first time in a long time, Ulster enter a season with high hopes and expectations. I complete a full pre-season and am primed for fourteen of my life's most pivotal months. Senior internationals will get about five weeks off at the end of the season before reporting back to Ireland camp in preparation for the 2011 World Cup in New Zealand. As director of rugby, David Humphreys has made a raft of good South African signings: Johann Muller, Pedrie Wannenburg, and my old Under-21 rival Ruan Pienaar. Darren Cave has established himself in Ulster's midfield and younger lads, such as Craig Gilroy, Nevin Spence and Willie Faloon, are proving their worth.

The season begins with wins over Ospreys and Aironi. Away from the action, I commit myself to the province after signing a new IRFU contract. There is an upward bump in wages but the main reason I am staying is that David has me really sold on his vision for the province. We are building a squad that can challenge for trophies each and every season. I celebrate the deal by tearing into Edinburgh, at Ravenhill, as we pick up another win. A knock incurred next time out, against Connacht, means I miss two home wins, but I return in time to face Biarritz at Parc des Sports Aguiléra.

We have lost eleven of our previous twelve competitive fixtures in France and never look like bucking that trend. I get over for a last-minute try but it is meagre consolation in a 35–15 defeat. December will bring a Heineken Cup double-header against Bath. If we take both games, we could bridge an eleven-year gap and reach the knock-out stages for the first time since 1999.

Ulster stumble in the league before November brings a break in that competition. I am back in the Ireland squad for a series of Tests that offer us a crack at the All Blacks.

First up, South Africa avenge their defeat from the year before by turning us over in the first game at the revamped Aviva Stadium. Rob Kearney scores a try with six minutes to go but Ronan O'Gara misses the conversion. We lose 23–21. I replace Jamie Heaslip in the second half of our 20–10 win over Samoa. As soon as the final whistle blows, our focus switches to the world's best team.

People would often ask me, when teams like New Zealand came to town, if I thought there was a chance of beating them. I believe there is a chance in every game, especially internationals. Even if you have lost ten matches in a row, you never pitch up thinking you are going to lose. If you play for Italy or Scotland, who have been poor for the last decade in the Six Nations, you do not go into a game with the sole intention of hanging in there for eighty minutes. If either of those sides wins their first Six Nations game, for example, they happily entertain the notion of winning a Grand Slam.

We know our squad has a number of world-class players. It is about those players – and I include myself in that group – peaking and the entire squad fronting up.

'Let's show these guys how good we are.'

We get off to a great start and land some high-impact tackles. Owen Franks, one of the All Blacks' propping brothers (the other is Ben), takes possession in midfield. I step out of the line and absolutely smash him. It is like hitting a brick wall but I put him down.

We are both getting to our feet when he puts a hand on my shoulder and whispers into my ear, 'Jeez, bro, good hit.'

Crap. I gave him everything I had and there he is, thanking me for it. I stopped him in his tracks but he, and his mates, keep coming. It is surge after surge of New Zealand pressure. Dan Carter is knocking over each kick at goal he is offered but Johnny Sexton keeps us in touch. We are 9–6 down, after thirty minutes, when I score my first ever Ireland try.

It is one of the best team tries we have scored all year. We make so many strong carries. David Wallace crashes it up, Johnny gets on the ball and finds myself and Jamie Heaslip out in midfield. That is something we want to do, as a team: use the back rows to add some width to our attacking moves. We are often guilty of lapsing into that Munster style of just crashing it forward, keeping everything tight and only the backs getting hands on the ball out wide.

We are told that we have to put in the hard yards and go through the phases but, when we get into attacking positions, to get out wide and open up space.

The ball comes and goes through Jamie's hands. If it goes to a video replay, it may be called back, as Jamie's hands pushed it slightly forward. The referee, Marius Jonker, is happy with the pass. When a move goes like that and everybody gets their hands on the ball, it is always a shame to call play back.

As soon as I latch on to that pass, I take off and beat Richie

McCaw on the outside. As I near the line, Mils Muliaina is haring over and, as I dive, tries to knock the ball out of my hands. There is no way he is jarring it loose. Try.

Johnny's conversion makes it 13–9 but Carter gets his fourth penalty, and for the second time in two years the All Blacks score a try right on half-time.

When Kieran Read and Sam Whitelock score further tries right after the break, we look finished. We regroup under the posts and are determined to give it everything we have until we hear the last whistle.

We have Tom Court playing tight-head and other lads – Sean Cronin, Mick O'Driscoll, Devin Toner – that come in and step up to the plate. Drico gets a sublime try, where he picks the ball off his shoelaces, on the run, and dives over. That gives us hope, late in the piece, of getting something out of the game but it is not to be. The final score is 38–18 but that does not reflect the performance we put in. Walking off the pitch, we are disappointed with the result but not deflated. We have not been hammered or played off the park.

It is only after the match, during a corporate question-and-answer session with sponsors, that I am reminded I have scored my first senior try for Ireland. The enormity of it sinks in and, ever so briefly, I am stuck for words.

A 29–9 win over Argentina the following weekend sees me score my second Test try. I finish off a good move that involves Jamie and Tommy.

We were not far off the best team in the world so, with some confidence still in reserve from that stand-out year of 2009, we head into a World Cup year with a degree of optimism.

*

My international form carries into the Heineken Cup, and I find the Ulster lads well up for the battle. We beat Bath 22–18 at home after trailing 15–3 in the first half. Our statement-making performance arrives at the Rec eight days later. Adam D'Arcy and Nevin, who goes head over heels doing so, score our tries but we still need Ian Humphreys' nerveless kicking to seal a 26–22 win.

Biarritz are beaten by a last-minute Aironi drop goal and need to turn us over at Ravenhill in January 2011 to have any hope of reaching the last eight. Our league form has faltered but we know we control our Pool 4 destiny.

The match is tied at 6–6 with two minutes to go when Ian steps up and slots over a 51-metre penalty to win it for us. Unbelievable.

Despite losing two of their five games, Biarritz have already accumulated five bonus points. It means we need to secure a bonus-point win against Aironi, in Italy.

Fifteen minutes into the second half we have a scrum on their 5-metre line and have already scored three tries. Our pack, with Tom, Rory Best and Deccie Fitzpatrick up front, are roasting Aironi's. We get over the line, from the scrum, and the referee puts his hand up. Try. Penalty try. Off he runs, under the sticks.

The scrum is still wheeling around and, me being on the flank, I spot the ref and raise my arm in celebration. My left knee is slightly flexed, though, and their tight-head prop and hooker both fall into it. Pure bad luck.

My knee folds in. I have already torn my cartilage on that knee – some of it has been taken away – so it is probably still vulnerable.

'Fuck! My knee.'

I am helped to the sideline and try to walk it off.

We close out a 43–6 bonus-point win and reach the quarter-finals. We will face Northampton Saints in April.

For me, the worst-case scenario, I calculate, is four weeks out. But the knee gets worse, and I end up going for an operation with Richard Nicholas, who operated on my knee after that Second Test against Argentina in 2007. I cannot get any movement out of it. It is constantly sore, but all the scans are showing up bony trauma. I just need to let it settle down. After a few weeks, we know the knee needs to be sorted. They remove a bit of gristle that had grown inside my knee joint, where my cartilage was. That eases the pain.

Once I get that out, rehabbed and strengthened, the knee is better than ever.

Even if it had been spotted immediately and I had had surgery in the days after the injury, I still would have missed the Northampton game. Who knows if my presence would have made much of a difference?

I travel over to Milton Keynes, where the game is taking place, with the lads. Dorian West, Saints' forwards coach, comes up to me and says, 'Sorry to hear about the injury, but it was music to our ears when we heard you were not playing today.'

'Thanks for making me feel better.'

Our set-piece is dominated and we fall short. Still, we have chances to win it. Adam D'Arcy drops the ball, over their try-line. Last chance of the game, literally dropped. We lose by 10 points.

The lads rally well in the league and finish third, which is good enough for a semi-final place under the new system, which was thankfully introduced the previous season. But we go into our semi against Leinster, at the RDS, without myself, BJ, Paddy Wallace, Dan Tuohy and Andrew Trimble. Leinster beat us 18–3, although they go on to lose the league title to Munster.

Of course, I also miss the 2011 Six Nations. I pay a couple of visits, in January and February, to Carton House. Declan Kidney likes the injured lads to dip their head in, to check in with the medical staff. Defeats to France and Wales end Ireland's championship challenge, but a 24–8 demolition of England, in a Grand Slam match that went badly wrong for them, gives the lads some hope heading into the World Cup.

Towards the end of the season, I start to think about taking a short break. I am sitting in my car, pulled into a lay-by near Moira, on the way home, when Deccie rings.

'How are you?'

'Not too bad. Just trying to get a holiday sorted here.'

'You're going on holiday?'

'Yes. The season is nearly over and I haven't been away anywhere, or seen any sun, in months.'

'Well, I would maybe like for you to stay at home.'

'Deccie, my head is turned. I need to get away. I need to get some head space. This whole knee injury thing has got to me.'

He mulls on that for a moment. 'Still,' he says, 'I think it would be best for you to stay at home and rehab that knee.'

'Right, OK, Deccie. That is your opinion, but the knee is coming along really well and I think the time away would do me more good rather than sitting at home.'

'If that is what you feel, then OK. It is up to you in the end. But I would prefer you not to go.'

Here I am, sitting in this lay-by for twenty minutes, arguing with the Ireland coach. Pleading with him and giving the reasons I should go on holiday. Back and forth it goes. I can see where he is coming from – he wants me right for the World Cup – but I know I need the break. If I get away, I can come back refreshed, mentally, and bring myself, and my knee, through a good pre-season. Deccie does not share my viewpoint.

If I am forced to stay in the country, I will go straight from one season to the next. Because of the World Cup, 2011/12 is shaping up to be an eleven-month season, ending with a three-Test tour back in New Zealand.

A lot of people do not understand that aspect of the game. Older players often tell you touring tales. 'Back in my day we played fifteen games in a row, blah, blah, blah.' OK, but you did not have that weight of pressure and expectation the lads have on them now. You are playing in front of 50,000 and 60,000 people, as well as millions watching on TV, with every slip or fumble analysed to death.

You need to switch off mentally, as well as physically. I am at that stage, leading into the World Cup, where I need to take a break or I will melt down. When you are mentally not right, it affects you physically. Seeps into your game.

Playing rugby week in, week out is the easiest part of the game. Pitching up on a Monday morning for training, pitch sessions, weights, then a Thursday run-out and a game on Friday night. Win, lose or draw. No worries. Pick up your cheque.

That is the easy part.

But when you are on your own it is different. Having to train one-on-one with physios. Having to do extra weights, alone. You are injured and you see a guy coming in with a medial ligament strain. Six weeks later he is gone and you are still there. Next guy limps in on a broken ankle, and a few weeks on he is back playing. You are still there, in this injured players' group. It is so frustrating.

As soon as I get off the phone to Deccie, I ring Michael Webb at Ulster.

'Michael, what is more important to me – another two weeks of rehab or two weeks of getting my head showered, going out to America and chilling out?'

'Stevie, what are you talking about?'

I recount my conversation with Deccie.

'Leave it with me,' says Michael.

A couple of hours later, my phone rings again. Deccie tells me he has spoken with the medical staff but explains that he is still not happy.

I feel like nutting my head off the wall.

'You've spoken to the medical staff. They think it's a good idea if I take a break.'

Deccie eventually gives his blessing and I am off to America.

It is great to get away from it all – rugby, rehab, World Cup worries. And before I fly out, I learn that the court appearance for myself and my brother, Dave, dating back to the fight in September 2009, is set for Tuesday, 21 June. For twelve days and nights, I try to put it all behind me. Darren, Chris Henry and Paul Marshall join me on the trip away. We head to Orlando for a week and meet up with Andy Maxwell, our old team-mate, who owns an Irish bar there, and go round to all the theme parks. We have no guide in Las Vegas, for our final five nights, but it is not too hard to find the craic out there.

*

The courts in Belfast have been on strike, on and off, for more than a year, so our court appearance has been put back on a couple of occasions. The legal fees kept rolling. Eventually, the date in June was set. Once it went on the books – Stephen Ferris, Belfast Crown Court, 21 June – it became a news story.

Many people automatically assumed I had given a couple of boys a beating on a night out. Wrong. There were ten lads and four girls standing around as a couple of the lads kicked the head off my brother. I intervened and was bottled, punched and slapped. It was a joke. No one on the other side was charged. I still have a scar above my eye from where the bottle struck. We did not press any charges against them but because a member of their party had been knocked out, and had his nose broken, we were looked upon as the guilty party.

We sought legal advice back in early 2010, when it became clear that the incident might go to court. I had been told, 'We'll just make sure, Stevie, we get you out of this and leave it at that.'

Let it all be brushed under the carpet and not another word said. I had nothing to hide.

I thought, 'Why the fuck are they not getting done?'

A couple of days before we go to court, I am at home, in bed, when there is a knock at the door.

'I'm not answering that.'

An hour and a half later, knock, knock, knock on the door again.

'Flip sake.'

My dog, Bailey, is howling, wanting to see who it is.

I go down to the front door and pick Bailey up so he will not run out. I open up and there is a reporter standing a few feet back. A Mondeo is parked out the front.

'Hi Stephen, how are you doing?'

'Hi, how are you?'

'I'm just here from the *News of the World*. I wanted to ask you a few questions about the fight that you and your brother David were in.'

'No, sorry, no comment.'

I close the door. Somebody is in the back of the Mondeo taking pictures. I make the cover of the newspaper, standing there in my boxers, holding the dog.

I am livid.

We go to court and Dave pleads guilty for actual bodily harm. He holds his hands up. He was deemed to be the attacker. The guy he struck was badly hurt in the initial altercation.

I plead not guilty to the same charge. In my eyes, and those of my lawyer, all I was trying to do was save my brother. I did not start the fight and I did not intentionally punch somebody without provocation. There were so many people there and I was just trying to get Dave out of the situation. My take on it is, 'If your brother, or sister, was getting a kicking, would you stand by and wait for the police to come or bail in and try to get him out?' That is how I explain myself to the judge, and how our lawyer presents my case.

The trial is initially set for November 2011, after the World Cup, but does not actually go ahead until February 2012. We go through the whole case again, both sides making their arguments. The judge agrees with our take and Dave, as the guilty party, gets the brunt of the punishment. He pays £2,000 to the court, for charity, as a goodwill gesture but the judge has his mind made up: Dave is ordered to complete the maximum community service hours, 240, and has a criminal record for two years.

Dave was in the wrong and deserved to be punished but, in my view, the sentence is harsh. Apart from our scraps, as brothers, he has never been involved in any other altercation in his life, nor has he ever had an issue with the police. And yet he is given a stringent sentence.

Why? My take on it is because 'Stephen Ferris, the rugby player' is involved. And because the rugby player is getting off lightly, they have to make sure his brother does not.

Dave is not far off getting locked up. The judge says, 'For this offence I could put you in jail.' He is shitting himself. There is a lot of stress on Dave, on myself and on our family.

He makes up the hours over the course of a year, each Tuesday, in a charity shop. He works long hours in his own job but never once complains during that time. From the moment that fight occurred, in 2009, he is a changed man. He moves out to the suburbs, settles down and starts a family.

The case proves a talking point over the summer of 2011. Ulster Rugby support us through the entire process, but when a solicitor's bill of £19,000 arrives, Dave has no chance of covering the costs, so I do instead. In the end, he would have been better off seeking legal aid as all the solicitors, consultations and meetings stand for little. The fact that Ulster publicly back us, and give me their support, however, means more than money ever could.

Nonetheless, the conclusion of the case does not arrive for another eight months. In June 2011, I walk out of court, not guilty but not free of suspicion. I have to dismiss all thoughts of the case from my mind as I have a World Cup to prepare for. Fortunately, there is another distraction, leading up to the tournament, and it changes my life for the better. The incredibly better.

I meet Laura McNally through my Ulster team-mate and friend Chris Cochrane. His girlfriend, Zoe, is from Portrush and is close with Laura. Chris and I are both injured and doing weights in the gym.

'Does your missus have any single friends?' I ask. 'I need to go on a few dates.'

'Leave it with me.'

A week or two later, he texts to say one of Zoe's friends is single and that I should drop her a line. Facebook is a wonderful thing so I add her as a friend and message that we could hopefully meet up soon.

One night in June, Gemma Bell, Rory Best's sister-in-law, calls up and tells me about a party bus heading to Portrush, from Belfast. Gemma works for Diageo, the drinks company, and they are having a promotional night up at Kelly's nightclub.

'Do you and three or four mates want to go up? There will be free drink all night.'

The boys from home are up for that. We get the train into town and the bus picks us up. There are another fifteen or so already on board. I know some, while others are strangers. I have a whale of a time. We are all in good form by the time we reach Kelly's.

I spot Laura on the dance floor and, hesitantly, say hello as she is walking off it. She strolls straight past me. So much for Facebook.

I walk over to one of the bars, with the boys, to get a drink and start talking to the bouncer. 'Look at you. Are you on steroids or something? I'll arm-wrestle you for twenty quid.' It is my old party trick whenever I have had a couple of drinks.

'Piss off.'

'OK, I'll arm-wrestle you for free then.'

He is not at all keen but eventually agrees.

Snap, I beat him like that.

'Have you another one in you?'

'Na,' he says, 'it's over.'

The boys have wandered back to the bar.

'What am I doing arm-wrestling this guy when Laura is here?'

I get another drink – for courage, perhaps – and find I am lucky to bump into her. She is out for the night with friends. They all live in a student house in Portstewart. We get chatting and spend the rest of the night hanging out.

After that night in Portrush, we agree to meet up another few times. The travel, between Belfast and Portstewart, is tough and means we do not get to see each other as much over that summer as we would like to.

Laura's dad, Owen McNally, was a professional motorbike racer who was once described as 'a man who got to you, likeable to the extreme'. His dream was to win the North West 200, his home circuit. He fulfilled that dream in 1997. Owen began racing in 1988 and went on to become one of the most popular riders in the sport. He had an infectious personality and always had time for the fans; not only this, but his skills on the 125cc and 250cc bikes were second to none.

He started out as a porter in Coleraine Hospital, but had to pack it in when he became successful and simply did not have time for both. He decided to open a Dyno business which tuned motorbikes; people would travel from England to have their bikes tuned by him. It was a testament to his knowledge and success. Owen had no fear and would test bikes in a T-shirt and jeans, 150 miles an hour up the back roads near his house.

Laura grew up on the North West track; she was very much a daddy's girl. She went to a lot of the races with her mum Tonia and little brother Gary. She helped her mum do the pit boards and played with all of the other racers' kids. It was a very close-knit community of friends and racers who all looked out for one another.

Owen bought Laura a 50cc petrol scooter when she was ten. She was practising in a field one day and drove straight into a fence. Her dad ran over.

'Are you alright?'

'I'm OK. Not too bad.'

He told her where she had gone wrong and offered some tips. Her mum took the scooter straight off her that day.

Owen died in 1999 racing the Ulster Grand Prix, on the Dundrod circuit. I was at the event that year with my friend Darren Gamble and his dad. We were there for a few hours but headed off early. We heard on the radio during the trip home that there had been a bad crash and someone was critically ill. Owen was winning the race and put the foot down to get a little extra yardage; he did not need to but that was how riders of Owen's calibre made those extra split-seconds count. On the last corner of the last lap Owen was thrown from his bike into an adjacent field. He sustained severe head injuries and passed away, in hospital, six days later, on 27 August 1999. He was thirty years old.

Tonia witnessed the entire crash and has tried very hard to

block this memory from her mind. According to Laura, her mum had a bad feeling that morning and decided not to bring her and Gary even though she begged to go. Laura was about to embark on her first year of secondary school at the time. It was tough on her, as she was incredibly close with her dad. She still likes to go to the North West, as it brings back fond memories. So does her mum. It is a way of life. Even if that crash had not happened, her dad would be racing to this very day. He had a love and a passion for road-racing, as all those guys do.

I wish I had gotten the chance to meet Owen. He liked a drink, the craic and was a bit of an eejit, just like Laura. It has been difficult for her. There is not a day that goes by when she does not think of her father, but she is a strong girl and lets nothing faze her. She loves talking about her dad and does not get upset about it. She is proud more than anything.

The only positive that can be taken from this awful tragedy is that Owen's life saved three others through organ donation. This is something that Laura takes comfort in – knowing three other families still have their loved one in their lives.

Laura's family are based around Portrush and Coleraine and have strong bonds. She was very close with her granny, who sadly passed away this year after a short battle with lung cancer.

Years after Owen passed away, Tonia met a builder called Ivan Morrell, who is also into his motorbikes. They talk of building a house together.

I meet Tonia and Gary for the first time at the family home. They are watching a film when myself and Laura arrive.

Tonia does a double take. It is something I have grown used to since breaking through with Ulster. It is like, 'Hello . . . oh, here, that's that bloody rugby player.'

It is only fleeting, though, as Tonia quickly comes over and says hello.

'Tea or coffee?'

'Um, coffee please.'

Tonia starts chatting away and that is that. Very easy; never awkward. Welcome to my home.

CHAPTER 15

My two aims ahead of the World Cup are to get strength back into my knee and to make at least one start in the four warm-up games. I need to prove to Declan Kidney that I can stand up to the rigours of weekly Test match rugby.

I do not see myself as a shoo-in, certainly when it comes to Deccie's starting fifteen. David Wallace, Sean O'Brien and Jamie Heaslip are all playing well and were teamed up during the Six Nations. Shane Jennings is knocking at the door and Denis Leamy is still on the scene. Even though I have played a lot under Deccie, I know I have to prove myself again after missing that Six Nations.

My main competition for blindside is to be O'Brien. Aged twenty-four heading into the World Cup, Sean excelled in Leinster's latest Heineken Cup triumph.

We first played against each other at Under-19 inter-provincial level and landed a couple of big hits on each other. Sean is another rarity in the Irish set-up – someone that has come through the club system, rather than Schools rugby. A bit like myself, he is a real power athlete. Extremely explosive. An unbelievable ball-carrier and one of the hardest guys I have ever had to tackle.

Tommy Bowe loves playing with him. As soon as he sees Sean get the ball, Tommy says, he takes off up the wing and trails him because Sean will get an offload or pass away. He played a lot at Number 8 as a teenager and in his early twenties but has shifted to blindside. He is one of the most talented and physical rugby players I have ever played with, and against.

We have six weeks together, at Carton House, before the squad is due to leave for New Zealand. The weather is brilliant for most of our time there. Myself and Phil Morrow, Ireland's strength and conditioning coach, have a good relationship from our time together at Ulster. After every single session, I do extra fitness exercises with him. Sometimes I do not take part in any of the on-field sessions with the lads. I seek out Phil to get my fitness, stamina and S&C up.

It is torture sometimes. So hard; so tough. Phil runs me into the ground but it is exactly what I need, as I have not played any rugby in six months.

The lads are in pre-season too, but they are doing fitness games – not as much running as I am. It is not any easier, but at least they are together. For a lot of my preparations, it is just me. If I am lucky, I have Phil for company.

I get there in the end and get back with the guys. My first group session is a game of touch rugby. We are playing two teams; width of the pitch. I score four tries in the game. Sprint 60 metres and leave a couple of the backs for dead.

Phil, my personal cheerleader, is on the sideline. 'Holy shit, he's back. He's flying, he's flying.'

I have to manage myself so I don't take on too much over that first month. It is great being down at Carton House in the lead-up to the tournament. Most evenings, after training, myself, Mick O'Driscoll, Denis and Rory Best head to the car to get the golf clubs out. We stroll over to the golf club and hop in a buggy or two. Each evening we get in at least nine holes. Ulster boys versus the Munster boys, with a bit of money thrown in to make it really interesting.

Even though those weeks are tough – we are pushed to our limits and we are in camp for so long – it is enjoyable. That team environment – a togetherness – is there from the start. Being at the hotel, and so well looked after, helps, but so does Deccie, by giving us free rein to go for a game of golf or to get away for the odd night.

Munster's Niall Ronan and Kevin McLaughlin from Leinster are in camp too. Niall was highly rated from a young age and Kevin is settling into a run of games after some injury problems, like myself, early in his career. Good players, but I feel that if I am fit, I am on the plane. Once I prove my fitness and play in a couple of the warm-up games, I will be OK.

I sit out our away defeats to Scotland and France. On 20 August, I am on the bench for our return against the French at the Aviva. We start well, with a Johnny Sexton penalty and a Cian Healy try, but France lash into us for the next hour. The same old faces are there, Dimitri Szarzewski and Pascal Papé. Both lads have been subbed off by the time I come on, after sixty minutes. We are deservedly beaten, with Johnny and Sean getting late tries to make the game seem closer than it really was.

Time for handshakes and the guard of honour. Again, being the man I am, I extend my hand to each of the French players. Szarzewski does the same trick again, like a fucking two-year-old.

Pulls his hand away. Again, I am called a fucking dickhead. This time, I shove him in the chest.

'Say that again.'

Szarzewski is not backing down. In fact, he is puffing out his chest like the big man. Paul O'Connell is fast on the scene. He clamps a hand on to Szarzewski's shoulder and looks fit to explode.

'You don't mess with Psycho.'

Szarzewski backs down; steps away. Johnny is in front of me so turns round and asks what the hell that was all about. Paulie checks if I am OK. The lads are all asking about it in the dressing room. I remind them about the eye-gouging incident.

'He thinks I've done over his mate, Attoub.'

'For fuck sake.'

I start against England the following week. The plan is to get fifty minutes in and see how I am feeling. I end up playing eighty as Wally injures himself, in such an awful way. He is tackled by Manu Tuilagi, twenty minutes in, and his leg catches on the pitch.

Nobody knows just how bad Wally's injury is. It looks worrying, the way that he has gone down. If he has badly tweaked his medial knee ligament, he may yet come back from that. Once we see the stretcher come on, the seriousness of his injury dawns on us. Still, we never think it will effectively end his career.

Felix Jones has already injured himself, against France, and is out of contention for the tournament. Geordan Murphy is back in the squad.

It is difficult to lose lads we have worked so closely with.

Heading into his final World Cup, Brian O'Driscoll, our captain, has seen most things. He reasons that you are always going to lose somebody. If you have four battle-hardening games before you play a World Cup, chances are you will lose one guy. We lose two, and they both go down at the final hurdle.

To lose Wally is hard but the comfort, cold as it is at the time, is the knowledge that we have a good unit – myself, Sean and Jamie, with Jenno backing us up – to go to the World Cup.

Wally would have had a massive part to play in that tournament. Myself, Sean and Jamie play well together but he could easily have slotted in. Ireland could have had one of us coming off the bench, to make a massive impact. It would have made a huge difference.

I get to meet up with Laura on my final trip up to Belfast before setting off to New Zealand. We have stayed in touch by phone and online. I really like her but know it would be foolish to rush into any sort of serious relationship before setting off to the other side of the world for two months. We agree to keep in touch. I drop in on my folks, Dave and his girlfriend before meeting the lads back in Maynooth. Then on 30 August, flight EI176 takes us out of Dublin and on the first leg of an epic four-leg trip to Queenstown.

Arriving in New Zealand, our first week effectively goes under the radar. There is not as much expectation on us as we performed so poorly in the warm-up games. We know a strong start is needed against the USA on 11 September, but before all that we make sure we have our stuff together and that we are a team. One guy who is vital to all that is Paul McNaughton, our team manager. He is exceptional at making sure there are things for us to do: golf, kayaking, whatever. He is crucial; Deccie's right-hand man.

Another factor that makes such a difference, following on from the 2007 World Cup, is bringing our own chef. Ruth Wood-Martin, our nutritionist, and Sean Dempsey, executive chef at the Fitzpatrick Hotel, arrive in Queenstown a couple of days before us. They sort out all the food, have the menus organized and make sure the local staff know what they are doing. Once that is taken care of, and we are settled and happy, they move on to our next destination, in advance, and do it all over again. Getting good-quality food makes such a big difference to our squad.

There is a running joke among the lads, during the flights down, that the best way to get over jet-lag is to go out and get hammered. You get up the next day and you have to forget about it pretty sharp. So they claim.

Even though we do go out on a few nights, in Queenstown, we still train hard. It helps that our training ground is amazing. Spectacular. The pitch is not the best but the surroundings are breathtaking. These steepling mountains, their peaks covered in snow. When we arrive, it is 2 degrees. We get out of the bus and look around, trying to take it all in.

There is a picture of Jamie and me that captures exactly how I felt on arrival. I have my arm around him and we are pointing off into the distance; stupid grins. In the background, rising up into the clouds, are these big, magnificent mountains.

'This is the World Cup. This is New Zealand. Let's friggin' enjoy this.'

We go bungee jumping and I dive off the biggest one, the Nevis Bungee – 134 metres down, from a cable car suspended in the middle of a glacial canyon. Myself, Paul, Jamie, Keith Earls, Fergus

Right: Jamie Heaslip and I take in the stunning scenery in New Zealand ahead of the 2011 World Cup.

Below: Queenstown was a fabulous place to train (as well as party!) and my strength and conditioning work had me at the peak of my game.

Above: Clearly an important tactical discussion with Brian O'Driscoll before we get things underway by beating the USA. He was an inspirational captain.

Below: What a back row that was: O'Brien, Ferris, Heaslip. Seanie and I had an absolute blast out in New Zealand, on and off the pitch!

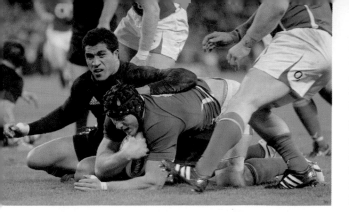

Left: My first Ireland try had come against the All Blacks in November 2010. We could have beaten them.

Below: We knew we could match Australia too, having drawn 20–20 with them at Croke Park in 2009, a game we should have won.

Below: And then this happened. Picking up Will Genia at Eden Park in 2011 sent shockwaves round the world. I love Paulie's face in this photo. What a game.

Above/below: The lowest point of my Ireland career – being yellow-carded for tackling Ian Evans of Wales. I think Wayne Barnes got that one wrong.

Clockwise from top left: More great memories from Ulster's run to the final of the Heineken Cup in 2012: having a laugh with David Humphreys, then celebrating with Rory and Brian McLaughlin after giving it my all against Edinburgh in the semis. The final was just one game too far.

Above: Getting ready to make my comeback against Scarlets after nearly a year and a half out of the game. What an atmosphere there was that night at Ravenhill.

Below: I took out all my frustration by dragging Kristian Phillips back a full fifteen yards. Man and ball, Stevie, man and ball!

Above/below: When the time finally came to say goodbye to Ulster Rugby, I at least knew that I could not have worn the shirt with more pride.

Left: Life after playing rugby does tend to involve a fair bit of time on the golf course. My game is improving!

Below: The only thing that really matters is your family and friends. My girlfriend Laura is my rock.

McFadden and a couple of others. We get the bus that takes us up a windy road. You have to hop into the cable car and get pulled out to the middle so you can jump.

Paul O'Connell is 6 foot 7, 114 kilograms. An absolutely massive man. He is standing there, ready to launch off, and his hand is shaking uncontrollably. He turns round to us.

'Lads, lads, I don't know if I can do this.'

We roar him on so he turns back. You are supposed to jump out, to get the full effect of the fall, but Paul is rigid. He starts to tip out and his knees just crumple on him. He falls over the edge but lives to tell the tale.

Next man up is Ferg. I turn round and there he is.

'What the fuck are you doing?'

He is stripped. Bollock naked. He is sitting in the chair, with the boys tying the noose around his ankles, hands covering his privates. He skitters over to the edge, looks down, hands up in the air. 'Woohoo!' and out he goes.

You can see everything hanging out in the photos.

We do a helicopter ride one day, and all climb aboard the Shotover jet-boats, racing up and down the river. There is another bungee jump at the Gondola, in Queenstown. We all give sledding a go. Essentially, it is like go-karting but downhill. Coming down that course is dicey. Twenty rugby players bombing down the same track in these wee things that are designed for kids. A week before the first game of the World Cup. Trouble brewing.

You have Mike Ross coming down in one kart and myself and Paulie not far behind. It is great craic. We shoot around the corner, at one point on the course, and there is chaos ahead. Jerry Flannery, who is a bit of a mad man at the best of times, has torn into it and flipped his kart. He has ripped a leg off his tracksuit bottoms.

That is the least of his worries as there are ten karts, with hefty lads behind the wheels, coming straight for him, with no intention of slowing down.

'Get out of it, Jerry!'

Jerry manages to jump over the first couple of karts that are shooting by, scrambling to one side and off the track.

You zip by him. Give him a wave.

'What are we doing here? We're playing the USA in five days' time and we are flying down the side of this mountain at 30 miles an hour in these bloody go-karts.'

You wake every morning and clap your hands at what is in store. There is always a trip and a mini adventure to be had. The training is great too. The temperatures are low but the sun is still shining most days.

Myself, Isaac Boss, Shane Jennings and Tony Buckley spot this boat out on the lake, across the road from where we are staying. The water is fucking freezing so, as the team bus pulls back from training one day, we get a notion.

'OK, lads. Recovery time. Let's go over and hop into this lake. It'll be good for us.'

Bossy's idea, no doubt.

I grab my bag and walk over. We meet the guy that owns the big boat – not multi-million-pound stuff but a really nice yacht. He knows who we are and beckons us on board.

We are happy to oblige. We head up on to the deck and start plunging off. There are more great pictures of that. Bossy doing back-flips off the thing.

We make a couple more visits. That is our recovery session. Hard to beat.

*

It does not matter who you walk around the town with – Paulie, Rory, Tony, whoever – as we all get on so well. We get the minibus to the leisure centre and it is always a good laugh. Harmless stuff. Lads pulling pranks, farting until we cannot breathe.

It has not yet made it to the press but England have already been through Queenstown and gained some local fame for taking part in a spot of midget throwing. We have a couple of quieter nights – a few beers – but there is one big blow-out. We head down to a bar called Ballarat and check out a band that are doing some decent live numbers. Andrew Trimble is really, really good on the drums so we are all hollering at him, to get him up there. Trimby is having none of it but we are not taking no for an answer. Eventually we get him up. Trimby is playing away and is unreal. The band are delighted; not sure what their original drummer thinks, though.

The owner of Ballarat is very flamboyant. A real character. Myself, Jamie, Sean and a few others are out and it is crazy. There are girls flocking from everywhere, all over the lads. It is insane.

The barman turns round to me and says, 'If you get your top off, and get dancing, I'll get you all a free round of drink.'

Off comes the shirt, in two seconds flat. I am dancing away like that, shirtless, for about an hour before I stick it back on. Get all the lads the free drink.

The bar has a really low ceiling so myself and Jamie, wherever we are crouching, are banging the roof to the beat of the music. Mumford & Sons.

Boom, boom, boom.

Next thing, one bang too many: Jamie's arm goes straight through the ceiling and plasterboard starts falling everywhere.

Jamie whips round to the barman. Nothing for a few seconds, then he shrugs his shoulders.

'Fuck it,' he must decide. 'It's the World Cup.'

That night turns into a messy one. A couple of the lads meander on to the Ice Bar and trail out of there near daylight. We push on until three or four in the morning before we start dandering our way home. Unfortunately, Fergburger, this famous burger joint, is closed.

It is an unbelievable night – drinking too much free booze, putting too many holes in ceilings and chatting up too many birds.

New Plymouth, then, is a bit of a shock. We had so much fun in Queenstown and it was such a beautiful place, then, bang, we are in an industrial estate, staying in a hotel that is pretty much a two-star bed and breakfast.

I am rooming with ROG, who spins around when he sees the place.

'What the fuck is this? This place is a fucking joke. We're the fucking Irish team and we're staying in this shit-hole. I bet the USA team are off staying somewhere fucking nice.'

It is what it is. We train at New Plymouth Boys' High School and the seating, around the pitch, is carved into the side of a hill. It is spectacular. Training is about ten minutes out of town, which is quite industrial. You walk out of the hotel and there is a car parts centre, next to a shop that sells paint. Beside that is a place that sells tyres, and bars. Endless. But to go to that school, and that setting, is fantastic. All of the kids come out to watch us train. They are giving stick down to us and giving it a bit of craic.

Deccie is always mindful of me doing every single thing in

training. He often tells me that I do not need to do one part or another of a training run, or drills. There might be one session a week where it is intense – tackling or something like that. He sees me as a strong tackler so I am spared. Instead, I take part in some restarts or run some moves with Alan Gaffney and the backs. I am not wrapped in cotton wool but am well looked after.

The United States are coached by Eddie O'Sullivan. The match is played out in mizzly rain – wet ball, constantly, which leads to a lot of handling errors and scrums. The US score a try, through Paul Emerick, in the last minute to take some of the gloss off it but it is a solid performance.

My first World Cup match, after all the frustrations of four years ago, all the fight to get on the plane to New Zealand, is a game I really revel in. They are a hugely physical side and have a second row, Hayden Smith, who ends up playing for Saracens, then moving on to the NFL. I run into him a couple of times and know I am in a friggin' match. It is not a great spectacle but it is a game where we just have to do a job. We do not set the world on fire but we have our winning start.

After the game, there is a good buzz; a great feeling. Phil has a lot to do with it. He stalks around the changing room, screaming our praises.

'Woohoo, woohoo! Fucking hell, Stevie, you were unbelievable!'

He walks around, high-fiving people.

'Jesus, Paulie, look at the size of you, you're huge!'

He is a motivator, really intense. It is brilliant.

Deccie and Phil must have a discussion beforehand as, on our way back to the team hotel, we get off the bus at a spin studio. We walk into this dark room and are told to hop on the bikes. The more you spin your wheels, the more these fluorescent lights flash around to the music. Thirty-five lads in this room, listening to 'Champagne Supernova', cycling at full tilt. Phil loves Oasis and has selected the music. We are all singing, at the tops of our voices.

The whole place is pumping. Twelve o'clock at night. It is surreal. We work up a bit of a sweat, get the blood pumping through the legs, and jump back on the bus to the hotel. Myself and Seanie then head out into New Plymouth. They have a massive beer tent, a huge fan-zone, which is good fun. There must be about two thousand Irish people and expats in that tent and us two, a couple of lads who have just played in the World Cup. People are offering us beers and asking for photographs.

I bump into a lad who is dressed in an all-in-one spandex bodysuit. The green part of the tricolour; his two mates are the white and orange. He lets out a roar and peels back the hood.

'Jesus hell, John, what about ya?'

It is John Kerins, a lad from Cork that I had played with for Ireland Youths.

I catch up with John and his mates and end up chatting with a group of girls, a couple of whom are Americans.

New Plymouth is not the type of place where you can walk out and get a taxi; they are in short supply. When Sean and I go to leave, with the American girls for company, we have no luck getting one. We have only had a few beers and have our wits about us. We have a massive game against Australia the following week. We eventually flag a taxi and go back to the B&B.

I send a text to my room-mate. 'ROG, I've got a girl back. Any chance of you fucking off?'

He texts back, 'No worries, mate.'

He gets his bags and moves out of there pretty quickly. He texts Drico: 'Big man's got a girl back, any chance I can bunk in with you?'

He does the right thing. Next day, I buy him lunch. Myself and Seanie are back on the mission to ensure we play well against Australia.

CHAPTER 16

We will face Australia at Eden Park, Auckland, but staying out at Waipuna brings back memories of 2007. It is near a bay, a good bit out from the city. The Aussies, of course, are staying downtown; right in the mix. The highlight of their media interviews that week is their big Number 8, Radike Samo, saying he has never heard of Seanie. He has not heard of any of the Irish guys apart from Drico. In fairness, when I played against the USA I did not know every single player on their team. But I made sure before I played them that I found out everything I could about them.

Myself and Seanie find the local shopping centre and pay that a couple of visits during the week. The build-up is low-key but the training is tough. There is an edge to it. Lads laying down big hits; snapping at each other. We have a few guys repping Australia's big threats. Geordan Murphy is Kurtley Beale – contesting aerials with Rob Kearney. Jenno running around, going mad and trying to get into breakdowns. He is mimicking David Pocock – their poacher. I absolutely smash him a couple of times as he is getting over the ball. He jumps up, eyes wide.

'Great work Fez, great work.'

'I absolutely ploughed you out of a breakdown and you're telling me well done?'

Everybody is in it together. Boys are acting like Quade Cooper and trying to step people. Opposition defence coming up and closing out the space. We have it down to a tee. We know exactly what we are doing and are confident going into the game. We know we have good set-pieces and that, if those click, it will probably win us the game.

There is a major setback that week, however. Jerry Flannery has hurt himself against the USA and his tournament is over. He has fought back for over a year to get here and now it is all over after only one game. A couple of days before we take on the Wallabies, we have just finished a training session out at Mt Smart – home to the New Zealand Warriors rugby league side – when Deccie asks Jerry to do one final task for the squad. No one is expecting it. We are sitting in a circle. Deccie stands.

'Guys, this is going to be pretty special here tonight. Jerry is going to present the match jerseys to you.'

Paulie hands Jerry each jersey and he passes them out to us.

Jerry is crying his eyes out, handing out the jerseys. We are shaking hands with him and some of the guys hug him. You just know how much it means to him. I embrace him for a few seconds and sit down again. To be honest, there is probably a tear or two running down my cheek. It is very emotional. I am close enough to Jerry but for some of the Munster guys it is surely tough to see a player they have played with for the last ten or fifteen years standing in front of them and knowing this could be the end. When the final jersey is presented, Jerry walks out of the room, but we sit there. Deccie says, 'Look how much it means to Jerry. It has to mean the same to you.'

Our World Cup could be over at any moment. We know we just have to go out there and enjoy it. That gesture, handing out the shirts. Jerry knows that he has played his last game for Ireland.

The game itself is a fascinating encounter. It is one of those matches that never seems to get going as there are so many scrums. It gives me a lot of time to look around, take in the match and the whole night – noise, atmosphere, colours, and rain clouds as they sweep in. From the first scrum, Cian has Ben Alexander under so much pressure. The scrums generally go like this: one, two, three, four ... ball in ... five, six ... Cian would get a nudge ... seven, eight ... another nudge ... nine, ten ... PEEP! Ten-second scrums, all the time. A tiny edge and then a whistle. Cian screws him. It is quality. To be on the flank and having to give it to the props, give it to them and give it to them, and to see the Australian boys crumple, it is brilliant. Each time, I pull Cian up, slap him on the back.

'Awesome. Awesome!'

I keep filling him with praise.

Dominance in the scrum does not mean we have the run of the entire game. We are level at 6–6 after half an hour. We are kicking our restarts deep but Cooper and Beale are taking turns attacking our line, with James O'Connor shooting in from all directions. We are lined up to defend with myself in midfield – our spread is Jamie, Seanie, myself, Gordon D'Arcy, Drico, Tommy and Rob at full-back, covering the field. They are running the ball out of their own red zone – the 22 – and I get caught out on a couple of occasions. The Aussies target me. The biggest gain they make is when Beale catches me on the outside. I want to push him wide but he steps inside and catches me out. They get up to the halfway line but our cover defence is good. We choke-tackle them, hold them up and are back into another scrum.

Our game-plan is not to go out and choke-tackle every single time. However, when you scent blood, you have got to keep doing it. As soon as we choke-tackle once or twice we think, 'Boys, we can do this all day. Keep kicking these penalties over.'

The referee, Bryce Lawrence, favours us as we are the more positive of the two sides. We have more carries, passes, clean breaks, possession and territory.

I get the benefit of the doubt on a play that makes my name in the tournament. Just before half-time, Will Genia feeds the ball into the scrum and, immediately, Cian is right into Alexander. Eoin Reddan has already taken a couple of nips at Genia. That is my red flag. I take a big step around and am on Genia the moment he touches the ball.

I pick him up, drive him back 6 or 7 yards and throw him to the ground. Within two seconds, the seven other guys who are in the pack, scrummaging, are piling over the top of me. Paulie and Donncha O'Callaghan come flying in; props who are getting out of the scrum, dive in. Lawrence could easily penalize us for going off our feet but, because we were so much more positive, gives us the scrum. We have all of the momentum. I am on top of Genia, pinning him down. Donners is on top of the pile. He is in my ear.

'Fucking give it to him, Fez. Fucking give it to him!'

It is not my character to grab somebody and put him in a head-lock. I stand up and walk back to my position. 'What's next?'

The lads are all off the subs' bench, screaming and cheering. Genia is the last to emerge from the mass of bodies on his 22. I am pretty sure he has got the message.

Of course, still pumped from that, I knock on after the next scrum and it is half-time.

We are charged. The talk is, there is no way these lads are beating us. We just need to keep doing the same thing. They will have to do something remarkable to change this game, the way it is going. Johnny missed a couple of kicks so we could have been further ahead.

We keep plugging away in the second half but are always aware of Australia's dangerous backs. We have the upper hand up front but they can easily single out the likes of myself or Seanie and get around us. That does not happen, as we are clued in to the tactic. Cian decimates Cooper when he tries to run the ball out of their red zone in the last ten minutes.

Cooper then attempts an out-the-back-door flick, with two minutes to play, but Tommy intercepts and sets off for what looks to be a length-of-the-pitch try. Somehow, though, O'Connor chases him down. Just short, but the break means we know we have the game won. That does not mean that we go easy on Tommy.

'Jeez, was it the quicksand got you down that corner?'

We frustrate Australia so much. They must walk out of Eden Park thinking, 'Fucking hell, we just didn't play.' Their big-name players did not turn up. At the final whistle Conor Murray jumps into the air. That image stands out.

I take my jersey off as I am walking into the tunnel and this guy catches my eye.

'Jersey?'

I think 'Aye, what the hell' and throw it at him.

He has my number 6 match jersey. I wonder where it will end

up. I do not know the name of the fella. I hope he looks after it.

Back in the dressing room, Phil Morrow finds a new level of pumped.

'Fucking yes! Well done, boys.'

We do not walk back to the changing rooms expecting to win the World Cup. Deccie re-emphasizes the point. Makes sure our feet are on the ground. He tells us that 10,000 people have been watching the game from 7.30 a.m. back at the O2 Arena in Dublin. Deccie always brings it up – people back home are up at the crack of dawn watching us play. 'This is what it means to the country. It's a massive boost to Ireland and a massive boost to the whole economy.'

It is not just about us, but about the whole of Ireland. It is about friends and family, the people that you love.

I nod my head in agreement before allowing myself to wonder if life could get any better than how I feel, right here and now.

About an hour later, I am sitting on a bike, spinning my legs, when Paul McNaughton comes up to me.

'You're a bloody lucky boy.'

'Why?'

'Oh right, you haven't looked at your phone then, have you?'

'No, Paul. Why, what's wrong?'

'There's pictures of you going to be released in the paper. First thing tomorrow morning. You with your top off, in Queenstown, in a bar.'

Ballarat.

'No way.'

My heart sinks. Apparently the English media thought we were going to get beat by Australia. They're releasing the photos to take a bit of the heat off England, as they have been in the papers so much. The idea was: Irish boys out partying in Queenstown, then they lose against Australia, World Cup hopes are up the left – in tatters.

'Paul, it was only free booze for the boys. There wasn't any harm in it.'

'Do you know what? It doesn't matter. We won tonight. Forget about it.'

Imagine if we'd lost. The pictures appear in the paper the next day of me, and Seanie O'Brien with his arms around two girls. Denis Leamy, Jamie and Geordan all out too. It would not have looked in any way good.

I decide to deal with the phone-calls and texts, and slaggings, in the morning. We have a big World Cup win to celebrate – 15–6 against the Wallabies at Eden Park.

Myself and Seanie meet up with two girls from Dublin. Seanie has met one of them before and says, 'Stevie, will you come with me? She's got a friend.' I go as his wingman. Nothing happens with these two girls but the rumour around the squad is that me and Seanie have two World Cup girlfriends. We meet up with them three or four times, down in Rotorua, on nights out. Everyone thinks we are pulling them but we are not. We do try to, now and again. Everyone believes Seanie and I are up to no good, for hours and hours, but nothing happens. All that time and effort. It is good fun, though, when we are bored with nothing to do. We meet up with the two girls in Auckland, have a bit of food and dander around.

Basking in our triumph, we hit a bar down at the Viaduct area. Some of the Irish media are there too – Gerry Thornley, Michael Corcoran and a few others. It is a really good drinking session. Even with the Irish media, everyone is in it together. Not like the

English media, trying to stitch you up when you go on a night out. The night ends when morning arrives, seven a.m., and the sun is coming up.

It is later that Sunday, before we set off for Rotorua and a game against Russia, that I get the latest from home. Images of me rag-dolling Genia, the world's best scrum-half, are being shown everywhere.

'Oh my goodness,' says Mum. 'You should see the newspapers back home. You lifting that wee fella Will Genia up and running back with him.'

I flick on to Twitter, and within two hours I have picked up ten thousand new followers. #StephenFerris is trending worldwide, all because of a moment that lasted two or three seconds in a match. It was a game-changing moment, but at the time I was unaware of the impact it made. After my defensive lapses, I was just pleased to be doing my share. Getting the victory, how-ever, means I can take a moment out to look back on these video clips and enjoy them.

A couple of weeks later, myself and Seanie are down at a café in Wellington. We spot Radike Samo a couple of tables over, casually dressed, wearing flip-flops. The Aussies are in town to play South Africa. We have a good laugh over our food that day.

'I bet he knows who we are now.'

When you get momentum going, you want to keep playing. However, I know that if anyone is going to get rested for the Russia game, it is going to be me. Deccie is managing my playing time after the knee injury. Paulie is rested as well. Leo Cullen captains the team. Keith Earls grabs a couple of tries and Isaac goes in for a great try against the post. There is a brilliant atmosphere. Earlier in the week we trained on the pitch, at Rotorua International Stadium, and it was immaculate. It was beautiful to run on; felt like a sponge. Getting a feel for the pitch made me want to play. At the same time, it is not a bad idea to get rested so I am ready to go again against Italy. I have a feeling that even if Jenno scores ten tries against Russia, he has little chance of being picked ahead of me. Myself and the lads are chilling, up in the stands, and the boys run in some great scores to win 62–12.

We are under the main stand afterwards, in a room off to the side of Ireland's changing quarters. I am lying in the corner, texting Laura and a few people from home, when it starts to get really cold. Paulie and the rest of the lads are lying in other corners, waiting for the guys to get showered and changed. There is a really old chin-up bar in the corner. The room must have been a gym years ago. I get up, as I am freezing. As I stand, and stretch my arms out, I faint. I hit the deck with a thud and do not remember anything for a minute or so after. Everything turns pitch black.

Eventually, I hear my name being called.

'Fez, are you alright? Fez.'

'What? What?'

Paulie shouts, 'Get the doctor.'

Eanna Falvey comes running out. 'Stephen, are you alright?'

'I don't know. I think I might have fainted. I'm OK.'

Eanna sits me down in the corner, gives me some sugar and puts my leg on a stool. He takes my blood pressure. A couple of hours later I am fine; back to myself. It is very strange. The first time I have ever fainted. People say when you are light-headed, do not put your arms up over your head. Maybe that is what happened, but it is bizarre.

That is the highlight of my Russia game.

*

Onwards, to the tip of New Zealand's South Island. Dunedin, and the match against Italy, which we need to win.

There is a barbershop next door to our hotel, the Scenic. A few days before we face the Italians, I pop down for a haircut. I am sitting in the chair as the barber is tidying up around the back and sides when a horde descends into the town. From a distance, but getting closer, their horns blaring.

Beep . . . beep . . . beep, beep . . . BEEP . . . BEEP, BEEP, BEEP, BEEEEEEP!

The barber looks out the window and tells me there are camper-vans coming up the road. I look out the door and there they are. Must be about twelve, in tow, beeping as one. Names and numbers painted on the front and sides.

No.1 Healy, No.2 Best, No.3 Ross . . . A few seconds pass and 'No.6 Ferris' scoots by. I start cheering and waving at them.

It is class – all these Irish people getting camper-vans and painting the names of the team on them. I finish my haircut and go back to the hotel to tell the lads. Lo and behold, we see them another few times along the way.

The Scenic is a nice hotel – big team room, a casino in the building and two minutes from the centre of town. The Octagon, as they call it. We train a couple of times at Otago Stadium. Even without a crowd on top of you, the pitch feels tight; confined. The locals call it 'The Glasshouse': there is a clear roof on top. As the sun goes down, I get a sense of how great the atmosphere could be on game night. I cannot wait to get out there for it.

On the Friday, two days before we face Italy, Deccie names his team. Paulie, Drico, myself and a couple of others are back. Conor Murray will start at scrum-half, beside ROG.

I am interviewed by Michael Corcoran, from RTÉ Radio, after the announcement. I get really emotional. This game means so much to me. Michael sets the scene.

'Stevie, I'm standing here in the hotel, and I'm looking at you, and I can tell how much it means. It's unbelievable how far Ireland have come, and unbelievable that you're standing here in front of me. I can hear the trembling in your voice.'

'You've no idea how much hard work we've all put into this and how much enjoyment we've had out of it.'

That night, myself and Geordie Murphy go to a restaurant. We are supposed to meet Martin Castrogiovanni, the Italian prop. Himself and Geordie are Leicester Tigers team-mates and good friends. I have played against Castro before, with Ulster, and have gotten to know him a little through Geordie. We go to a quirky little restaurant and find Castro and a few of the Italian boys sitting across the table. It is strange, as we will be playing them in forty-eight hours. But that is rugby for you. There are no enemies as such.

During the game, I feel we are in control. Italy never look like beating us. Personally, it is one of my best performances for Ireland. Work rate and getting ourselves involved in midfield are key for our back row. We pour everything into wearing Italy down in the first half.

They have such a good scrum. If we start giving away scrum penalties the game could turn against us, as it had for Australia in Auckland. We have to ensure parity there, at least. With about fifteen minutes gone, and the score 3–3, I lay down one of the most satisfying hits in my career, on Castro. He takes the ball and comes round the corner of an Italian ruck. I blindside him. We smash off each other, with his big hair flying. He comes back at me and I crack him, again, to the ground. That sets a tone. We are eager to make good hits, carries, and positive impacts early on. We make sure we do not let Italy out of their own 22 without scrapping for it. We make them play deep and, given that they are not the most skilful team in the world, they find it very difficult to do.

Only 9–6 up at the break, but we sense they are close to breaking point. Drico scores a try early in the second half, then I help to deliver the killer blow. On fifty minutes, Gordon makes a great break off a line-out move and we are right up into their 22. I am making myself available for carries. Carry, go round the corner, carry, around the corner again. I hop up from the second carry and sprint to the wing, just inside Keith. Rory carries the next one and pops his AC joint doing so. We come back again, hit a pod in the middle, come out wide and hit me. I am one-on-one with Andrea Masi but bump him and offload for Keith in the corner. He touches down, then comes over and jumps at me.

'That was unbelievable. That's the fucking work rate we need. Unbelievable.'

I am absolutely punctured, having carried twice before sprinting out to the wing and getting the ball away. That is what we have been working hard on. It is shown the following day in our video review, me working hard and getting out to the wing. That is exactly what we need, going into the quarter-final against Wales.

The Welsh have rebounded well after their opening loss to South Africa. Whereas our victory over Australia has thrust us into the spotlight, they have plenty of time and space to get themselves set for our match.

Our training that week goes so well; it is brilliant. Jenno is running around, warbling. Boys are killing him and he is getting up, clapping them on the back.

'Brilliant, well done, lads.'

Our line-out work is going really well, our maul defence too. We are hurtling into each other in training. No injuries, nothing.

There is always a talking point in the media – O'Gara or Sexton? Again, Deccie goes with Conor and Ronan as his half-backs. Johnny and Eoin are left on the bench.

There is so much chat during the week that the Irish back row is the best in the world. The true test, we are told, will be against this Welsh back row – Dan Lydiate, Sam Warburton and Toby Faletau. We are told to talk up the Welsh back row during media interviews. I am sure they are instructed likewise. Heading into the game, none of us feel the result will be decided in that one battle. There are match-ups all over the park that we need to dominate.

We have been relatively lucky with injuries in all areas but one – hooker. Rory hurt himself badly in the Italy game and is a massive doubt. It looks for all the world that Sean Cronin is going to start but Rory grits his teeth and gets through a final fitness test. Fair play to him, I do not know how the hell he did it. That is Rory for you, utterly selfless and completely committed to the cause.

Myself and Seanie are sitting in our hotel room, before the game, and all you can hear is singing, down below.

'Stand up for the Irishmen, stand up for the Irishmen.'

Then, really low: 'Sit down for the Irishmen, sit down for the Irishmen.'

Louder again: 'STAND UP FOR THE IRISHMEN, STAND UP FOR THE IRISHMEN!'

We look out the window and there are about two hundred

people outside the Intercontinental Hotel, around the team bus, and we are four or five hours away from kick-off. It keeps going and going, for hours.

Seanie looks at me. 'Fez, we can fucking win this thing today. If we can get France in the semi-final we can win this.'

There is a feeling, though nobody says it aloud. We do not say it in a team meeting. But if myself and Seanie are talking about winning the World Cup to each other, then there are bound to be other guys saying the same thing.

We are guilty of looking beyond Wales and thinking about France or England in the semi-finals.

In the warm-up I do not feel nervous. The stadium in Wellington, 'The Cake Tin', is not conducive to great atmospheres. The crowd in Dunedin was on top of us. You could stand on the sideline, turn round and say hello to a supporter. You were that close. Wellington, though, is odd. The crowd feel distant. It does not feel like a World Cup quarter-final.

We go out, fired up and focused, yet find ourselves 7–0 down after two minutes when Shane Williams scores in the corner.

'Hello, wake up. Let's get back at this.'

We build our way into the game. Williams then holds Seanie up over their try-line. We have a move off the line-out that works perfectly, and ninety-nine times out of a hundred Williams could not hold Sean O'Brien up over the line. We glance around at one another. 'What the hell is going on? How the fuck are we going to get through here?'

It is one of those matches; we cannot break them down.

At the end of the day, it is the captain's call to kick penalties for the posts or to the corner. It is our job to ensure his decisions are the right ones. We believe, each of the three times we kick to the corner in the first half, that we will score. We have practised a lot of moves during the week in training and use a couple of them in the match. We are camped between their try-line and 5-metre line for huge periods of time, but Wales hold firm.

Seanie, myself and Jamie do not get to carry as much ball as we need to. Wales start to get the upper hand in the scrum and put us under pressure. We are not getting clean ball there or at the breakdown. When we do get our hands on it, they are chop-tackling us. One going for your ankles, the other for your neck.

There is one occasion when I charge at their line and Sam Warburton flies into me. He goes that low with his tackle that I try to jump over him. He clips my heel when I am in mid-air. I manage to land OK, just about, and spin on, but I am off balance and am hit straight away with a follow-up. That is exactly what they are good at – hunting in pairs, low chop-tackles. They are very, very physical. Shaun Edwards, their defence coach, has them well drilled. Their kicking game is better than ours. They pin us back.

For all of our struggles, we level the match early in the second half. I am out in the wider channel again, forty-five minutes in. I make a carry, out on the left, and the play looks like it is sweeping right. We have a penalty coming our way. Conor throws a pass back in my direction but it falls short. It is bobbling around on the ground and Tommy is wrapping around me. Mike Phillips, the Welsh scrum-half, is up on me quick and surely figures I will go to ground. Instead, I flick it up for Tommy, who passes to Keith. Phillips swivels and makes a desperate lunge but Keith gets it down, in the corner. ROG nails a touchline conversion to make it 10–10.

That should be our catalyst but, instead, we go into our shells. Wales start to put the squeeze on us and Phillips gets over for a try, six minutes later, that bursts our tyres. They beat us 22–10 and it should be more. Rhys Priestland misses three kicks at goal.

We are just not on form that day. Over the years I have heard players warn, 'Don't let a game pass you by.' I allow the game to pass me by like the click of my fingers. For me, it is over before it really starts. I am on auto-pilot the whole game. There is never one stage where I feel we have the beating of Wales. It is a strange sensation. It is not a one-off, but these days are extremely rare. One that got away. Out of the World Cup without ever hitting our stride.

Any other day, myself, Seanie and Jamie would back ourselves to get the upper hand on Lydiate, Faletau and Warburton. We feel we have too much power and physicality. You can go around chopping boys all you want, trying to get on the ball. But the amount of firepower that myself, Seanie and Jamie have, we could have done it. That is what I tell myself, at least. 'Give me another shot at these guys.'

Wales go out to France in the semis but the All Blacks claim the glory. Even before I board a flight for home, just like the Lions, I am targeting the next World Cup. 2015 cannot come fast enough. The squad will be brilliant. Johnny and Conor as half-backs. Rory will make another one, and you can never put it past Paulie. Seanie, Jamie, Rob Kearney, Andrew Trimble, Tommy Bowe. Guys who have been there, done it and got the T-shirt. To go on another World Cup, experience the same craic that we had, the same friendships that we made, and try and frigging win it.

September 2015 – mark it on the calendar.

*

I kept in touch with Laura during the tournament. We had decided it would be foolish to make anything exclusive before I set out for New Zealand. Still, I looked forward to her calls when I was away.

I meet up with Laura a couple of weeks after returning home. It does not take long to feel comfortable with her again, to pick up where we left off.

'I missed you. I missed your company; the craic.'

We go out for a few more dates and make it official. Still, for seven or eight months, the travelling is a nightmare. Laura is working for a bar, running PR events and working late nights. She wants to get a job in Belfast. I am keen, too, as I hardly get to see her. I suggest she moves into my place, a half-hour out of Belfast. First job she applies for, she gets. The rest is history. November 2015 will mark four years together.

The reason I was initially drawn to her was because I liked going out, partying. She is the exact same. If we went out this Saturday, she would want to stay out later than me. That is what attracts her to me, her fun-loving attitude. She likes to relax. Nothing fazes her and she does not get stressed out. That is exactly what I need in my life. In years to come, when times get tough, she will be a rock for me.

My mates often slag, asking when I am going to pop the question. I feed them a line, or tell them to mind their own business, but I know. She is definitely the one, 100 per cent.

CHAPTER 17

While myself, Paddy Wallace, Tom Court, Andrew Trimble, Rory Best and Ruan Pienaar are off in New Zealand, Ulster start the season like a house on fire only for it to turn to ash. Top four in the league is already looking unlikely and we are barely a third of the way into 2011/12.

Between Brian McLaughlin and David Humphreys, however, we make some good additions, and the younger lads are ready to step up as regulars. Once we get everyone back, after the World Cup, we feel capable of putting a good run together, and giving the Heineken Cup a good dart.

The South African guys really add a lot to our squad. Johann Muller is into his second year as captain and has a lot of respect from the guys. Pedrie Wannenburg brings real physicality at Number 8, and Stefan Terblanche, a former South African international, provides some great experience at full-back. Stefan arrives in late October after Jared Payne's first season at the club is ended by an Achilles injury.

The squad is bolstered by another World Cup winner – John Afoa. John is not renowned as an amazing scrummager as over in New Zealand they rarely scrummage twenty times a game. Still, he proves a real asset. His wife moved back home early enough into his first season and he spends the next two on his own in Belfast, but he's an easygoing lad and he fits in immediately. When he gets out on the pitch, he never lets the side down.

I make my Ulster return in a home league win over Connacht then line out for my second match in our Heineken Cup opener. We have Clermont, Leicester and Aironi in our pool. We know we have a good side and can go far if everyone stays fit and healthy. Getting to the quarter-final the year before has given us the belief that we can do it again and, maybe, go a few steps further.

We have Clermont at home, first off. Trailing by 2 points, with twenty minutes to go, I land a big hit on Lee Byrne, my old Lions team-mate. From studying Lee's game, I know he steps off his right foot most of the time. He gathers a kick from Ian Humphreys but, as soon as it left his foot, I was on my bike, closing down space. Lee is left-footed but is not shaping to kick the ball back our way. He is coming my way, I guess. I know he is going to step back towards me so I launch myself. It is a good shot and he bounces back.

Ian scores a cracking try down the left. We end up winning 16–11 but Clermont take the losing bonus point as they have finished within 7 points of us. It is a good game and a cracking atmosphere, and after this winning start we have the appetite to keep doing well.

Lee later texts and asks if I can do anything about getting my tackle on him taken off YouTube.

The hit on Byrne is a further sign of a greater defensive responsibility I am taking on. It is more through the progression of my game than conscious design. Part of a game-plan is to get the ball into my hands as soon, and as many times, as possible. I also set out to be our top tackler in games. Now, when possible, I want my tackles to be impacts rather than soaks (merely halting the runner) and I often seek to follow up by counter-rucking to win turnover ball and get us moving forward. Line-out jumping is not my forte, while I consider my rucking and mauling as fine, but areas to improve. A growing strength, I feel, is my being able to read plays. With growing regularity, I can see what the opposition are planning and am able to time my runs so I make impact tackles.

You can talk about getting your line speed up or introducing a pillar defender (to cover gaps at the ruck), but when it comes to the crunch, it is one individual against another. It is up to you to make a tackle. If you miss it, your team is up against it. That is where you need a team-mate to anticipate eventualities and step up. For me, it is about timing. It is not about sprinting across the pitch and screaming 'I'm on him', it is about getting yourself into the best position to make the most effective tackle. My aim is to come out of the defensive line, close down the space and, as soon as the guy catches the ball, I am there before he can make a plus pass and move the play along. I want to nail him from the out-side-in so, if he is stepping back in, he is heading into traffic. If you are going for the hit, it has to be full-blooded because if it is not, forget about it. Ratchet it back and you will end up getting bounced or hurt. Of course, that does not happen all the time. But my success rate is climbing.

We have a defensive play called 'WOLF' where I shoot the line to make a tackle. The guys in behind me then know to pile in behind for a counter-ruck. We used it for a couple of Heineken Cup games but the lads know me so well now that they can also tell when I am lining up a big hit.

*

Ulster's belief is not shaken after a 20–9 loss to Leicester, at Welford Road, and bonus-point wins over Aironi leave us in good shape going into the New Year.

Our fate is all but decided when we annihilate Leicester at Ravenhill.

With the score tied 7–7, their giant Samoan winger, Alesana Tuilagi, sprints down the wing. Andrew Trimble tackles him and rips the ball out. But, as he does so, the ball takes an odd bounce back into Tuilagi's hands. He passes the ball back inside to Anthony Allen. I have tracked the ball, and that move, all the way across the pitch. I track, and track, and as soon as Allen takes the ball I clothesline him with a tackle across the chest. Truth be told, it is a bit high. Allen knocks the ball on and we have our turnover.

If I do not make that hit, they score and go 14–7 ahead. Craig Gilroy picks the ball up, starts a counter-attack and makes 30 metres. From that, we are awarded a penalty that Ruan converts to make it 10–7. We go on to win 41–7.

Being there at the right time and making an impact – nothing gives me more pleasure.

Before we play our final pool match, against Clermont at Stade Marcel Michelin, we know we are in the quarter-final. Myself, David Humphreys and a good few of the lads are in our team room, watching Gloucester's match against Toulouse on someone's iPhone and someone else's iPad, which is flicking in and out. Toulouse lose and Harlequins are shocked by Connacht. When the final whistle blows we are off our feet, jumping around.

'Yes! We're in the quarters!'

It makes our sleep the night before the game much easier.

We wake the next day and our match preparation is good. There is an upbeat feeling about the place. The way we see it, we can go out now, free from worry, give these boys a good game and see what happens. If we win, we get a home quarter-final. If not, we are away to Munster at Thomond Park. It does not matter if we get a losing bonus point or not as we would still finish eighth seeds.

Before the game, Johann stands up and delivers one of the best speeches I have ever heard. 'At the minute,' he says, 'we have an economy ticket to the quarter-finals. Now, which one of you guys wants to go business class?'

'What?'

'If we go business class, we get a home quarter-final. We play Cardiff at home.'

'Go on, yes. We want to go business class!'

Johann is a great speaker and has that gift of making you believe in what he is saying, and how it will happen.

We go out and play some really good stuff. There are a couple of chances at either end. In the first ten, twenty minutes it is like, 'Holy Moses'. We make a line break, they hit back with one of their own. Crazy.

Nathan Hines, Clermont's lock, is up to his usual tricks. After one ruck, he grabs hold of my ankle. I am screaming at the touch judge.

'Can you see this?'

I cannot shake free. And he has hold of Dan Tuohy with his other hand. Strong fella.

Morgan Parra is unbelievable for them. He kicks all their goals and controls the tempo very well. Brock James takes up the running when he comes on.

A refereeing decision costs us. Just after the hour mark, Chris Henry is being held in, at the side of the ruck, by Hines, and their hooker, Ti'i Paulo, crashes over in the corner and scores. Chris was trying to get free to tackle Paulo but Hines had him pinned. It should be a penalty our way but, instead, Parra converts and they go 16–9 up.

We have a couple of chances to score again – Ruan and Parra trade penalties – but it is not to be. We get the losing bonus point but know we should have won.

Munster await at Thomond Park.

In March 2008, we played Munster at Musgrave Park and were badly beaten. Alain Rolland was refereeing and before the game, in the changing room, he came in for a brief chat. I approached him.

'See Alan Quinlan, I've been watching him all week. At the breakdown he has been doing this, that and the other.'

Rolland turned round. 'Stephen, just you concentrate on your own game. I'll deal with everything else. Zip.' He mimed zipping his lips and walked off. I never said anything to a referee ever again.

Munster ended up pumping us and Quinlan got away with blue murder all day. It was not worth antagonizing the referee, I found. But I always got on with Rolland, he was a good referee.

Wayne Barnes, I would argue, is not at Rolland's level. He is a referee that likes to be centre stage.

The first time I encountered Barnes was playing against Treviso in the Heineken Cup back in January 2006. It was his first European match as a referee. Afterwards, we were chatting away at a dinner table in the post-match function. It was very casual, and he seemed like a really nice bloke. I am sure he is a really nice bloke. But as his refereeing career has advanced, he has seemed to me to believe he is above everybody, that he is superior to all the players and coaches. I know referees need to present that image of certainty, as teams often question decisions, but he has taken it to the point of dismissiveness. When you pick up a paper after a match, you are not reading about the best scores, tackles or players, you are reading about some decision Wayne Barnes made. Yellow-carding somebody for a fair tackle or missing clear penalty calls. It is never about the two teams; always about him.

Ireland's first game in the 2012 Six Nations is at home to Wales. If you win that first game, your first thought is, 'We are going to win all our games.' But if you lose, it takes everything away from you and you are fighting. Yes, the trophy is still up for grabs but it is out of your hands. It is in Wales's hands if they can beat us then win all their games. There is a lot of talk about rivalry and hatred between the camps but it is blown out of proportion. I have no issue with the Welsh lads and am still in touch with a few that I met on the Lions tour.

We are the better team on the day, by a long way, but we are not clinical enough on a couple of occasions. We are 21–15 up when George North dives over to cut our lead to a solitary point. We restart, kicking it long, and Wales run the ball out of their own 22. They are making yards for fun in the last five minutes. It is bizarre. We are leaking yards with every phase. There is a minute left on the clock. Mike Phillips picks out a first-up runner, Ian Evans. I line him up for a hit. We need to stop their momentum. I dip low, heave into Evans, wrap my arms around his leg and drive him back. The whistle blows and I see Wayne Barnes signal a penalty for Wales, 30 metres out, in front of the posts.

Wales are going to win. Evans and Rhys Gill, the Welsh prop, have some words for me.

'Unlucky, mate. Unlucky.'

Evans should be penalized for slapping me on the back of the head. For being unsportsmanlike.

When the yellow card is shown to me, I put my hands on my head. 'This cannot be happening. That was not a dangerous tackle. It was not even a penalty.' Those thoughts are going through my head as I walk to the sideline. Leigh Halfpenny knocks the penalty over and Wales lead 23–21.

I can only watch on as Wales claim the restart, go through a couple of phases and kick the ball out. Their celebrations rub it in even more. The entire Welsh bench runs on to the pitch as if they have won the World Cup. Jumping all over each other, hugging each other. I turn and walk to the changing room.

'This can't be happening.'

Declan Kidney comes up to me soon after.

'Stevie, I was wanting somebody to get up and make a positive impact and that's exactly what you did.'

It is the lowest point of my career, even compared to all the injuries. When you let your team-mates down, guys who have put their body on the line for seventy-nine minutes and are within touching distance of getting a win, it stings. It is the fourth yellow card of my career and the third time I have been flashed one by Barnes.

'If we could go back and replay that moment,' Deccie continues, 'I would want you to do exactly the same thing. Listen, don't be getting down on yourself, don't be getting hurt.'

Of course, after the yellow card it soon follows that I am cited.

I am summoned to a disciplinary hearing, in Heathrow, with our team manager, Mick Kearney. We have a solicitor with us. We go through the video evidence and I give my explanation. Barnes does not even show up to it; he is on speakerphone. Barnes says I tipped Evans's legs beyond horizontal. That is completely untrue: when we go back and look at the video footage, his legs do not go above horizontal. And one of the legs was still on the ground; the studs of one boot were still on the ground. If I had lifted both his legs off the ground, that may have been a reason for the call, but that did not happen. Both myself and the solicitor argue that it was never a penalty and it was certainly not worthy of a yellow card. At the end of the hearing, Antony Davies, the Englishman chairing it, addresses myself, Mick and the solicitor. His exact words are, 'I am sorry that the referee's bad decision has cost you the game and potentially the championship.'

I already feel shit about letting the team down and letting the whole of Ireland down. Instead of going on Twitter and reading about how well you played, you log in and read about how much of a dick you are.

You let Ireland down.

What a fucking stupid tackle.

What was Ferris thinking about then?

I stopped reading after the first hundred. Ah shit. My rugby career is going the opposite way. To top it all off, and be told that it was not even a penalty, never mind a yellow card, is even more upsetting. But the public does not know that. There is a personal apology but nothing appears in the papers. There are no headlines saying 'Wayne Barnes makes wrong decision'. Never. Why? Because they back their referee.

Mick tells me that I should not mention the apology if I am speaking to the press.

'Look, Stevie, don't be saying to the media that they made the wrong decision because there is no point in getting into a war of words.'

One newspaper gets wind of it and runs a story, which the committee and the IRB both deny. The whole hearing is on tape so they should know better.

I am cleared to play France, in Paris, but the officials make a balls-up of that too. We are just about to walk out of the changing room, pumped, full of caffeine, bouncing off the walls, ready to smash some French boys. We are in a huddle, ten seconds before we have to head out, and Deccie sticks his head in.

'Lads, the game's off. The pitch is frozen.'

Fuck sake.

We suspected as much in the warm-up: the pitch was hard as a plank of wood. It is a joke. They should play it the next day but fans have made travel arrangements and cannot stick around. It is farcical.

We beat Italy 42–10 and, two weeks later, are back in Paris to play at a thawed Stade de France. We get off to a great start and lead 17–6 at the break, thanks to two tries from Tommy Bowe, an intercept and a chip and chase. France hit back, really strong. I lead the tackle count, at fourteen, but everybody is throwing themselves into a defensive effort. In forty minutes of rugby, you usually get one shot at a penalty, at least. Not once in the second half do we look like scoring. It is not like we are under unbelievable pressure for the second half or they are camped on our line. We just make too many mistakes to build any sort of forward momentum.

Rory Best clatters Dimitri Szarzewski at one stage and, soon after, I repeat the dose.

We win a penalty.

'Take that. One-nil to me.'

Two Parra penalties and a Wesley Fofana try even the game up, 17–17, and the final twenty minutes are strangely subdued. No side can sustain pressure.

With six minutes to go, France work their way up to our 22 and the ball is flung back so Lionel Beauxis can go for the drop goal. As blindside, I see it as my job to get out there and block it. I am away as soon as the pass is released and launch into a dive as Beauxis pulls the trigger. The kick is blocked and we go again. We eventually retain the ball but knock on. Julien Malzieu has a go up the left wing but is bundled out. Game over, and a draw that feels like a defeat.

I offer Szarzewski my hand at the end. He walks by. I suppose I will never learn.

The team is struggling to get over the finish line but, from a personal perspective, I feel at the top of my game. When I am fit, nobody can challenge for my jersey. That may sound cocksure but I believe my coaches feel the same. When I am fit, it is Brian O'Driscoll, Paul O'Connell, Rory Best, Rob Kearney, Stephen Ferris. First five names on the team-sheet. That is the way you have to think; to believe you are good enough. Kevin McLaughlin is doing a good job for Leinster and Peter O'Mahony is on the up with Munster but I do not sense them breathing down my neck. Coming up to the 2007 World Cup, I am sure Denis Leamy and Simon Easterby had the same thoughts. It is your job to stop those questions being asked and other names being mentioned.

The draw with France has effectively ended our championship hopes but there are still two games left, against Scotland and England. I am running around in the warm-up, before we face the Scots at the Aviva Stadium, and my left ankle locks.

I go to ground and signal for Eanna Falvey.

'Eanna, my ankle's locked. It won't move.'

I strapped my two ankles most of my career, always for that extra protection. This has never happened before.

'Come on in.'

He helps me into the dressing room, injects me with local anaesthetic and gets the joint moving around. I run out and play eighty minutes, making the most tackles I ever had to in a Six Nations match – eighteen. Peter comes in and has a great game at openside. He goes off after sixty-five minutes, absolutely shattered. I help set up Trimby's try in the corner. We win handily, 32–14.

Back in the dressing room and Peter is knackered. He will get up to speed with Test rugby, I know, but it will take another few games. I have sailed through the match and feel I have another eighty minutes in me, right now. Then the local anaesthetic wears off. The ankle stiffens again.

'Oh shit.'

Our final game is against an England side that are starting to show signs of life under caretaker coach Stuart Lancaster. Wales are set for a Grand Slam and we only have pride, and our final standing, to play for. The memory of our 2010 win at Twickenham is strong and we are eager to finish on a high.

I pop my AC joint after five minutes. I plough into Mouritz Botha and he hits the deck. My right arm is hanging there, barely any feeling in it. I am struggling for a while but I suck it up. I have been here before and know adrenalin will get me through. I could easily walk off and say, 'No, not for me,' but I stick in there. I have to grind my teeth to get through scrums. It does not help when we are going backwards at a rate of knots.

We are 9–3 down and conceding a raft of penalties when Mike Ross goes off. Tom Court comes on in his place. Mike was having a tough time before he went off. In my opinion, it is very easy for him to walk off the pitch, rather than dig in. If there is any possible way he can tough it out until half-time, we may still have a chance. At the very least, he can give Tom some tips; a pep talk even. I feel so sorry for Tom as he has not played tight-head prop for a while. He is up against Corbisiero, one of the best loose-heads in the world, and a massive English pack. He is expected to come on, at Twickenham, when we are already losing, and somehow hold his own.

Tom puts his body on the line for fifty-five minutes and not once does he complain or feel sorry for himself. I am not saying Mike does it deliberately, but walking off the pitch with a sore neck undoubtedly saved him a lot of grief that day. Mike is a bloody great player and he has done some awesome work with Ireland. He does not get the recognition his efforts often deserve. Still, that change is disappointing. If he stays on, we have a better chance of winning that game. It is one of those moments. Mike gets injured, Tom comes on at tight-head and gets absolutely shafted.

In the middle of all the carnage, Dylan Hartley bites my finger. We have a ruck out wide. I tackle him, to clear him out. My arm is draped over his shoulder as we hit the ground. He latches on to my wee finger and sinks his teeth in. I hop up – 'What the fuck?' – and hit him a couple of slaps on the head. 'You dirty bastard.'

He denies it, in his New Zealand accent.

'Yeah, whatever.'

There is another scrum being set. I jog over to Nigel Owens, the referee.

'Ref, look at my finger. Dylan Hartley just bit me.'

'OK, hold on a second.'

He calls the two captains over. 'Now, we've had an accusation here of biting. I didn't see anything but it will be looked at afterwards.' End of story.

Donncha O'Callaghan is arguing with Nigel. 'Look at his finger, you can see the teeth marks in his finger.'

That sums Hartley up. Roger Wilson, who played with him at Northampton, tells me he is a really good lad. I am sure he is a decent fella, but he is dirty on the pitch. I do not hold any grudges. He is a good rugby player who manages to get himself into a bit of trouble too often. On this occasion Hartley's punishment, when it is eventually handed down, sees him banned for eight weeks.

With no action being taken during the game, I have to shake it off. I look at my finger, teeth marks deeply set, and think, 'That's another disciplinary hearing I'll have to go to.'

Whenever we run a move, and England force us into turnovers or penalties, we pack down, each man to the pump. They shunt us back and win a penalty or a penalty try. We kick off and go through it all again.

Tom gets taken to the cleaners by the media afterwards. 'This guy is a joke. This guy is not an international prop. This guy is useless.' It is unfair.

There is some discontent within the camp about the coaching set-up. Some of the senior players are keen for a change of direction. They want someone who would have more of an influence on game-plan, training and everything else, rather than leaving it to the backroom staff.

As director of rugby at Ulster, David Humphreys has his mind made up that Brian McLaughlin should take charge of the academy, and of the younger guys coming through. When Shane Logan was introduced as Ulster chief executive in 2010, he placed a massive emphasis on the academy structure and making sure we got Ulster players to break into the first team, rather than bringing lads in. Two years on, both Shane and David feel Brian is the ideal candidate for the job. Only problem is, Brian has turned out to be a great coach, one that, after getting us to the league play-offs the year before, now has us in the last eight of the Heineken Cup for the second season running.

As players, people may be surprised to learn how little we know about the behind-the-scenes goings-on at the club. The rumours had started around the turn of the year.

'If Brian doesn't win one of these trophies, he's gone.'

'What?'

'Yeah, that's the word on the street.'

Next thing, you go for a coffee and people are asking, 'Here, is Brian on his way out?'

'That's news to me.'

It is all you can say but it does not stop us talking.

Brian says nothing to us but I am not sure if he knows any better himself. It is tough on him, personally, and it must be tough on his family. He left teaching to come into the professional set-up.

Some of the senior players, myself included, on occasion, chat about Brian's future and where the club is going. We are under the impression that, if Brian goes, he will be replaced by a top-class international coach. Myself and Rory debate whether Ulster will hire the former South Africa coach Jake White or Michael Cheika, who did so well with Leinster. That is the standard of coaches we are talking about.

A month before we even play Munster, the axe is swung. Brian will remain in charge only until the end of the season, when he will take up the academy role. A couple of weeks later, David tells me we are getting in Mark Anscombe. I know little about him. David assures me he is a great coach.

'What's wrong with the one we have?'

I roll my ankle in a league win over Aironi in late March, and set my sights on the Heineken Cup quarter-final the following weekend. The *Morning Telegraph* begins 'Stephen Ferris: Ankle Watch'. I am able to train fully in our final session, at Newforge, and know I should get the number 6 jersey.

Ian Humphreys and Paddy Jackson are fighting for the number 10 jersey but, for the Munster game, Brian goes with Humph. We have a pretty strong pack – full strength. Tom Court up against one of our old Ulster colleagues, BJ Botha, Rory Best against Damien Varley and John Afoa taking on Wian du Preez. The second rows pitch Johann Muller and Dan Tuohy against Paul O'Connell and Donnacha Ryan. I am in the back row with Pedrie Wannenburg and Chris Henry. Munster go with Peter O'Mahony, Tommy O'Donnell and James Coughlan. We have Craig Gilroy and Andrew Trimble on the wings, Paddy Wallace and Darren Cave in the centre, Ruan Pienaar at scrum-half, beside Humph, and Stefan Terblanche at full-back.

There is a good buzz, and feeling, about the place. We know we have a chance. We kept ticking along in the league matches leading up to the game. No major new injuries. We stay down in Limerick the night before – do the usual stretches, exercises to keep loose, and have a meal together.

There is such a huge travelling support. Chris Henry tells me there are three busloads coming down from Cregagh Road, Malone Rugby Club.

'They can't even see straight and they are not even in Dublin yet.'

The way the seats have worked out, three sides are Munster and, as we walk out, the stand to our left is all Ulster. It is mad. People going nuts. It is like a concert.

I feel really good, really strong, in the warm-up. Minutes before kick-off, I start getting cramp in my left foot as my strapping is too tight. I collar Gareth Robinson.

'GG, could you snip there and there on the strapping so I get some release?'

Once he does so, everything is OK.

I head into the changing room to get sorted and get the final words from Brian and Johann.

We run out and everything seems to go our way. Tom and John are getting the upper hand, at scrum time, on BJ and Wian. We start getting penalty after penalty and Ruan has his radar tuned in. He is kicking them from 50, 55, then 60 metres. Nailing them.

Not many people would realize just how windy it is out there.

It is really swirling. But whatever way Ruan strikes his kicks, they go dead straight. You can see the ball going left, then right, in the wind before straightening up and going over. We are standing behind him as he kicks. Fifteen heads weaving one way, then the next.

'Wooaaa, woooaaa, wooooooooaaaa, yes! It's over.'

He kicks them true, and it pays off.

We get into a 17–3 lead. It is a great team performance that features a super individual try from Craig Gilroy. It is brilliant play, even though he should pass two or three times beforehand. It is a great individual try but, fuck, he should pass. Humph is on his shoulder a couple of times and could have got over under the posts, making for an easier conversion. If Gilly had not scored, he probably would never have played for Ulster again. That may be a bit harsh, but if he had been caught – even if Munster had given away a penalty and 3 points – it might have been a different story.

They force their way back into the game when Simon Zebo scores in the corner. It is extremely clever play from Munster. They pretend to hit it up but go out the back. Our defence has closed in, which means there is a load of space outside. We probably should stop it but, in fairness, it was good play.

It is a game that you do not want to end. I shoot in to tackle Munster's openside, O'Donnell. He carries the ball into me and I strip it off him, like a baby.

'Oh, thank you.'

Everyone is still set in the defensive line; they do not know I have the ball. The minute I snatch it, I go to ground. Johann is running around, to get into line. I scream at him: 'Johann, Johann!'

He looks and spots that I have the ball, so comes in, over the top, and cleans out.

There are a couple of times when I kick the ball away in the second half, just to relieve the pressure and give us a chance to regroup.

The home support do not have too much to cheer about. That is a great fillip for us, as we know we are keeping them quiet. We got off to a good start, as we had talked about beforehand. All season, when we got off quick we were in games right until the very end.

I am thrilled with my contribution. I counter-ruck, carry, smash the Munster boys. Every tackle I make, I seem to stop them dead in their tracks. Paulie must make around twenty-five carries, yet every time he gets the ball, I launch myself at his ankles, as hard as I can. There is no point hitting that big guy up high. At one stage, after a tackle, he lands in a heap, on top of me. I can see it in his eyes.

'Oh, you again.'

Bang, bang, bang. We are not backing down.

David Wallace, not long back from his knee injury, comes off the bench for what turns out to be his last game for Munster. I do the same with him. He only gets the ball a few times but we chop him at the ankles. Take the big guys down.

The feeling at the final whistle is sheer euphoria because not too many sides win down at Thomond. I put my arms up in the air. Adrenalin is coursing through every part of my body. We head over to the Ulster support and they are going wild. Such a good buzz, such a good feeling.

In the changing rooms, we have the music pumping and the dance beats going. I head out for an interview. The reporters are telling me it is one of our best ever results, coming down to Munster and turning them over. I could not agree more.

It is our best team performance in the last ten years. When everything works, you usually win. Everything has worked so, so well today. It is great to be a part of it.

We meet the Munster players at the post-match function, over a chicken curry and a few beers. We catch up with Donncha O'Callaghan, Donnacha Ryan and BJ. Donnacha says, 'Well done, lads. Make sure you go on and win the thing.'

That is the general sentiment among the Munster boys: 'Go on and win it.' They probably believe they would have reached the final, and won it, had they beaten us.

We face Edinburgh in the semi-final in Dublin. I get about fifty-five tickets for a reduced rate of around €25. I pay for them with my credit card and have to run around collecting money off my mates. A couple of tickets go unpaid for but, forget it, this is a once-in-a-lifetime opportunity.

No disrespect to them, but when you have Edinburgh at home, you back yourself, ninety-nine times out of a hundred, to beat them. We do not play in any way well in that semi. Deccie Fitzpatrick starts at tight-head as John had been cited for what was deemed a dangerous dump tackle on Felix Jones. It was an absolute joke of a decision but he was banned for three weeks. Deccie packs down against Geoff Cross and scrummages him off the park. That is one of the big keys to our win – our scrum dominates them. We play OK. We do what we have to do. Edinburgh score a try in the final minutes to take some of the gloss off, but by that stage a party has broken out in the stands.

There are 46,000 fans there and most of them are Ulster. White and red everywhere.

A busload of people, about forty-five, come from home to watch the game. All friends and a few family members. After the game, I walk out of the stadium with my kitbag in hand and jump into a taxi. Brian has given me the all-clear to go home with them.

The traffic is still so bad that the taxi creeps about 500 yards in fifteen minutes. I get a phone-call.

'Stevie, where are you? This bus is looking to leave.'

They are at the first roundabout, near the docks. I get out, pay the taxi driver €10.

'Cheers. I'm walking.'

With my Ulster tracksuit on and kitbag over my shoulder, I walk all the way from Lansdowne to the docks. Given the numbers we have down in Dublin, just about every car that goes past has an Ulsterman in it. Beep. Beep. 'Wooooo!'

There I am, picking up into a run to get the bus. I get there, nearly more out of breath from that run than from the match. I climb the steps to a cheer and, the moment I do, I am handed a bottle of Buckfast.

'Here. Get that down your Gregory.'

Laura is there. My brother Dave and his wife, Rebecca. More friends and family. We have a great time on the way back home, stopping off along the way to get a few more drinks; pee-stops in between. It is brilliant.

Whenever I take to the pitch, I want to be the best. I believe I am the best. Maybe some guys do not believe that – they go out to do their job and help their team along. I want to do my job, do the hard work, be man-of-the-match, get 10/10 in the paper.

I never go on about myself or my game. In interviews, I say how pleased I am with my form and look ahead to the next game. I would like to think that people – supporters, team-mates and coaches – see me as grounded.

I never walk out for an interview, having won man-of-the-match, and tell reporters I am looking forward to winning another the following week. If I have a bad game, I come straight out and say it. If I have a really, really good game, I acknowledge it, say how pleased I am, and turn the focus to the team.

But to finish an interview at Thomond Park, having beaten Munster, and have Paul O'Connell shake your hand after you are presented the man-of-the-match award . . . life as a rugby player does not get much better.

I want to be the best player in the world. As far as I see it, what is the point of being one of the best players in the Ulster team? I want to be one of the world's best.

In 2012, it is getting to that stage. It is myself, Johnny Sexton and Rob Kearney vying for European Player of the Year. I am talked about as one of the best back-rowers in Europe and the world. My name is thrown out along with the likes of Jerome Kaino, Kieran Read, Jamie Heaslip, Sam Warburton, Sergio Parisse, Richie McCaw. That is right where I want to be. I have no interest in being an average rugby player.

Winning the Heineken Cup with Ulster would be in no way average. It would be the ultimate dream.

Whether it is down to player management or injuries, I have never played against Leinster, away, in my career. With the final at Twickenham nearing, it is not a game we are shitting ourselves about, thinking, 'We are going to struggle to win this.' We have a lot of belief that we can beat anybody. Knocking over Munster at Thomond Park, in Europe, does us wonders. We deserve to be in the final.

In the lead-up to the match, we chat to Pedrie and are amazed at the number of deciders he has played in, with the Blue Bulls. He has never lost one. In every cup final he has played, he never lost. When you hear that, just as you are gearing up to face Leinster, it gives you confidence. 'We've got guys here who have never lost. We have Johann Muller, a World Cup winner. Ruan. John. Pedrie – Mr Unbeatable.'

Humph was out-half for the quarter-final but Paddy Jackson started the semi against Edinburgh. Paddy being selected as out-half for the final is not that much of a shock and the players are happy enough with the decision. Humph is very good at exploiting space but has struggled with a couple of concussions. Brian may have that in mind and figures it is best to have him as back-up. We know Paddy is a great young player coming through. Does he have the big-game temperament, at that age, in an 82,000-seat stadium, in a Heineken Cup final? Who knows. Time will tell. With Ruan on one side and Paddy Wallace on the other to protect him, 'Jacko' is in good company.

7–3 down after twenty minutes of the final, in front of a crowd of 81,774, I tear my calf. Seanie and Kevin McLaughlin, playing blindside for Leinster, tackle me. The ball is offloaded to me and I take it from a standing start. I drive into the lads and twist, to present the ball. I feel a massive pop.

'Oh shit, I've pulled something here.'

It hurts like hell but I tell myself to dig in. There is an hour left to play but we need to make changes soon or we could wind up getting thumped. We do not have a Plan B. We thought we were going to go out there, throw the ball around, make a couple of line breaks, put Leinster under pressure, use a couple of mauls and score tries. Our scrum is not going well. Cian Healy is giving John an absolute hiding. Our maul defence is shite. Seanie really steps up to the plate. He is immense. We make it too easy for him; give him a platform. Brian O'Driscoll is getting offloads away and Sean is coming up with 60-metre breaks.

Under pressure, Paddy makes some errors. He is not the only one underperforming. Not at all. The forwards get dominated. The backs are dominated. We are getting done all over the pitch. Healy gets over in the corner, after a couple of phases, for a converted try. It is too easy for them. Ruan lands a penalty, with the last kick of the half, and we are back in the game. Eight points down.

I am getting medical treatment on my calf, not even sure if I will be able to play on.

Brian walks into the changing room. I bolt upright.

'Brian, we have to change something. If we continue to do what we're doing, we are going to get beat.'

'OK, Stevie. Hold on, hold on a second.'

'No, Brian. We need to do something. We need to change something so we can turn it around and win this game.'

One of the other lads says, 'Stevie, it's alright. Calm down.'

It is far from all right. I am far from all right.

He listens, but he is more concerned with trying to quiet me down. It is as if he would prefer not to make a scene. I start welling up. Not with anger but with frustration. We cannot break Leinster down. We are on the verge of losing the game within forty-five, fifty minutes. We need to do something dramatic.

Player power is massive. Within other professional sports, football and the like, I do not know how big a part it plays, but within rugby it is huge. In the big games, though, everything happens so quickly. There is no time to alter things drastically on the pitch. It is not like I can go up to Rory and say, 'Right, we need to change this up. Come on into this huddle here, boys.' That does not happen. The moment to make any major changes is half-time, and we do nothing.

Ulster's style of play has not changed that much over the last eight years. Munster's go-to, at times of real pressure, is to get around the corner, work hard, work hard. Work the opposition. That is not really Ulster's strength. Our strength is getting the ball into the wingers' hands and trying to get space. It is not crash, bang, bang. Ronan O'Gara kicks it into the corner. Bang, bang. It is simple but effective. That style may have critics but at least it is a fall-back option. Plan B.

Brian sends us out, lined up the same. Encourages us; tells us to be more clinical; to clear them out at the breakdown. I run out for the second half, thinking, 'Right, OK. We're going to run the exact same plays here.' Within minutes of the restart, Leinster win a penalty, kick for the corner, claim a line-out, maul us over and get a penalty try. 21–6.

My head drops. You cannot help but feel that Leinster are too good a team for us to come back from 15 points down, especially with me hobbling around. The injury is the last thing on my mind, though. I am running into contact on one good leg. Stupidity. The calf is filling up with blood and is getting bigger and bigger. It is like a rock.

Ireland have a summer tour to New Zealand – three games

– and there I am, running around with a torn calf. I am sure Declan Kidney is sitting up in the stands tearing his hair out.

'Why is he still on the pitch?'

Brian changes it up but he does it too late. He brings on Humphreys with thirty minutes to go. We trail 24–9. I dislocate my thumb in a ruck. We score a try through Dan Tuohy and are within 10 points again. 'We might get a good run at this.'

Then Stefan, in his final game for Ulster, gets yellow-carded and the wheels come off. Heinke van der Merwe gets over for a score and, in injury time, Sean Cronin, their hooker, runs in another, over in the corner. It is embarrassing. 42–14. The biggest ever defeat in a Heineken Cup final. Thirteen long years since we last got to a final and we let ourselves down. Players, management, everybody. We fail. We have given so much to get here and to be beaten in such a resounding manner is an anti-climax.

It is tough to take but, some days, you have to hold your hand up and admit you were second best. We go around the Leinster squad and shake their hands. Isaac Boss knows us well, from his time at Ulster, so he comes over for a chat. We head back to our team hotel in London and, as it is the last game of the season, have a few beers.

Nobody takes it beyond that and goes out on the town. With my calf injury, I am limping about. I just want to go to bed. There are times when you want to get pissed and forget about a defeat, but I have the New Zealand Tests to think about.

The next day, I have Deccie calling up, asking after the calf.

Brian has a lot more to offer the Ulster senior team. A lot of the players feel that way as well. After he is moved, or, as I put it, sacked, anyone you talk to struggles with the logic.

'Here, was Brian McLaughlin shafted?'

'Brian McLaughlin was done over,' I often hear.

The only man to bring Ulster consistency and get them challenging in Europe again.

The reason people are so upset and annoyed is because he is from here. He is from around the corner. A home-grown, local man, and he has made Ulster a team to be feared again.

In my opinion, he was not shafted, but he definitely had a lot more to give. A decision had already been made by David to bring somebody else in. Professional rugby is what it is, but Brian could have, easily, been planning for the next season with us. Instead, he is settling into his new role at the academy.

For a week or two after the Heineken Cup final I am down in Carton House, and as I am supposed to be heading away on tour, I get my calf scanned and the medics tell me they will draw blood out of the injury. It means a six- to eight-week lay-off. It is not going to heal overnight.

'Fuck sake. That tops off a shitty few weeks.'

I go from a guy up for European Player of the Year to winning nothing, personally or with Ulster, getting injured, not going on tour and getting an operation on my thumb that summer.

Sometimes life just smacks you in the face.

CHAPTER 18

Maybe we do need to walk around with a bit more swagger. We were Heineken Cup finalists last season and showed we could mix it with the best.

A snippet from a pre-season interview I give at Ravenhill Stadium on 31 July 2012, in the newly built grandstand. The sun is shining, we have new jerseys on and new sponsor logos. Rory Best is over giving interviews by the bar and Tommy Bowe, who has re-signed from Ospreys, is down the far end, smiling away for the cameras. Roger Wilson is also back, from Northampton, Jared Payne is fit again, and Mark Anscombe has brought in former Auckland Blues wrecking ball Nick Williams. My pre-season started a couple of weeks late but I am targeting a return in early September. The sessions under Mark have some pace and bite to them. He has arrived from New Zealand having led Waikato Chiefs to successive Super Rugby titles.

There is genuine belief that this is the year we will take the final step to becoming European champions.

Saturday, 15 September 2012

We hit the ground running and win our first three games in the league. The day after the third of those, I am not long home from an early-afternoon training session with the Ulster lads. We beat Munster 20–19 the night before so Jonny Davis and Jonny Bell go easy on us; gently put us through our paces.

'Come on,' I say to Laura, 'we'll drive into town and get some dinner.'

We head to the Fitzwilliam Hotel, in Belfast, for a bite to eat. We are shown to our seats and are looking over the menus when I get a call from Davey McGrath, who we all know as 'Scraf'. He must be inviting me round for a game of darts, or a few beers. We are settling in for the meal so I hit the silent button. He rings again.

That is unusual.

He must be out, drinking. I cancel it. Two seconds later, it rings again.

'Laura, I better answer this and see what he wants.'

'Scraf, what's up?'

'Stevie, have you heard the craic?'

'No.'

'Listen, I don't know how to tell you this.'

'Mate, what's wrong?'

'You're not going to believe this, but Nevin Spence has died.'

'What the fuck are you talking about?'

I am his team-mate and yet this is a friend from home ringing me up to tell me.

'What are you on about?'

'There was an accident at his farm. Stevie, I wouldn't lie about something like this. I'm just ringing you to give you a heads-up.'

'Right. OK.'

I do not even ask him how he found out or knows. I hang up and look at Laura.

'Nevin Spence is dead.'

'That's not funny . . . Wait, you're kidding me?'

Next minute, the phone rings again. It is John Dickson, the photographer who works for the Cornerflag sports management agency. I pick it up.

'Don't tell me this is true.'

'Stevie, it is. Nevin has passed away.'

'What the fuck happened? What happened?'

John explains the circumstances. He does not go into all the fine details but lets me know Nevin, his brother Graham and his dad Noel have all passed away. Noel had gone into a slurry tank on the family farm in Hillsborough, County Down, to rescue the pet dog. Nev and Graham, and their sister Emma, had tried to save him but the fumes were overpowering. Nev, only twenty-two, and Graham, thirty, had died. Emma was in danger too.

'Laura, let's go.'

We make our excuses, leave and hop into the car. I head up the road a bit before I get back on to John. I do not know why. I need John to explain it all to me again. I am trying to get my head around it.

David Humphreys then rings. 'Look, Stevie, we are going to get all the lads in tomorrow. To go through everything and get everyone together.'

This cannot be happening.

Laura is probably in more shock than me. I know grieving affects people in different ways. With the John McCall passing, one minute I was bawling my eyes out like a youngster and the next moment I was OK. 'I'll deal with it. I will be fine.' Then I was crying my eyes out again.

It is completely the opposite with Nev. I do not shed a tear. I am completely calm about the whole thing. You can understand exactly why he dived into the slurry tank, to save his family members. I would have done exactly the same thing. I could understand why he died. With John, I could not understand why.

Nonetheless, it is very, very hard. Some of the guys at Ulster are in bits. Some of the young lads, or guys that have played only one or two games with Nev, are taking it so hard. Bawling. Not knowing who to turn to or who to talk to.

I drive in the next morning and still cannot get my head around it. Twenty-four hours before, I was with Willie Faloon and a couple of guys kicking a ball around the car park. Nev was there as well. Twenty-four hours later and the guy is in a box, ready to be buried in a couple of days' time. A few of the guys are in turmoil. Reverend Thompson, the Ulster chaplain – he would be in three or four times a year – comes in and chats to us. There is nothing much that anyone can say but it is good that we all get together. We have breakfast together.

From the moment I hear Nevin has died, it is all a bit of a blank until he is buried. Time seems to go by in a flash. Before I know it, I am sitting in a church with three coffins, side by side, at the front. This does not happen to any family anywhere across the world. Why is it happening? Why is it happening to us? I know Nev and his family were church-goers and they believe. But I am not sure what I believe. 'How could anybody take three men away from a family like that, in one clean sweep?'

Three or four days fold into each other. I get on to a coach, outside Newforge Country Club, and an old team-mate of ours, Jim Nagusa – the Fijian Flyer – is there. He is playing in France, with Montpellier, but has flown over for the funeral. I attend the funeral but do not go to the graveyard. That is not my thing at all.

After, we pay a visit to Ballynahinch Rugby Club, where there is a book of condolences for the Spence family. I am in a line, and when it comes to my turn, I just stand there. Bryn Cunningham, another former team-mate and now a sports agent with Cornerflag, is in front of me. He writes something along the lines of 'So sorry for your loss' and adds that himself and his wife, Veronica, are thinking of them. A nice message.

I get the pen and just stand there. I start reading all the messages. I keep reading and reading and reading. Flipping the pages back.

'What do I write here?'

There is a queue of about ten people behind me. Flick over another page, then another. It starts to sink in.

'Oh my God, he's dead. He is buried; in the ground. I am never going to see him again.'

I was not best mates with Nev but I talked with him every day. We slagged him because he was completely rare. He would come in with a stupid, rare joke every day.

'Nev, will you frig off. Go away, get out of here.'

'OK, OK.'

And he would go off out of the physio room, smiling away.

I keep reading and reading. Eventually I write something stupid. Three or four words. Something like 'I'm so sorry' or 'Sorry for your loss'. I have been reading all these lovely words, and tributes, and prayers. Still, that is the best I can come up with.

That is it. I sign it off 'Best, Ferris' and get back on the bus.

We have a memorial service at Ravenhill. There are 4,500 or so at it and they fill the whole of the old stand. The Rev says some words and Rory Best has a speech. Crazy. Just crazy. I do not know how Rory is able to get up and give a speech like the one he does. So heartfelt. Capturing what we are all thinking. Madness.

That is the kind of man that Rory is, being able to get up and speak like that. I certainly could not have done it. The words he says sum it up perfectly – what Ulster meant to Nev and what he meant to us. The whole service is perfect, the way it goes down. The weather is cold. Everybody is sitting on the stand but it is not raining. There is an air that he is definitely with us. It is bloody tough.

It shows the character of the squad that we are able to come together and end up putting in a run of great performances. Every shirt we play in, after that, has N.S. embroidered on it. Of course we wear black armbands for a while as well. Nev is sorely missed off the pitch but missed on the pitch, too, as he was so talented. He was class. If you needed somebody to make a big hit or make a charging run, do the simple things right, you would look to Nev. He was always there.

Time is a healer. Every day we go to work and we talk about him. Six, eight weeks later we are talking about it as much. You try to put it to the back of your mind but he is never far from your thoughts. Conversations still turn to 'Remember when Nev said that? Remember when Nev did this?' Paddy McAllister, who was best mates with Nev, visits his family every Saturday. When Jimmy Nagusa is over, Paddy takes him up to visit the family.

I do not know who took the photo, Nev's face-plant against Bath, in 2010. That photo summed him up right there. We were trailing by a point. Paddy Wallace ended up giving him the pass and he went over in the corner. No regard for his own safety; he wanted that try for the team. We won that game.

His ability on the pitch was exceptional. It did not matter if he was playing for Ballynahinch, Ulster or Ireland A. He had what it takes. There was a match he played against England, for Ireland A, at Ravenhill. He was man-of-the-match and Ireland won 20–11 or something. He was in the centre.

All the lads were like, 'Did you see Nev?'

I missed the match but watched it back. Nev literally handed Manu Tuilagi off like he was a rag doll. He sent him flying, in the centre of the pitch, and ended up setting Denis Hurley up for a try underneath the sticks. 'Right,' I thought, 'this guy has so much ability.'

I can testify to his physicality as he ended up fracturing my cheekbone in training, in May 2010. Not too many people had ever sent me sprawling like that.

I try to remember all the good things about Nev. He scored two tries against Dragons away. At the halfway line, he literally just steamrolled over the top of this guy. Then he looked at the fullback and went, 'I'm fast enough to get to the outside of you.' He took him on the outside, skinned him and took the corner. Bags and bags of potential. He also played football for Northern Ireland Under-16s. He was a good footballer, even if he had trouble kicking rugby balls. He had a lot of sporting potential. Just a pity it was all taken too early. We come up against things in life and thankfully Ulster honoured his memory in such a positive way.

When you lose a team-mate it is immensely tough.

Unfortunately, I have lost two over the years that I played. That is the way of life. The way Mum and Dad put it to me, if you work in a bank with forty, fifty or sixty colleagues, it is inevitable that somebody is going to get sick, somebody might die. In any workplace, in any environment, there is always going to be bad news coming at different stages. It is exactly the same in rugby. Guys getting cut, having to retire at a young age and, in the tragic cases of John and Nevin, passing away. Life is about dealing with it and trying to move on.

We stuck together and, through it all, had that winning streak of thirteen games and played some good rugby for the rest of that season.

As for me? Well, I was not involved in any of those games.

Friday, 2 November 2012

The eventual medical diagnosis will read:

> Torn retinaculum. Partially torn and stretched lateral and anterior ankle ligaments. Boney bruising with ankle joint trauma.

At the time, with my forehead dug into the Ravenhill turf and rain sheeting down from on high, all I can feel is intense, searing pain. My ankle is on fire. Allan Jacobsen and Andy Titterrell are back on their feet. I can feel the November internationals slipping away. Gareth Robinson and Davy Irwin assess me on the pitch but my night is over. This feels like a different pain to any I have experienced before.

I am helped off the pitch. I turn my face to the night sky and feel flecks of rain on my cheeks.

'Please don't let this be it. I'm not ready to go yet.'

CHAPTER 19

As an injured player, all you want is a date. Something to circle on a calendar. An aim.

My immediate predicament, following the disaster against Edinburgh, is figuring out what the hell is wrong with my ankle. The Game Ready, the icing machine, does nothing for the swelling. Two days later and I am down in the Sports Surgery Clinic in Santry. The medics suspect a torn ligament but my ankle is so swollen that they cannot fully determine the issue. I stay down in Ireland camp and try, with ice, and the physio, to reduce the swelling.

While I am down, I use the swimming pool at Marian College. It is right across from the Aviva Stadium. Ireland physio James Allen joins me. He feels the light work-outs may get the swelling down. Less than two weeks after my injury, I am doing aqua jogging sessions. They are really intense. James is a good motivator, and tells me how well I am doing. After about fifty minutes in the pool, sweat is pumping down my face.

'Holy shit, that had to do some good.'

I ease out of the pool and look down. The ankle is still black and blue. Still swollen.

As I hobble out and back to the car, my thoughts are dark.

'This is just not right. There is something really wrong here. It doesn't feel good.'

It takes ten days before they can get a decent scan of the ankle. It shows a tear of my deltoid ligament. It is significant. Everyone's ankle is bound by three lateral ligaments and, most importantly, the deltoid ligament. Damage to that severely restricts movement and function. Once that joint is exposed, through a tear, any friction can cause an intense burning sensation. Crudely put, my ankle feels like I am being jabbed with a dagger every time I put pressure on it.

I am ruled out for six weeks. The November internationals are gone, as are Ulster's back-to-back Heineken Cup matches against Northampton. My first comeback date is circled on that calendar as 4 January 2013. A league match against Scarlets, at home.

My last Ulster and IRFU contract had been the most lucrative. I had signed a two-year deal, before the 2011 World Cup, and it saw my take-home pay increase again. It was ridiculous, unbeliev- able money. I had to pinch myself when I was getting my pay cheque through the post.

Talks about a new contract have been going on since just before my injury. Ankle trouble has weakened the bargaining position of my agent, Ryan Constable. The IRFU's offer is way below what I have been on. I have the potential, still, to earn what I was once on but that would depend on me playing each and every Ireland game. It is, by no means, guaranteed money.

I have been one of their most consistent performers for the past five seasons but they are not willing to place their faith in me. I have seen them do this with Tommy Bowe, before his move to Ospreys, and they are doing it to Johnny Sexton too. There is talk that Johnny may move to a Top 14 side, in France. The amount of time and effort I have given to the IRFU and they have given me this offer.

I ask Ryan to sound out other clubs.

Clermont Auvergne are interested. I speak to Vern Cotter a couple of times, by phone. He is keen to get me over to France. Gerhard Vosloo, their South African flanker, is struggling with niggles of his own. Vern sees me as a replacement for him. Gerhard, I hear, is on about £500,000 a season.

In late March, an offer arrives from Japan. Coca Cola Red Sparks are based in Fukuoka and play in Japan's Top League. They have a couple of southern hemisphere boys on the books. They offer £140,000, tax free, for an eight-month contract. I do some research on Japan and the Red Sparks set-up. Jerome Kaino and Shane Williams send messages with tips and recommendations. It looks like a beautiful part of the world. I am ready to go. Spread my wings and see the world. Laura is just as enthused about the possible move and committed to joining me for the new adventure.

I go back to David Humphreys.

'Humph, what's the best you can do?'

'Stevie, what do you need to stay?'

'I need the same deal as I was on if I'm going to stay here.'

'Well, that's not going to happen.'

The next day, I walk in. 'I'm sorry Humph but I've signed for Coca Cola Red Sparks.'

'Stevie, I respect your decision. Hopefully we'll get you back in a year or two, whenever you decide to come back. We respect your decision and I wish you all the best.'

'Thanks very much.'

I want to make a fresh start. Ideally, I will play eight months in Japan and, with Clermont still asking to be kept in the loop, sign with them for two years and make my case, with Ireland, for the 2015 World Cup.

Word about Japan leaks. It is not from our side and definitely not from Japan. That tells me I have made the right decision.

As soon as I get into rehab, the problems begin. Any movements I try, or weight I put on my ankle, cause it to pop. It is throbbing. Killing me.

'Why is this swelling not going away?'

And as soon as I do a calf raise or walk on the treadmill, the back of my ankle joint pops. We figure the inflammation is causing it.

Another scan reveals the retinaculum – a little pillowcase the peroneal tendons sit on – has torn. Every time I was using my calf muscle, the tendon had been popping out over the ankle joint. The result is extreme soreness and an unstable ankle.

There is me in a swimming pool, aqua jogging, with this serious, debilitating injury. A medial deltoid injury, tweaked lateral ligaments and a torn retinaculum. The joint had been given a really bad going over.

Michael Webb and Eanna Falvey – the doctors at Ulster and Ireland, respectively – and Ulster physio Gareth Robinson bang their heads together.

'Right, OK, surgery is required here. The only way to get this fixed is surgery. You are not going to be able to play with a torn retinaculum.'

I go to see Johnny McKenna, a surgeon who works out of the clinic in Santry. He too believes an operation is required. I get a second opinion from another orthopaedic specialist, Andy Adair in Belfast.

'Look Stevie,' he says, 'there are a couple of procedures you can do. There is one where you cut away a sheaf of bone, put the tendon back in and a sheaf of bone over the top. Obviously the tendon is not going to come out, but it's a long lay-off. You will potentially miss the Lions tour.'

Another route involves placing in some carbon fibre to take some of the load pressure off the joint. It is not advised if I want to continue as a professional athlete.

I take that in on the trip home. Thankfully, I have the all-clear to drive. I pull into a garage a mile from home and call Michael.

'What do I do here? All I want is the best medical advice. I don't know if this surgery is the best for me or which surgery is the best.'

'We can only provide you with options, Stevie. It is your decision which surgery you want to get done.'

'OK, no worries.'

I hang up but have that sense of déjà vu. My call to make, again, but what is the right call?

I want to play for the Lions again. To do that, I have to play in the 2013 Six Nations. That is the driver, but Ulster and Ireland have huge games coming up too. Truth be told, I want to get back, and playing, as quick as I can.

I discuss my options again and go with the operation, with Johnny, in Dublin. I wake up from surgery, in early January 2013, with the retinaculum stitched back together. Two weeks in a protective boot to help it heal. While I am down, I stay at Carton

House with the Irish lads. With the boot on, I am able to walk about. The stinging pain has passed. However, when the boot comes off, I find a badly swollen ankle. The ache returns. No movement in it, no dorsiflexion.

My left ankle has brilliant dorsiflexion. There is a simple test that requires you to stand a little bit away from a wall and, keeping the sole of your foot flat, flex forward. On my left leg I can stand 20 centimetres away and flex forward so my knee tips the wall. My right ankle has minus 2 centimetres of dorsiflexion. Even if my toes are touching the wall, my knee sits slightly back.

Eanna joins me, a couple of weeks after the operation, at Johnny's surgery.

'This isn't great, Stephen, is it?' says Johnny.

'No. It is killing me.'

'I'm not really sure there is much more we can do.'

'Right. But how do I get back playing rugby?'

He tells me I need to take time off to allow everything to settle down. The Six Nations is no longer a possibility. The Lions is a long shot. It will require Ulster getting into the knock-out stages again. The lads are still going strong on two fronts. I resign myself to missing out on Ireland and focus on 30 March – a league match with Leinster, a week before the Heineken Cup quarter-finals.

I go back to Ulster and, with Gareth Robinson, we find a shallow pool at La Mon Hotel, in Belfast. The water buoyancy takes a lot of weight off my ankle. I am doing nothing more than walking back and forth, and a few stretches, but the flicking at the back of my ankle persists. I tell GG it is starting to niggle.

'Oh right, we'll just leave it. We will do a couple of lengths, you just kicking on your back. We will get a bit of blood flowing through your joints and see what happens.'

We leave it at that, but three days later, when I try some calf raises, the flicking returns.

More surgery, relatively quickly this time, in March. Ulster are in the Heineken Cup quarters, away to Saracens, but I am of no use to them. They lose 27–16.

Surgery number two is to remove from the front of my ankle joint some osteophytes (bone spurs) which were causing extreme discomfort. I am happy to see them go but the procedure, inevitably, has caused more scarring to the joint. There are more medical consultations, MRI scans, ultrasounds. A lot of time sitting in the house, icing my ankle, getting physio treatment and feeling like I am getting nowhere. I am up against a brick wall, all the time. It is soul destroying. You go in and get an operation, you think you are going to be fixed. You are obviously going to be sore but you are going to get better, and better. Before you know it, you are back. It happened with my knee. It happened with my thumbs. It happened with my cheekbone. There was always light at the end of the tunnel. With my ankle, it is pitch black.

The next doctor I see is Malcolm Crone, who works in the Ulster Independent Clinic. He carries out a moving ultrasound, which tracks the movement of joints and ligaments in motion. When the ankle is stationary, everything looks fine. However, as soon as I begin to move, the peroneal tendon is subluxing (flicking out).

'Stevie, obviously the first operation didn't fix the initial problem, but it is not just the tendon.'

I have so much scarring and damage to the front of my ankle joint that it needs to be looked at, as soon as possible. I fly to London and meet another surgeon who recommends the same operation Andy Adair had initially suggested. I fly back home and book an appointment with Andy.

'OK, Stevie, we will get this done. We will do our very best to get it sorted out.'

As I sleep, the bony sheaf comes out, the tendon is placed back and the bone is reinserted. I wake up and feel no immediate sense of pain relief. The three operations, in January, March and May, have left behind a lot of fibrous tissues – scarring. Of course, the rehab then starts again. Rehab one, rehab two, rehab three. This is my fourth go at rehab after the initial injury.

First signs are good. The problem with the back of my ankle feels like it has eased. I spend nine weeks in a cast. If there are no adverse reactions, when the cast is removed I can focus on pre-season for 2013/14.

That summer, Ulster enjoys a heatwave. Temperatures are over 25 degrees, most days, for about four weeks. Still in a cast, I hobble around on crutches, try not to get the plaster wet in the shower. It is important not to bear weight on the ankle and to keep it elevated.

Laura gives me lifts in and out of Belfast but if she is not around, I get a taxi – £20 in, £20 home. I just make sure I am there for training, get my weights done and never make an excuse.

Off comes the cast, in early July. The girls in the Ulster treatment room remove it. The stink is incredible.

Zero movement. The front of the joint is locked. Every time I try to force it, pain pulses through my body.

My mind is racing. 'What next?' pushes to the front.

I admonish myself for not going with Andy's suggestion of the bone sheaf surgery straight away. Perhaps that would have fixed the problem, without the stitching down in Dublin. The major scarring around the joint is now the issue. Three surgeries in five months. All that rehab. All those exercises and routines. Taking six weeks off after the injury, rather than rushing for a solution, would have been better. The slower route may have proved the safest. There is no way of knowing, however, so I have to shelve those thoughts.

'What next?'

The only option is to push on. The ankle soreness is a daily companion. I try not to complain.

The support of Jonny Davis, at Ulster, is incredible. I often come in at six a.m., for leg weights. I run on the Alter-G (anti-gravity) treadmill. Ulster have bought it to help me with my rehab – it costs about £50,000. It takes a lot out of me so I am forced to rest for several hours. I work on upper-body weights at eight p.m. Jonny is there for every single session. GG too. Eanna, Johnny and Andy, everyone at the IRFU and Ulster – they are all invested in my return to play too.

'Just give it a chance, Stevie,' says JD. 'Time is a wonderful thing, especially with injury. Your body is healing itself.'

JD is a friend, too, so does not just fill me with positive words. We talk about my future. Retirement is mentioned. I prefer to cling to his words about time healing wounds.

The mental side of my time on the sidelines is just as tough. You are getting paid for sitting and doing nothing. Some days, I go to the swimming pool to try to flush out some of the inflammation. I go home and sit on my arse, three o'clock in the afternoon, with ice on my ankle. I take anti-inflammatories and painkillers and hope they are the ones that will do the trick. I doze off and wake to the news or a TV quiz show.

Laura will tell you, I am a terrible patient. Go and do this. Get this for me. Go and get that for me. I am just sitting there, my ankle up, ice on it.

I start getting depressed; really down. If Laura or a couple of mates talk me off the couch for a night out, I am not much company. Laura is an unbelievable girl, great craic, loves going out and socializing with friends. But after an hour or so, my ankle begins to throb.

'Get off your feet, get off your feet, get off your feet.'

I prop my ankle up on a table. It works, for a while.

'Laura, any chance of us getting out of here?'

'The night is only getting going.'

That is usually when I pull my trump card. I roll down my sock. My ankle is the size of a tree trunk.

'OK. One more drink.'

That always means two. She needs the nights out too. It cannot be easy living with me.

It does not help, either, that I get the odd sly comment.

'Fucking hell, what are you doing out drinking? You are recovering from an ankle injury, what are you doing out drinking?'

'Hold on a minute here, everyone has to chill out at some stage and get away from it.'

I go for a coffee.

'Aw, big man, when you back?'

Walk into the butcher's.

'How's that ankle? When will we see you out there again?'

Go in to get a tyre fixed.

'When are you back, big man?'

Aaahhhhhh.

Next thing, all you hear is, 'Here, I heard Dublin fucked up your ankle.'

'Where did you hear that from? It's not true.'

Soon after my third operation, another rumour does the rounds: 'I hear you are definitely retiring.'

Oh my God. People making up their own minds from what they read in the papers.

In work, away from work, somebody else asking about my ankle. A fucking nightmare. It is driving me insane.

I try not to bring it into work. Hide all signs of weakness. I head in, each day, with a smile on my face.

'How's the ankle?'

'Stevie, what's going on with your ankle, mate? You back soon or not?'

'Ach,' I reply, 'it's not too bad today.'

As soon as you start saying to the lads your ankle is fucked, you are done. That is it.

Guys I am close to, like Rory Best and Chris Henry, reckon I am quieter than usual, but the reality is we do not mix that much. Injured players have the rehab group, everyone else is out on the pitch or in the gym together. I try to stay positive in work but find I bring all this crap home.

I am honest with my brother, Dave, and particularly with my parents. If they ask about my ankle, or how I am feeling, I tell them the truth.

I never like dealing with sports psychologists. I always think they are talking shit. I prefer to think I can deal with everything on my own.

I have dealt with three operations on my own. I can deal

with the rumours. I can deal with the moods. I am a big enough man.

With this comeback bleeding into a new season, however, I think perhaps I should seek out someone to talk to. Ulster often provide psychologists and therapists to lads that request them. It might help me deal with the constant questions. I tell myself I will, in another couple of months, if things do not improve. For now, though, I can handle it.

The rehab group, for all its support and good intentions, is the hardest to take. When you feel yourself improving and can see the light at the end of the tunnel, it is easy. You have a goal and you know you are getting closer. With my other injuries, there was always a time-frame. Something to work towards.

In July 2013, I am approaching nine months out injured. Lads come into the group with torn knee ligaments, fractured ankles, dislocated shoulders. Six, seven weeks later and they are out again, back training with the boys. You are still in the group. It feels like my life is spent on the physio bed.

I sign a new deal with Ulster and the IRFU. I could have easily bluffed Coca Cola Red Sparks and played a couple of games, later in the year, but I keep them fully informed about my injury and treatments. I do not want to let myself, or them, down. They appreciate the openness and tell me the door is still open, in the future. I am gutted. I was chomping at the bit to get over there, to have that chance of a change in lifestyle.

Instead, I knock on Humph's door again. He approaches the IRFU on my behalf. They offer a six-month contract for £100,000.

I have until 31 December 2013 to prove I can be a rugby player again.

Rory finds a project that proves a welcome distraction. As part of the new stadium build at Ravenhill, which is soon to be christened Kingspan Stadium, we get a new team room. I am placed in charge of sorting it out. I get coffee machines into it, pick all the sofas, the pool table, TVs, PlayStations, get a dartboard up. I make it my responsibility – my mission – to get it done. I know that if Ulster Rugby were to do it, there would be one TV in the corner and a couple of beanbags. There is a budget put in place, from the players' social fund. I make sure to utilize it as best I can. I am flying around, handing over my match jerseys to companies in return for discounts. I get all the lads to sign my jersey from the Heineken Cup semi-final against Edinburgh. That is handed over for a 30 per cent discount. We get some nice sofas in return. It keeps me busy for a while.

On we go into the new 2013/14 season. The only thing new for me is setbacks. Every step forward is followed by two steps back. Each one shreds at my ankle. I go through weeks of strengthening exercises only for the ankle to swell when I put my full weight on it. I go back to the start, build up to running in a straight line. The joint flares up. Then I can put my weight on the joint and run in straight lines. But when I try a side-step or lateral movements, it is back to square one.

I have never spent so much time alone, in my own company. While friends and family work, train and play, I brood. I try to plan for my future but it is a daunting expanse. I ask a lot of questions of myself.

'How am I going to get back from this?'

'What am I going to do after rugby?'

I have no plans for after rugby. I have my hands in a couple of investment and business enterprises but that is not going to get me much of an income. I want to start a family in a few years. I will have a mortgage to pay, cars, insurance. Medical bills, more than likely. I will have to look after my parents.

I have my surly moments and pick fights. Both Laura and my mum can quickly move on from a quarrel – usually one that I start – but I brood for twenty-four hours. Perceived injustices. I can be terrible to get an apology from. Mum says I get it from Dad's side. He, of course, says it is the other way round.

I am a stubborn bastard. It is a quality that has, already, prolonged my rugby career. I could have easily quit after the knee injury, against Aironi, but there was no way I was missing the 2011 World Cup. The same goes for this ankle. I am not letting it beat me.

Still, I am proud of myself that a switch never flicks. That I never go AWOL. I make sure to surround myself with people I like, whether that is Laura, friends from home, my parents, Dave, Rebecca and their wee girl, Daisy. Get out to a restaurant in Banbridge and catch up with mates. My internal dialogue is a mere whisper when I am in good company.

Match nights are a bitter pill. As you are injured, and not playing, you have to do public relations work. It is the one thing I would like Ulster Rugby to change. It is easy for the guy with the broken finger. He can turn round and say he will be back in six weeks. For the guys with long-term injuries, it is a trial.

You have to walk into a group of fifteen to twenty people, in the corporate boxes, and have everyone ask the same questions. How is the foot/knee/ankle/back? How is that torn hamstring? When are you coming back? You give, more or less, the same answer to everybody but you should not be put in that position. It is to keep the sponsors happy. It drives me insane.

Knock at the door, Ricky Andrew beside me, in we go.

'How are things? I'm Stephen Ferris. If you need anything, just speak to the girls here and they will sort you out. By the way, this is Ricky Andrew. He has played fourteen times for Ulster and is on the up.'

You stay and chat for a while.

Next door.

'Hi everyone, I'm Stevie. This is Ricky Andrew. On his first senior contract but we are expecting big things. If you need anything at all, just give the girls a shout.'

Shake hands. They introduce themselves. I get everybody involved, have a conversation. Tell a few jokes, slag some of the players. A prediction or two. Pretty soon, the chat turns, not to Ricky, this young kid coming through, or the game. It is my ankle.

It is fine if you are doing that for three home games in a six-week period. By March 2014, I have been doing it for seventeen months. The same boxes. Bumping into the same people. It wears you down. I feel like I am hiding something.

'Hi, I'm Stevie . . .'

'Ah, good to see you again.'

'Yeah.'

'How's your ankle, big man? Are you any closer to coming back?'

A few times I am supposed to do PR, I do not show up. I cannot stand the thought of doing it again. On a couple of occasions, I watch the boys at home, on the TV. I make some notes and arrive in on Monday.

'This is what we are doing right . . . but we did these things wrong.'

I am met with a £50 fine; £100 when it happens again. I get on well with Sarah Sherry, the team administrator. She drops by.

'Stevie, you missed your PR. I'll let you off this time but you are going to have to make it up during the week.'

I jump in my car a few days later and show up for a photo-shoot at Ulster Carpets in Portadown. I pose for a couple of pictures, sign some autographs.

'So Stevie, how is the ankle? You coming back soon?'

'Aye, aye. Hopefully. It's feeling good today.'

CHAPTER 20

I get a six-month extension on my six-month extension: 31 May 2014 is the new deadline. A stay of execution.

3 January. Big win over Munster. 7 February. Ospreys defeated. Two more targets missed. Matches the guys win without me. I say 'without', but I put in a couple of good performances in the corporate boxes. Ulster are also flying in Europe. We win all six pool games to set up our first home Heineken Cup quarter-final in fifteen years. Rory Best, Tom Court and Tommy Bowe, for a second time, are Lions, having played a part in a successful tour to Australia. Ireland, now under Joe Schmidt, are on course for a Six Nations title. Peter O'Mahony is doing a top job in the number 6 jersey.

Some of the conversations I have at Ravenhill are turning to a life after rugby. Pundit, spokesman, coach, salesman. People are throwing job suggestions at me. It makes a change from telling them my ankle is fine and then hobbling to the next room.

People now ask, 'Why are you feeling sorry for yourself? You've played for Ireland thirty-five times, you've been on the Lions tour. You've played for Ulster 106 times.'

They cannot understand. I want to play for Ulster 206

times, win seventy caps for Ireland, go on three Lions tours.

On 28 February, however, I show my face, pump the hands and beam smiles in every direction. There has been progress on the training ground.

The past year and a half has been horrendous. It has been an almighty struggle, the fight to get back playing.

Beating Jonny Davis in the progressive sprints and setting a club record as fastest player shows I still have that speed; the explosive power. 9.98 metres per second. I am faster than our quickest backs – Tommy, Craig Gilroy, Andrew Trimble, Paul Marshall. My opening 20-metre bursts are quicker than that of two-time Olympic 100-metre champion Usain Bolt. I am sure he would smoke me over 100 metres. Kick a rugby ball up the touchline, though, and I fancy my chances of getting there first. Clearing out whoever happens to be there too.

JD could not have missed the final strides of those sprints, however. Running at full speed, my ankle joint obliges. When I am on my toes and sprinting, it is not too bad. Slowing down, and that lack of dorsiflexion, is the problem. Decelerating causes the joint to dig in. The force of 109 kilos pushing my knee forward while the ankle joint bites down. I have to limp, and hop, to slow.

Straight-line speed is not an issue but I need rapid deceleration for change of direction and tackling. And, in rugby, you are not alone for long out there. Get another guy jump on you, in a tackle, and that is 220 kilos going through the ankle joint.

I tell JD I will be fine. Getting out there and testing it in match conditions may be the best solution.

I am not the only person entertaining the notion. Family, friends, coaches, medical staff – all agree that if I can get back and put a few games under my belt, I could well turn the corner. In reality, all I can think of that night is 9.98 metres per second. I want to get back out there with the GPS units and hit 10.

After months of him asking if I am good to train with the squad, I am finally able to say yes to Mark Anscombe. He has yet to see what I am capable of and, in our contact session, I am glad to show him something other than the lad he has seen on YouTube.

On Thursday, 13 March I am named in my first Ulster squad of the season. We face Scarlets at Ravenhill, on Friday night, and a win can press our case for a home semi-final in the league. John Afoa and Nick Williams also return to the squad. Johann Muller calls us all in for a team-talk, following the captain's run at Ravenhill. Stuart McCloskey is there, Rory Scholes and Sean Doyle too. Lads I have not had the pleasure of playing with yet. A nod at Ricky Andrew, the twenty-three-year-old full-back – my corporate-box partner in crime.

A couple of sentences in and I get that tingling sensation. I have missed Johann's rousing speeches. If only we could play Scarlets right now.

I do not face the press but Ruan Pienaar tells everyone I am 'raring to go'. Always understated, is Ruan.

I go to bed on Thursday feeling like a kid waiting for Christmas. I am up early for breakfast but convince myself to go back to bed for an hour after. I grab a sandwich and take Bailey for a dander around Moira Park. It helps get the blood flowing in my legs. I drive to the ground, park across the road at the grammer school and sign a few autographs before meeting up with the boys. Physio table reserved for S. Ferris. With the help of Gareth

Robinson, I strap knees, ankles and feet. Craig lies on the opposite table. The revamped ground is so new. It is gleaming.

On the wall, in GG's physio room, is a quote about Nevin Spence. It is taken from Rory Best's touching tribute to our team-mate.

> He was born in Ulster, he came through school in Ulster, he played rugby for Ulster, and all he wanted to do for the remainder of his career was to stay here, win trophies and be successful with Ulster.

As my ankles are given a final once-over, I clasp my hands together and close my eyes. The familiar sounds of countdown.

Cowboy throws me on with twenty minutes to go. Tommy and Paddy Jackson linked up for a stunning try, late in the first half, but there has been little to get excited about since. A Scarlets try, just before the break, cuts our lead to 21–10.

I have not been an impact sub since my debut season but I am charged for the role tonight. The murmur in the crowd turns to a roar as the fans realize I am coming back.

The buzz threatens to die down as Scarlets win a penalty off our scrum. Craig is coming on too but he stands a couple of steps behind as I take in a lungful of air. The chant begins.

'One F in Ferris, there's only one F in Ferris . . .'

Olly Barkley makes it 21–13.

Enough of this shit. Time to get out there.

Roger Wilson switches to Number 8. I will play blindside but take up my place in midfield, and we put up the high bomb.

Kristian Phillips, a split second after clutching the high ball, feels every hour, minute and second of my time on the sidelines. I career into him and drive him back 10 metres.

'Welcome back, mate, that was a good hit.'

Class of him to say so.

The hit registers a g-force of 12.5 through the GPS unit in my jersey; 8–10 g is regarded as a very heavy impact. I can still feel the collision; it reverberates across my shoulders. It feels fantastic to hurt somewhere else.

I make a couple of good impact tackles, ball-carries, and claim a line-out or two. We lay siege to the Scarlets line. They concede penalties trying to stop us. The referee, Neil Hennessy, signals the last play of the game, no matter what happens. I tap the penalty and go, side-stepping one tackle. On the very next phase, Tom heaves over for a late try and we get the bonus-point win.

We take in the applause as we walk towards the Clock End.

I am in agony.

I have developed neuromas on my toes. They are caused when the nerve endings are damaged and thickened. It usually happens to women who wear high heels all the time. I have got them as, for the past few weeks, I have been running a lot on my toes. I did not want to close the front of the joint up with a flat foot. Now, I am paying the price. My left knee is hurting too. An old war wound mixed with the fact that I am not flexing it forward properly when sprinting.

Humph finds me in the dressing room, soon after the game finishes. He is thrilled for me. For his club. 'That's what we've been missing,' he declares.

His words hold a lot of weight.

Through it all, though, a dull pain that, as thoughts move to the next match, trumps all the others. The ankle and the knife that feels permanently jammed in there.

'It's still fucked. It's still killing me.'

When I made my comeback from the knee injury in 2011, we played France. The knee did not come into my thoughts once.

My ankle was constantly in my head.

Being surrounded by the lads again, taking in the roars and the laughs in the dressing room, at least proves a release. The relief, from pain anyway, comes from an ice bath.

All that hard work has finally paid off. I was able to get out and savour it. The YouTube clip of me coming on and the crowd chanting my name – that is something I will be able to show my kids and grandkids in twenty, thirty years to come. I have made my comeback after a massive injury and was able to get back out playing for Ulster. In the back of my head, I never wanted my last game for Ulster to be a fucking shitty wet night in Ravenhill against Edinburgh when I absolutely wrecked myself.

I wanted to have a couple more good memories.

Pain gives way to joy. Friday, 14 March 2014 is a great night.

The second game of my comeback features my first ever concussion in professional rugby. The lads hold on for a 9–3 win in my absence. Following the head-injury protocols, I pass all the necessary tests and am declared fit to face Cardiff Blues. The ankle is a different matter. Sore, aching, I am icing it at every opportunity. There are worries about their artificial 3G pitch and what it could do to me. Personally, I am looking forward to playing on a surface I know will not give way.

On the Wednesday, we are training down at Methodist College's Pirrie Park. I run a couple of plays and then ask Robbie Diack if he can step in for a couple. He does not need asking twice.

I am walking about on the touchline when I start to get a bit of a limp. I try to free my leg up by jogging a bit but my ankle locks. It sticks in a position where I cannot put my heel to the floor. As soon as I put any pressure on it, I am gasping and hissing. That is training done for.

I have to walk about 300 yards to get my car. Some of the lads call after me.

'You alright, Stevie? What the hell is wrong with you?'

'My joint has locked up, it's killing me here.'

I head back to GG, and he gives the ankle a look.

'Jeez, you know, you need to rest up.'

I am sick of hearing that. I head home and take anti-inflammatories.

Thankfully, the joint has freed up come morning. There must have been something there just catching it. Maybe a little bit of bone that was out of place, stuck in the ankle joint.

I am named at blindside for the Cardiff game. Wins are a priority so I throw myself into match preparation. Still, I flag the locked ankle joint with myself. If something like that can happen in training, imagine if it happens in a match and I am tackled. It could snap my ankle in two.

I feel really good in the warm-up for Cardiff. The plan is to give me the first forty minutes and see how I get on.

Running on my toes again, my feet are in bits. Whenever I try to flatten my foot, the ankle tendon begins to dig in at the front. We score the first try, through Darren Cave, but little else goes our way. We are 22–5 down at the break. Sean is going to take my place.

I sit on a bench and begin to unravel some of the tape that is struggling to hold me together. The boys rally to lose out 28–23 in the end, grabbing the consolation of a losing bonus point.

I am no different to other rugby players when results, and performances, turn. I question myself and my ability. I missed a couple of tackles out there. 'Oh my God, this is my comeback and we were getting hammered at half-time. The boys went out and nearly stole it. Am I at the races here? Am I so far off the mark, was it a shite team performance in the first half, or what?'

Another part of me – the confident guy that had claimed Ireland would win the World Cup – focuses on the good parts of my game. I made a couple of crucial hits. I came around the corner for one of them, and showed I still had the instinct to make it. It was on the short side, they put a ball outside them and went back in to Alex Cuthbert. Nobody was covering the inside. I saw the move unfolding in front of me and I got round. He was almost underneath the sticks but I grabbed him by the boots.

'Ah, you bollox.'

I play the tackle back, in my mind, that night. It gives me the confidence that I can do it again, and cut out the errors, against Saracens. They arrive in Belfast next week. Win, and we have another Heineken Cup semi-final at the Aviva Stadium to look forward to.

The fitness issues remain as we prepare for Saracens, coached by my former boss, Mark McCall, since 2009. The corner I am turning feels never-ending. I take part in a session, sit out the next, play a part in the following one. Cowboy might want me to start but he opts to place me on the bench.

Starting the quarter-final has been a driving force in getting back so missing out on the blindside spot, to Roger, stings.

Rory, as ever, has some kind words. 'Stevie,' he tells me, 'even you being named in the squad gives the boys an extra 5 per cent. That is how much you mean to us.'

The rest of the build-up is brilliant. Everyone enjoys it. We are number one seeds for the competition and aim to prove that in front of a sold-out Ravenhill.

It does not happen for us. Jared Payne is sent off after only five minutes. He chases an up-and-under from Paddy and collides with their full-back, Alex Goode. There is no ill intent there but Goode lands awkwardly on his head. Jérôme Garcès, the referee, must look at twenty replays but, I feel, his mind is made up when the stretcher comes on for Goode. Straight red.

We are fighting against one of the best teams in Europe with only fourteen men, and seventy-five minutes to play. Sarries exploit the space really well. Chris Ashton scores a good try as he bursts straight up the middle. Roger is forced to cover in the backline and there is a gap that Ashton bursts through.

I come on with twenty minutes to play and with us trailing 10–9. The lads have shown unreal character to stick with them. The crowd expect me to single-handedly turn the game. Jared is back on the bench, in a jacket, and pats me on the back. I try my best but find myself forced into more tackles than carries. Owen Farrell links up with Ashton for his second and, at 17–9 down with thirteen minutes to play, we look finished. Rory and Ruan are off the pitch, injured. We find another gear and Paddy kicks two penalties to give us a chance. We have seven minutes to find the winning score but they hold firm and keep their discipline. Garcès blows his whistle for the last time. 17–15, and we are out.

Garcès's decision costs us the game and, I am certain, a 10-point win. We are the better team but there is no planning for harsh decisions like that so early in the game. We are deflated. Jared is broken up about his sending-off but, as we tell him, he has nothing to be sorry for. It is a small consolation that the atmosphere that night is the loudest and most amazing I have heard in my Ulster career.

These fans deserve success.

A few days after our Heineken Cup elimination, I meet up with JD for lunch at a place on Ormeau Road. We pull up and I jump out of the car. Straight away my ankle is killing me, just from walking across the road. JD has been through everything with me for the past seven years. He waits until we get inside and takes a seat.

'What's the craic? Have you thought about your ankle, Stevie?'

'I feel like I am at a stage where I feel my time is up. I just can't keep battling it. I feel it is me up against a brick wall the whole time.'

'That is why we are here. You are wrecking your own head here. You could get back and play another two or three games, but what's the point? You have achieved everything that you can in rugby. You could go back and take another really bad bang to the ankle and you may not be able to walk again. You're in pain every single day. Why keep doing it to yourself?'

'JD, there is no need for you to tell me this. I know this. I have been thinking about this since I got back. Well before that I had been thinking about retiring.'

Everybody else is telling me it will come good. It will come good. JD has seen enough. He tells it to me straight.

'Look, Stevie, this isn't going to be OK. This is you for the rest of your life now. It doesn't matter how many strength and conditioning sessions we do, or how many running sessions, or if you can squat 250 kilos. If you cannot run, you cannot be a professional rugby player.'

'I know, you don't need to tell me.'

But he does. I need to hear that from someone else. Someone I trust. It is not worth any more stress or pain. I would rather retire and have the fans, and my team-mates, remember me for the player I was. I do not want to be that guy that plays five times a season and fades away.

I could have fought on to the end of the season if we had advanced in Europe, and the team still needed me, but now feels like the time. I settle on going to see the surgeon, Andy Adair, one last time. If he says there is a chance of playing on, I have a decision to make. There is still a league to be won.

Andy sees me later that week. GG joins me.

'Look, Stevie, your ankle isn't much different to what it was. It is not getting better. If anything, it will probably get worse the more you play.'

In his eyes, it is a medical decision that I should retire because my ankle will probably deteriorate further. It is impossible to go on as a professional rugby player. In a strange way, I am happy to hear him say, 'This is not going to get any better.' His opinion does not come as a shock to me. However, for somebody with thirty years of experience working with ankles to advise me to give up, that is closure.

I walk out of there with the weight off my shoulders straight away. As soon as I know, 100 per cent, I am going to retire, I feel an overwhelming sense of relief. There is no expectation on me now. I will go and enjoy the rest of my life. I had an absolute ball for nine years, playing professional rugby. I can just forget about it, forget about the ankle, about training, and just chill out and start to enjoy life again.

I head for home and prepare for conversations with my parents, my brother, and with Laura. I know they will be relieved too.

CHAPTER 21

The Ulster boys reach the league semi-final but fall short against Leinster. Another season of close calls. My last. I am down in Dublin to cheer them on but Leinster do not give them an inch.

My retirement will be announced once the season is over but everyone at Ulster Rugby knows this is it. There will be no send-off as I leave the pitch for the last time. I have witnessed the richly deserved fanfare around Brian O'Driscoll, who is also retiring at the season's end. I always liked to start games with a bang. I am happy to leave the stage quietly.

On 3 June 2014, Ulster Rugby release a statement, confirming the end. 'I have shared a pitch with so many talented players over the past nine years and I want to thank my team-mates at Ulster and Ireland for the support that they have given me.'

I am incredibly touched by David Humphreys' words: 'We knew from the day and hour that he walked into the academy that he was an exceptional talent. Through dedication and hard work he developed into one of the best forwards in the world game.'

I think back to that Stade Français Heineken Cup semi-final at the end of 1998. Watching Humph play that game, as a thirteen-year-old, eating crisps at my friend's house. We ended up on the same team, together. Absolute madness.

Sometimes you have to pinch yourself. Ronan O'Gara is an absolute legend of the game and I had the privilege of playing with him. Brian O'Driscoll – best Irish player of all time and one of the greatest rugby players the world has ever seen: I played with him, for Ireland, thirty times.

At twenty-eight, I am now an ex-rugby player.

I sign the Ulster Legends wall, in the tunnel out to Kingspan Stadium. My phone goes crazy – calls, texts, tweets, messages on Facebook.

Myself and JD had often set off on cycles around Castlewellan Forest Park during my months of rehabilitation. I have the mountain bike with me in the car today and I pull into a cycle store, Chain Reaction, on the way home. I take a few minutes to read some of the messages, and posts. 'You are the best player to play for Ulster Rugby.' 'You will be sorely missed.' 'You're an absolute gentleman.' 'If you need help with anything after rugby please get in touch.'

As the minutes pass, I am flicking through these, flicking, flicking and flicking. I must scroll down for ten minutes. There are more than five thousand messages and comments. My name is trending on Twitter. Facebook is still going mad.

A really positive message from Jerry Flannery, wishing me well. Texts from Ronan O'Gara, Brian O'Driscoll and Paul O'Connell, saying you will be sorely missed, you are one of the best we played with. It is humbling. I am overwhelmed.

People had been asking me, earlier in the day, about retirement.

'Has it sunk in that you will never play for Ulster again?'

I had a month, following the Saracens game and my consultation with Andy Adair, to get to grips with the fact that my playing days were over. Reading the messages, it finally hits home.

I am never playing rugby for Ulster again. I'm never playing rugby again.

I sit there for five minutes and fill up. Bawling again. Crying into my hands. I look at myself in the mirror and say aloud, 'Jesus! Look at the state of you. Calm yourself, big man, will you?'

A car pulls up beside me, moments later, and I am recognized. I take the bike from the car and have a conversation with them. We touch on the past, the recent past, but our chat is mostly about the future. It feels good.

About a week later, the players get together for an end-of-season dinner. It is a private Ulster Rugby affair, separate from the awards functions, at the Ivory restaurant – just a meal and a few drinks.

The speeches start. Tom Court is moving on to London Irish and Paddy Wallace, another guy who has had injury issues, is retiring. Chris Henry stands up and says a few words about Tom. He has had such a good career, considering where he came from – Pertemps Bees via Queensland Reds A side. Many people thought he was a piece of crap when he first arrived and was getting screwed in early matches. People at home were saying to me, 'My God, who is this guy that Ulster have signed?' Ten years later and he is an established international, plays week in, week out for Ulster, never takes a backward step. Called up by the Lions in 2013. I loved playing with him.

Tom is an emotional fella at the best of times so he wells up. A few tears start coming down his cheeks. He stands up and thanks his wife, Cath, for sticking with him through thick and thin, and his two kids, Madeline and Theo, who he has brought up in Belfast. I look around and there are tissues everywhere.

Now it is my turn. No chance of me blubbering away like Tom.

Rory Best, my greatest friend in rugby, has a few words to say. He introduces a highlights package of clips from my career. On it comes and there are some big hits, tries, tackles. In the background is this cheesy porno music. Slow motion of me smashing someone while a saxophone screams in the background.

I turn to Rory. 'Where did you get the music?'

'Don't talk to me.'

The video runs on. Despite the music, it is beautifully put together. A lot of effort has gone into it. Memories come flooding back. I feel myself choking up and, as a distraction, grab a beer.

Warm applause as the video finishes. A couple of lads shouting. 'Well done, big man. Nice one.'

Rory stands again. I am paraphrasing, but his heartfelt speech hits the spot.

'I thought Stevie would be doing this for me. I didn't expect to be up here saying Stevie is a great player . . . I expected him to be standing here saying Rory, you are thirty-six now, you need to give it up.'

I feel the tears rising. Take another swig of beer.

Rory presents me with a watch on behalf of everyone at Ulster Rugby. A TAG Heuer with 'S.F. 106' on the back, to denote my Ulster caps. It is a nice touch.

I get up. 'Jeez, I am a bit overwhelmed here, guys.'

Everybody from Ulster is in the room. Management, forty professional players, ten academy players and all the partners. Well over a hundred people in total.

I try to continue but Rory's words have tipped me over the edge. I am in tears. The hard man, who runs about bashing into people, is in tears. Sniffling as I try to have my say.

'I'd just like to thank . . . Tom, you set me off.'

A few years back, when Ryan Caldwell was leaving Ulster, he made a memorable speech where he thanked his wife, mum, dad, everyone else he had ever known.

'I'm like Calders up here,' I say.

That sets everyone off laughing, and gives me a ten-second breather. I pull myself together.

'I want to thank everybody. I could stand here all night talking about people who have come and went but I will catch up with all you guys in the coming weeks.'

I say how proud I am to have played for Ulster Rugby, my province, and leave it at that. All things considered, I have kept it together. Paddy cannot say the same.

Paddy is standing there, saying, 'Why is this so hard?' The tears are coming down his face. All the girlfriends and some of the lads see and the tissues are out.

You have played with these guys, given your heart and soul for Ulster Rugby for the last ten, twelve, fifteen years. Guys you have known.

GG Robinson is not here. He could not bring himself to go. He has been very close to myself, Paddy and Tom. The night would have been too much for him. We say our goodbyes, one on one, on another day. There are no tears.

'I'll see you soon,' I say. 'I won't be too far away.'

It is the truth. Already, I am looking forward to heading back to Ravenhill, as a fan, and cheering the boys on.

The cry-fest is a big source of amusement later that night. As we near two o'clock, Dan Tuohy hands me a tissue.

'You alright, Fez? Here, dry your eyes, big man. You OK?'

I catch up with Davy Irwin, the team doctor and an Ulster legend, at the bar.

'It's very embarrassing, that I broke down.'

'Stevie, it just shows how much it meant to you to play for Ulster for so long. Don't think for any reason that people seeing you standing up there and getting emotional is a bad thing. It just shows how much it did actually mean to you.'

It is a great team night. From the ground staff to the physios and coaches, Johann Muller, who is also moving on, the players and their partners. Everybody feels as one.

The summer passes and I have a great time, reconnecting with friends and family without having to worry and watch myself. The ankle still hurts, every day, but I am finding ways to cope. Being surrounded by so many great people helps.

I spend time with Dave, Rebecca and Daisy. Just over a year old, Daisy likes to be lifted in the air. I am warned off tossing her a couple of feet into the sky. Maybe I do not know my own strength.

I catch up with the Ulster lads at Callum Black's wedding and we have another couple of good nights.

Ulster's pre-season, for 2014/15, starts on 30 June. Part of me wants to head over to Ravenhill. Chat to the girls on reception; drop into the team room for a coffee and a game of pool. Instead, I hop in the car and drive to County Louth to talk about writing a book.

It is weird, because I thought it would just hit me. I thought I would wake up one day and think, 'Fuck, I'm not a rugby player any more,' but I haven't.

I would give my left testicle to be back out, playing rugby. Really would.

Part of me thinks, 'Frig, I wonder if my ankle was alright, would I still be able to throw my boots on, go out and perform?'

But, the way the game is now, I do not think I would have lasted another five or six years. I am twenty-nine, writing this book. I was twenty-seven when I injured myself. If I had made it, without that injury, to thirty, thirty-one, I would have been doing well.

Every Friday night you play a game of rugby and it is like being in a car crash. That is what it is like. Except when you are in a car crash, that is it. One car crash. When you are in a game of rugby, you might be in five or six. The hits . . . fucking hell. When you sit and think about it . . . fucking hell. If I go in to hit someone, it is 10 g. If I do that three times a game, how is that affecting my body?

Too many injuries. Too often. That was my problem.

Every year you hear 'Ulster are decimated by injuries', 'Ireland are decimated'. That is the norm, not the exception. Leicester, Gloucester, Harlequins, Leinster – every team is decimated by injuries. Every team has six or seven players that are out for months and months with bad injuries. Soft-tissue injuries – tweaks and pulls – are decreasing but serious injuries are on the up. Bones are getting broken. It is getting crazy.

When I started, David Humphreys, Tyrone Howe, Simon Best, they played just about every game. It is different now. Ten years ago, it would have been a four- to six-week injury period. Now, it is four to six months. Boys are having operations. Invasive procedures. Sean O'Brien, by my reckoning, has had about twenty surgeries and the guy is twenty-eight. Madness.

The one thing I have learned is, once you have an operation, on any part of your body, you are not the same. My thumbs are wrecked. My left one is fused. It is not the same; never will be. Constantly sore. My ankle is sore – bites all the time. My knee is banjaxed. My face too. Even when I am sleeping, the plates in my cheekbone press down, leaving indentations and bruises.

Never the same.

That is part of the game now. So many injuries, so many operations. The lifespan of a rugby player is dramatically shorter. There will not be many Brian O'Driscolls in the future – sixteen years at the top of the game. Thirty-five is no longer a realistic retirement goal. If most guys get to thirty, thirty-two, they are doing well.

There is an opportunity here to play professional sport and earn good money. In Irish rugby, you are hearing of the top guys earning anywhere from €400,000 to €600,000 a year. If you can get four or five good years, earning that type of money, that can set you up for life. Years ago, it was not like that. I often wish I was turning professional now, as those figures are frightening. So are the injuries, however. That wish is replaced by enjoying the life I now have.

2005 to 2014. I like to think I lived through a good age for rugby and that I made an impact.

In December 2014, I am asked along to Newforge for a Q&A session with Rory. We cover many topics – Neil Doak taking over as coach, league hopes (Europe has not gone well), Ireland's chances at the 2015 World Cup – before Rory is asked about the best player he has ever played with.

'I am not saying this because he is my friend, but Stephen Ferris.'

I am taken aback.

Rory continues, 'I've never met a player that can turn a game with one big hit, carry or clear-out. He always delivered a game-changing moment.'

I was not somebody who did the donkey work, although I enjoyed that side of the game. I was a game-changer. I am glad Rory saw that as that is exactly what I was aiming to do, every game. Those game-changing moments – I prided myself on them.

We agree to catch up for a coffee a couple of days later. I ask if we can meet up somewhere in Belfast. I have to head into town to drop off the TAG Heuer watch at the jeweller's. It has stopped working. When they picked out a watch for me, the lads picked one that took after me – broken down.

CHAPTER 22

As my first year out of the game ticks on, the only exercises my legs get are from rounds of golf, cycling and from walking the dog. I have not run since the Saracens game. I do not intend to run, ever again, because my ankle will not allow me to. It will never be the same again. Being in shoes all day is a nightmare. I put my feet up and it is like getting electric shocks in my toes. I still take anti-inflammatories to help the joint settle down. Getting up and down stairs is a nightmare. I cannot close the front of the joint. If I am going up a step, I must place the foot down and close the front of the joint up, before bringing up the other one. I often stay on the tips of my toes, and that has adverse effects on my nerves. The neuromas on my feet need to be looked into. I do not need to play professional sport any more so I will not rush the next step. Not again.

Most players have a year, after they retire, during which they can go in for operations and consultations that are covered by their insurance. After that, you are on your own. A doctor over in America was in touch with Michael Webb, at Ulster. He deals specifically in ankle trauma and would like to help. I tell him I will let everything settle for at least a year. If I am still having complications, maybe I will get in touch and see if there is another operation, or something beneficial, to make my everyday life after rugby easier.

'No worries. I'm always here. Give me a shout if you are ever over in New York. We will meet up and have a look at it.'

I meet people now and they want a selfie.

'What do you want a selfie with a retired old man for?'

'Oh, you're a legend!'

Myself and Laura go to Ulster's first game of the season – a friendly against Exeter that we, or they, lose at the last minute. I have a few pints and a catch-up with lads that are not playing, Chris Henry and Darren Cave. Everybody keeps coming up for my autograph and pictures, as if I was still Stevie Ferris the rugby player. I grab the other lads.

'Get the boys in there as well.'

That shows how much respect the fans have for me. It is really nice when you bump into somebody, in a hotel or a café.

'How you getting on, big man? What are you doing with yourself?'

'Ah, taking it easy for now.'

'Here, I was over at the Heineken Cup final in 2012.'

'Don't you mention that. You're not allowed to talk about it.'

You have a bit of banter, chat about the good times and the bad times, instead of talking about the injury.

I am in touch with Paul Magee, president of Dungannon Rugby Club, about getting involved with some coaching. I would love to give something back to that club.

BBC and BT Sport are also in touch and ask me into the studio for some work as a pundit. It proves a whole new challenge. As a player, you listen to what past players and pundits are saying, read the papers, speak to the media. They always seem so negative. 'The team is not doing well.' 'What's going wrong?' You think, 'For fuck sake. Why are they so negative? We lost a couple of games but we will win the next few. What's the big deal?'

There is Andy Ward on TV, saying we are in crisis.

'What does he know about choke-tackling? The game has changed.'

On the other side of the fence, I find myself being negative. I could not tell you why, because I hated it when I was a player. There are times, though, when I find myself veering that way if Ulster are struggling. I say struggling now, but if I was in the team, I would never admit it. With the media work, you try to say what you think as much as possible but it is often hard to criticize your friends.

Having been gone for less than six months, it is hard for me to sit there and say Rory Best's line-out throwing is rubbish and he should be dropped for the next game. That is not me. Of course, his line-out throwing may be off, but he is still going to play the next week. You can criticize players but it is just about the way you do it. The one thing I have learned is, it is very difficult not to be negative if you are sitting on the other side of the fence.

Some nights you might think, 'Darren Cave wasn't great tonight. He hardly got on the ball. It might be best to give Luke Marshall and Stuart Olding a go together next week.'

That may not be the question or subject you are asked about, so you just stay quiet.

'What about Dan Tuohy. He played well?'

'Yes.'

Ulster, in 2014/15, do struggle. They get beaten at home by
Toulon, in the new Champions Cup, and never recover. League
form is better but they have the odd blip. It is not because of
quality but because of the squad size. You cannot lose Paddy
Wallace, John Afoa, Tom Court, Stephen Ferris and Johann Muller
– five top-class international players – and bring in Franco van der
Merwe, Wiehahn Herbst, Clive Ross, Sean Reidy and Charlie
Butterworth. Franco is the only international of the five and his
only Test cap was in 2013.

I give a press interview and talk about Toulon attempting to
sign Richie McCaw, the best number 7 in world rugby. Ulster are
considering offering Clive Ross a permanent deal. No disrespect
to Clive, I say, but that is the difference.

If Ulster pick up a couple of injuries and Chris Henry is not
back, they have to scrape the barrel to put out a team. If one of
Toulon's back-rowers – Juan Fernández Lobbe – goes down, they
are able to bring on Juan Smith. If Ulster have their full team fit,
they are in with a chance. If Chris gets injured, they might bring
Robbie Diack off the bench. That is the gulf in class. A Heineken
Cup and league is not won by fifteen players, it is won by thirty-
five – by a squad.

I meet up with Rory Best soon after. He tells me Clive is down
in the dumps. 'I can't believe you ripped him out in the media.'

'Look, I was only saying what everyone else was thinking.'

I am not saying Clive is a bad player, but he is not of the level
of McCaw or Kieran Read. I am not someone for slagging for the
sake of it. As a pundit, I try to stick to the mentality I had as a
player. If someone has a bad game, I will say it and try to justify
it. I am honest. Maybe too honest at times.

*

When I first started playing professional rugby, I did not go out socializing with the Ulster boys. I went home and met the boys from Maghaberry. Played poker or had a night out in Banbridge. I could not give my friends the same time as my career took off. My friends began to settle down, start families, over my years in the game. Now I am free from my rugby commitments, it is me calling them, asking them if they want to go here, there and everywhere. Andrew Champion, my old work-mate from the paving company, now has a company of his own, installing drive-ways. He has three children.

I get in touch with the lads on Facebook one evening. A couple of them work abroad now and then but, near the end of the year, they are all back in the country. My brother Dave, old housemate Stephen Williamson, Crawford Beckett, Adam McMinn, David McGrath and his brother, Ricky. Andrew is there, as is James Coburn, back from Australia. It is a great get-together.

Another night, we are playing pool in my garage. Ricky, James Crooks, Mark Fraser and Chris 'Big Hands' Collins. Ricky hands me a beer.

'Steve, it's good to have you back, mate.'

'What?'

'It's good to have the old Steve back.'

They're all local mates. All guys born and raised in Maghaberry. Guys I was in primary school with from the age of four.

A bit of the old me is coming back. I am able to socialize with guys instead of worrying about my ankle and what is best for it. I can now worry about what is best for me. Relax, have a few beers on a Thursday night and play pool.

On other nights, I get down to the old local, the Maghaberry Arms. Coming home from the World Cup in 2011, myself and

Rory got a taxi up the road. We went to my house first. Outside the bar, from one lamp post to the other, was this big banner that read 'Stevie Ferris, Maghaberry's World Cup Hero'. The guys had had a whip-round in the bar and gave some other guys a couple of quid each to get this banner made.

A week later they invited me up to the bar and presented me with a trophy. It said 'Best World Cup Player 2011 Stevie Ferris'.

The guy who did it all, Alan Irwin, is an old next-door neighbour. I went to school with his daughter, Deborah. Mum and Dad know him well. He had sorted it all out. He is one of these guys that, when he gets a drink, says, 'I'm so proud of you.' And he is. He is just happy that someone local has went on and made something of himself. It was very cool that I could put Maghaberry on the map.

On Sunday, having taken it easy for the rest of the weekend, I drop in for a couple of pints. As soon as I am in the door, I am paired up with a lad and a game of darts. Doubles competition. I end up hitting four 180s during the day, including one in the final. To win, I need to check out on 61.

Bull. 3. Double 4.

Happy days.

The lad I am playing with asks what I am drinking.

'Ah yeah, stick on another pint.'

It is getting late but I stay on. No firm plans for the morning. I know life will not always be this way so, for tonight, I raise a glass to our victory.

Hanging up the boots has also given me a chance to get over to America and catch up with another friend, Rory McIlroy.

I have been away in America with him, socializing, having craic.

He is a mate. He will always give you a buzz to see what is going on.

He loves his rugby but he cannot get over too often. He gets home for around three weeks a year and always has his hands full. It must be tough. Imagine the number of people he has to see or go to. I will never say, 'Here, mate, free for lunch tomorrow? Fancy going out here?' If I get to catch up with him one or two times a year, brilliant. Reason being, he is in demand so much. Sponsors to answer to, too. This is a multi, multi-millionaire and he is still this run-of-the-mill guy from Holywood in Belfast. It is refreshing.

Myself, Paddy Wallace and Niall O'Connor have been over to see him in Florida. I always thought, as an Ulster and Ireland rugby player, that we were getting the VIP treatment. When you would go to a nightclub, Eddie O'Sullivan would make sure there was security there, to look after us.

'Don't mess with us, we've got security guards.'

These are just bouncers that have been hired for an extra night's work. You go out with Rory and he has a team of people with him. Two or three guys, driving in a minibus. All fully armed in case the shit hits the fan. These guys, walking around in their civvies. Blending in; having a pint of whatever. You just would not know they were security. They are there, looking after Rory.

You come out of the hotel and jump into a black SUV and they drive you wherever you want to go. We have a plan to head to Philadelphia so the SUV takes you to a private jet. All our luggage has already been packed in for us. We take off. No security check-ins, $7,500 an hour for the smallest jet. We are in this one as it is only a short hop.

We arrive in Philly and hop straight into another black SUV, with another tailing behind. We are taken straight to Lincoln Financial Field, Philadelphia Eagles' stadium, where a lovely woman comes to meet us. She brings us pitch side and we meet the head coach, this guy called Chip Kelly. We head into the dressing room and are introduced to a couple of players. Absolutely massive. They have so many players. Class. Into our own box – free food and drink all day.

The Eagles were doing well until we go to see them. They need to beat the Seattle Seahawks but they lose. Old Chip will be lucky if he keeps his job.

The owner of the Eagles comes in, looking to meet Rory. There is a cop nearby, decked out in full leather and looking as if he is about to strip off. Big shades on. As soon as the owner sees Rory it's like, 'Oh my God. Hi. Jeez.'

Holy shit, the world's number one golfer is in my stadium.

This guy is probably worth ten times what Rory is – investments all over the world, huge NFL franchise – and yet he is in awe.

For us, we just know him as Rors.

As soon as the game is done, we are straight back into the SUVs – airport, jet, back to Florida. He is staying in West Palm Beach – he has a couple of days' work there with Nike; we are in Miami.

Rory, being the guy he is, does not ask us for a penny the whole time. The way he put it to us is, 'Guys, it's all relative. It's irrelevant. You are mates of mine. If you invited me out for dinner, you would not expect me to pay for it.' Still, he invites us out there, pays for our hotel, nights out, dinners. It is all on him.

I pull him aside one day.

'Your generosity does not go unnoticed. There is no need to do this. We are more than happy to pay.'

He will not hear a bit of it.

The three of us do not head over because Rory is paying for it. If he had invited us over anyway, we would have went and paid our way. It is just that he is so generous and looks after his friends. He would do likewise for Harry Diamond and Ricky McCormick – another couple of friends. Australia, the Masters, whatever. Just so he is hanging out with a few guys he knows, and is close to, not just the golf guys. I can see where he is coming from. If I was touring with the rugby guys all throughout the year – the same faces – it would start to drive you up the wall.

Christmas 2014 is excellent. I am able to go up the north coast and play a bit of golf and relax. No commitments. The BBC contact me about working on 26 December and 3 January, for a couple of Ulster games, but I say no. For the first time in ages, I have no set plans and am able to chill out.

Get up in the morning.

'Ach, what will we do?'

Go for something to eat. Visit the relatives or a friend I have not seen in a while.

I do not have training to worry about or my life being dictated by Ulster Rugby.

Still, I would prefer to have it back the old way if it meant I could still play.

I am still asked if I miss the game. Would I like to be out there? I do not trot out a line but my response rarely falters. It comes from the heart.

'Look, I had a blast for nine, ten years in professional rugby. I haven't lost my leg. I've had a really good innings. Professional rugby is getting to the stage where if you get ten seasons out of it you are doing well. I look back on my time and say, "Jeez, I had a great time, met some unbelievable people on the way, lost some unbelievable people as well, but that's the nature of life." I keep battling. It is not going to end now. Somebody could die tomorrow, even myself, but that is just the way life goes. You got to deal with it in the best way possible.'

In 2015, I set off on the holiday of a lifetime, with Laura, that takes in Thailand, Australia, New Zealand and the United States. I do not catch any of Ireland's Six Nations games live but follow updates online and let out so many yelps, curses and roars on the final day as the lads retain their title.

Upon returning home, I do some more work with the BBC and find myself growing into the punditry role. Unfortunately, the night I truly feel settled is the same night that Ulster's Guinness PRO12 League hopes go up in smoke.

Leading 14–9 against Glasgow Warriors, in Scotstoun, Ulster have dominated the entire match and need only to see out the remaining four minutes. Glasgow knock on as they try to play out from their own 22, but the video referee is called in as Warriors' Niko Matawalu makes a meal out of a brush with Ulster prop Ricky Lutton.

Matawalu flings himself to the ground and George Clancy, the referee, ends up penalizing Ulster. The ball is kicked up the line, Glasgow secure line-out ball, and their winger D. T. H. van der Merwe gets over in the corner for a last-gasp try. Finn Russell converts and Ulster, kicked in the teeth again, are out.

Back in the BBC studio, analysing the game proves stressful. Ulster should have put the game away long before the referee made his call. They were the better team for seventy-six minutes, but the better team does not always win.

The cameras come to us after the final whistle. I always wore my heart on my sleeve as a player so, I tell myself, I should not change. I am going to be completely honest. I declare that Matawalu has made a fool out of himself, with his play-acting, and suggest he should get an Oscar.

In my mind, I am only saying what most Ulster rugby fans are thinking. A lot of pundits do not do that. They try to please the broadcaster, referee, players or league. That is not me. If George Clancy makes a wrong decision, in my opinion, I will say it.

Sometimes that honesty may get me into trouble, but at least I can sleep well at night.

It is an unwritten rule in professional rugby. You do not act like Matawalu did. Nothing against Clancy but, I feel, if Nigel Owens had reffed that game, he would have said, 'What are you playing at? This isn't football. Scrum Ulster.'

If I had been playing in that game and had taken a swallow dive like that, Rory Best would have hit me a slap in the head and I would have been fined by the lads.

Kev Geary, one of the strength and conditioning coaches at Ulster, loves getting a bit of banter going.

Nick Williams is insanely strong. There is a gym exercise known as the bench pull. You lie down, face first, on a gym bench. You then lift weights towards your chest until you get them up far enough that it rings off the metal underneath the bench.

Kev posts a video of Nick as he tries the pull. Up Nick jumps: 'I heard it. I heard it!'

I am not sure. The weights looked far enough away to me.

My record was 145 kilos and Nick has just done 145 kilos. I am tagged in the post, on Twitter. A club record equalled; gauntlet thrown down.

A part of me wants to get back into that gym and go for 150 kilos. 'Record that, Kev!'

I leave off. Instead I reply, 'I'm a retired man. Big Nick is far stronger than me.'

CHAPTER 23

Saturday, 6 June 2009

We are lined up across the halfway line at Vodacom Park, Bloemfontein. The high veld. Next to me stand Paul O'Connell, Andrew Sheridan, Ross Ford and Shane Williams. Irish, English, Scots and Welshmen.

James Hook gets the signal from Wayne Barnes. The third game of the South African tour but a first chance for many of us to stake a claim for a Test jersey. Three days ago, I made my Lions debut and scored in the final minute, rounding off a 74–10 win over the Golden Lions. A 75-metre dash to the try-line.

The Free State Cheetahs await James's kick-off. I am in the number 6 jersey, joined by Joe Worsley and Andy Powell in the back row.

Ford and Paulie are first on the scene as the Cheetahs receive the kick from James. I hover on the fringes, looking for that hit, that early impact to get into the game. Adriaan Strauss, their big hooker, tries to take the ball around the corner and I give him everything I have; stop him in his tracks.

Seven minutes in and just about every player squares up to each other. Euan Murray and Wian du Preez start flinging digs.

All the other forwards pile in as the backs look on. I am trying to wrench du Preez off Euan as Joe tussles with Heinrich Brüssow. Paulie has one Cheetah arm around his neck and is still going after another two.

Typical Psycho.

James bangs over a penalty, soon after, and we edge ahead.

Ten minutes in and we do some damage. Hennie Daniller, their full-back, tries to burst through the centre but is met by Joe and Luke Fitzgerald. They drive him back. I pile in, for the counter-ruck, and the ball spills loose. I am on it.

I pluck it, on the run, and just have Corne Uys, their centre, to beat. I do not bother with side-steps or veering wide. I trust my pace. Uys makes a desperate dive but merely flicks off me. I canter in the final 20 metres and dot down under the posts.

Five minutes later and we are 17–0 up. Donncha O'Callaghan claims a line-out throw, Harry Ellis finds James and his chip over the rushing Cheetahs defence is sublime. Keith Earls takes it on the charge and steps two men to run in a sensational try.

Lads are standing up over all the park.

The score is 20–0, midway through the first half, when the Cheetahs come to life. Tewis de Bruyn, their scrum-half, makes a great break. I spin and arc a run back to our try-line. De Bruyn looks odds-on to score but I get back, just in time, and blindside him with a hit. I swing round and try to get back on my feet to poach the ball. The whistle blows.

It is definitely a penalty. One hundred per cent. Is it a professional foul? No. Is it a yellow card? Probably not. Lee Byrne was covering from full-back so could have prevented the try.

Barnes calls me over and tells me it is a professional foul. He flashes yellow. I take my seat on the naughty chair for ten minutes.

Cheetahs score two tries in the space of eight minutes. All I can do, from the dug-out, is curse and cheer.

They nearly score a third try. J. W. Jonker is passed the ball out on the left wing. All he has to do is run to the corner. He runs the ball for 10 metres then chips it ahead. By the time he catches up with the ball, and dives to touch it down, it has gone dead.

'What the hell just happened? That guy could have just run in.'

I stand on the sideline for the final couple of minutes of my time in the sin-bin.

Unbelievable. From 20–0 to 20–14 in the space of ten minutes. I need to make it up to the lads.

I get the signal and tear back on. For the rest of the match, I play like a man possessed. I tackle every white shirt I see, make a couple of breaks and offloads. I put Keith through a couple of gaps. The oxygen is rare in Bloemfontein – it is 4,500 feet above sea level. I use every ounce of it.

We need a couple of penalties from James to keep them at arm's length. Still they keep coming. Big hits are needed. Paulie is blowing hard but there is no way he is coming off. At 26–17 it is far too tight for that. We cannot lose. We need all the momentum we can get, going into the Test series with the Springboks. I win a couple of big turnovers and make half breaks and carries and get us back up the pitch. We need a score to kill them off.

Nine minutes left on the clock and we have the numbers out wide. Harry finds Shane on the right wing. Leigh Halfpenny is inside him but James is wrapping around his outside shoulder.

Shane pops the pass but Uys is on it. Intercept try, straight up the pitch and under the posts. 26–24.

'Shit.'

We try to push the Cheetahs back but many of us are flat out. It is taking longer and longer to get back on our feet. It feels like my chest is being tightened in a vice. I spot a Cheetah edging my way and take him down. My legs are burning but I get back up.

All those sessions with JD at Ravenhill, building up my fitness levels, are kicking in.

Two minutes to go and we are not letting them get any closer than 30 metres. They sense it themselves and opt for the drop goal. I see the snap and set off for Louis Strydom. He goes for the kick, 42 metres out, and I am almost on him at the release. No block down, but I hope I have done enough.

I spin and there I stand, a metre away from Strydom, as the ball hurtles towards the posts. It looks good. We stand there, bobbing from one foot to the next, as slow motion seems to take hold. Strydom has the distance but the kick flies right and wide. Just.

There is just enough time for the restart but the Cheetahs are beaten as soon as that kick goes wide. We see the match out for a narrow, narrow win.

My name is announced as man-of-the-match. I swap jerseys with one of the Cheetahs but, overheating, stand shirtless for a few minutes.

That game had everything. I am the most exhausted I have ever been but I feel confident that is also the best performance in my career, to date.

Some of the Cheetahs come up to pat me on the back.

'Well played, mate, great game.'

I throw on their jersey for the man-of-the-match presentation – the gold kruger I know I will cherish for ever.

Who would have thought, even a few years ago, that a young fella from Maghaberry would be up on the big screen at Ellis Park, getting the plaudits and keepsakes?

Interviews done, I stand out on the pitch as the clear-up operation begins. I will head down to the boys soon but, for now, I want to take it all in.

This is the pinnacle of my sport. From Friends' School to the British & Irish Lions in six years, with some paving and jelly-packing in between.

I walk towards the dressing room with my shoulders and chest puffed out.

'I'm here to stay. I'm here to take this number 6 jersey and that is it.'

Most of the lads are half changed when I squeeze into the cramped dressing room. Ian McGeechan is in conversation with Paulie but gives me a thumbs-up. Paulie nods.

I fetch my kitbag from an overhead locker and place the kruger near the bottom, under a tracksuit top. I will give it to Mum and Dad to look after when I get home.

I grab a shower and allow myself to replay a few key moments. Live them again. The din of conversation has eased as I step out and grab a towel. I am one of the last ones out of the dressing room, buttoning up my shirt. Paulie will be saying a few words on the team's behalf, thanking the hosts.

I enter the function room and spot the lads, already down the back, joking away. Andy Powell shoots a mega-watt grin and ROG waves me over. The speeches will begin any moment now and I do not want to be caught at the front. I make my way to the boys, shaking hands along the way.

Playing for the Lions is the most thrilling experience of my life. Twenty-three years old and on tour with some of my heroes. There is no place else I would rather be.

ACKNOWLEDGEMENTS

I would like to take this opportunity to thank all the people who have helped mould me into the person I am today.

I can only start by thanking those who mean the most to me – my family. The support, guidance and love that my mum, Linda Ferris, my dad, Robert Ferris, my brother, David Ferris and my beautiful other half, Laura McNally, have given me, through not only the last ten years as a professional rugby player but my whole life, has been immense. I owe each of them a great deal for the part they have played in my journey.

I would like to thank all of my friends from Maghaberry who have supported me throughout my career. Friends you grow up with are friends for life. I hope I did you all proud when I represented not only my grass roots, but Ulster, Ireland and the British & Irish Lions.

Without every single player I have played alongside throughout my career, mine would not have been successful. To my Lions, Ireland, Ulster, Dungannon, Portadown, Lisburn and Friends' School teams, thank you. I enjoyed every single minute I played with you all. In each and every team, I have made friends. From the heart, it counts for a lot.

I had talent as a rugby player, but that alone does not see you to play at the top level. I was coached by a lot of great people. I would like to make a special mention of the coaches who made the biggest impact on my career by believing in me. These include Barney McGonigle (Friends' School, Lisburn), Thomas McGaw (Portadown U18s), Jeremy Davidson (Dungannon and Ulster), Allen Clarke (Ulster, Ireland U19 and U21s), Mark McCall (Ulster), Brian McLaughlin (Ulster), Neil Doak (Ulster), Jonny Davis (Ulster strength and conditioning), Kev Geary (Ulster S&C), Philip Morrow (Ulster and Ireland S&C), David Humphreys (Ulster), Eddie O'Sullivan (Ireland), Declan Kidney (Ireland) and Sir Ian McGeechan (British & Irish Lions). Words of thanks and gratitude must go to Ryan Constable and his team at Esportif (formerly Cornerflag).

I suffered my fair share of injuries in my career and, as a result, spent a lot of time with physios and masseurs. They helped me get better, invested their time and energy in me, and had to deal with my shite craic on a daily basis. Thanks to Gareth 'GG' Robinson (Ulster), Alan McCaldin (Ulster), Phil Glasgow (Ulster U19 and U21s), Brian Green (Ireland), Cameron Steele (Ireland), Willie Bennett (Ireland) and Dave Revins (Ireland). And last but never least, Paddy 'Rala' O'Reilly – Ireland's bag-man/psychologist/friend/story-teller/joker.

The first few pages of my autobiography include a foreword by my friend and golfing legend Rory McIlroy. His time and effort is much appreciated not only by me but by all involved in my book. A genuine guy who said to me when I asked him to write the foreword, 'No problem lad, anything to help a mate out.' That sums him up. Many thanks, Rors.

I would not have written this book if it hadn't been for my ghost-writer, and now friend, Patrick McCarry. His phone call

– to express his interest and excitement about telling my story through this book – was one I am glad he made. His enthusiasm, hard work and patience have added so much to my autobiography. I truly believe that, without him, my story would never have been told. Thank you.

You can have the best life story in the world, but if you do not have a publisher to back that story it will never be printed. Transworld backed me from the first minute I spoke with them. Myself and Patrick knew, instantly, that Transworld were the guys to make the book special. The relationship we had throughout this process was based on trust. Just like the way I had to trust every player I took the rugby field with. Belief comes with trust, and I believe Transworld have done me proud.

Lastly, thanks to all of my supporters and fans who got behind me, week in, week out. Without your support I would not have enjoyed the game of Rugby as much as I did. It was an honour to represent all of my fans and I hope I left some lasting memories of the one F in Ferris . . .

Index

Index